Philosophical Reflections
on Black Mirror

Also Available from Bloomsbury

Morality and the Movies: Reading Ethics Through Film, Dan Shaw
Stanley Cavell and the Arts: Philosophy and Popular Culture, Rex Butler
The Continental Philosophy of Film Reader, ed. Joseph Westfall

Philosophical Reflections on Black Mirror

Edited by
Dan Shaw, Kingsley Marshall, and James Rocha

BLOOMSBURY ACADEMIC
LONDON • NEW YORK • OXFORD • NEW DELHI • SYDNEY

BLOOMSBURY ACADEMIC
Bloomsbury Publishing Plc
50 Bedford Square, London, WC1B 3DP, UK
1385 Broadway, New York, NY 10018, USA
29 Earlsfort Terrace, Dublin 2, Ireland

BLOOMSBURY, BLOOMSBURY ACADEMIC and the Diana logo are trademarks of
Bloomsbury Publishing Plc

First published in Great Britain 2022
This paperback edition published 2023

Copyright © The Estate of Dan Shaw, Kingsley Marshall, James Rocha,
and Contributors, 2022

Kingsley Marshall and James Rocha have asserted their right under the Copyright, Designs
and Patents Act, 1988, to be identified as Editors of this work.

Cover design by Charlotte Daniels
Cover image: *Black Mirror* Season 4 Episode 6 (Black Museum, 2017) (© Netflix)

All rights reserved. No part of this publication may be reproduced or transmitted
in any form or by any means, electronic or mechanical, including photocopying, recording,
or any information storage or retrieval system, without prior permission in writing
from the publishers.

Bloomsbury Publishing Plc does not have any control over, or responsibility for, any third-
party websites referred to or in this book. All internet addresses given in this book were
correct at the time of going to press. The author and publisher regret any inconvenience
caused if addresses have changed or sites have ceased to exist, but can accept no
responsibility for any such changes.

A catalogue record for this book is available from the British Library.

Library of Congress Cataloging-in-Publication Data
Names: Shaw, Daniel, 1951- editor. | Marshall, Kingsley, editor. |
Rocha, James, 1975- editor.
Title: Philosophical reflections on Black mirror / edited by Dan Shaw,
Kingsley Marshall, and James Rocha.
Description: London; New York: Bloomsbury Academic, 2022. | Includes
bibliographical references and index.
Identifiers: LCCN 2021030316 (print) | LCCN 2021030317 (ebook) |
ISBN 9781350162143 (hb) | ISBN 9781350162167 (epdf) | ISBN 9781350162198 (ebook)
Subjects: LCSH: Black mirror (Television program)
Classification: LCC PN1992.77.B525 P45 2022 (print) | LCC PN1992.77.B525 (ebook) |
DDC 791.45/72–dc23
LC record available at https://lccn.loc.gov/2021030316
LC ebook record available at https://lccn.loc.gov/2021030317

ISBN: HB: 978-1-3501-6214-3
PB: 978-1-3502-7953-7
ePDF: 978-1-3501-6216-7
eBook: 978-1-3501-6219-8

Typeset by Deanta Global Publishing Services, Chennai, India

To find out more about our authors and books visit www.bloomsbury.com and
sign up for our newsletters.

Dedication

The editors and contributors dedicate this book to our colleague Dan Shaw, who passed away mid-way through this book project in March 2020. Dan Shaw is survived by his wife Vera Marie Shaw, son Patrick Shaw, daughter Anna Shaw, step brothers Christopher and Trenn Roberts, step sister Catherine Hansen, and his dog Lucy.

Dan Shaw *served as Professor of Philosophy at Lock Haven University, Pennsylvania, for over thirty years. He devoted much of his scholarship to film, served as the managing editor of* Film and Philosophy, *as well as authored the books* Film and Philosophy: Taking Movies Seriously, Morality and the Movies: Reading Ethics through Film, *and* Stanley Cavell and the Magic of Hollywood Films.

Contents

Introduction: Charlie Brooker's Artistic Vision *Kingsley Marshall, James Rocha, and Dan Shaw*   1

Section One Is *Black Mirror* Philosophy?

1 Through a Screen Darkly: *Black Mirror*, Thought Experiments, and Televisual Philosophy *Robert Sinnerbrink*   11

2 *Black Mirror* as Philosophizing About Immortality, Technology, and Human Nature *Lorraine K.C. Yeung and Kong-Ngai Pei*   31

3 Technology in Pastel Colors: An Alternative Take on *Black Mirror* *Laura T. Di Summa*   49

4 The Virtue of Forgetting in Nietzsche's Philosophy and *Black Mirror* *Dan Shaw*   67

Section Two Versions of the Self in *Black Mirror*

5 Free Will in *Black Mirror: Bandersnatch* *Sander Lee*   81

6 "White Christmas": Technologies of the Self in the Digital Age *Diana Stypinska and Andrea Rossi*   97

7 You Were Never Really Here: Representations of Artificial Intelligence in Charlie Brooker's *Black Mirror* *Kingsley Marshall*   114

Section Three *Black Mirror* and Relating to Others

8 "Crocodile" Going Too Far: Philosophical Reflections on Human Nature and Moral Character *Clara Nisley*   129

9 Rats, Roaches, and Rapists: "Men Against Fire" and the Propagation of Propaganda *Leigh E. Rich*   144

10 "Between Delight and Discomfort": The Act of Mirroring in the
   Age of *Black Mirror* Shai Biderman   168

11 The You They Love: Patriarchal Feminism and Ashley Too
   Mona Rocha and James Rocha   184

Conclusion *James Rocha and Kingsley Marshall*   200

About the Contributors   207
Index   211

Introduction

Charlie Brooker's Artistic Vision

Kingsley Marshall, James Rocha, and Dan Shaw

Black Mirror (2011–) is a science-fiction television series first broadcast on Channel 4 in the UK before being produced and distributed by Netflix from 2016. The show takes an anthology approach, presenting each of its stories as a discrete single drama commonly situated in dystopic, near-future settings. The episodes are orientated around three main themes: (1) the development, use, and exploitation of technology; (2) the ethics related to the deployment of this technology by members of the public and corporations; and (3) an exploration of the nature of what constitutes consciousness specifically related to artificial intelligence (AI) and robotic or cybernetic technologies. The show's format, atmosphere, and narratives of social commentary have been compared to the influential science-fiction series *The Twilight Zone* (Serling 1959), which initially ran between 1959 and 1964, and was subsequently rebooted in 1985, 2002, and, more recently, 2017 by CBS All Access. *The New Yorker*'s TV critic Emily Nussbaum described the show as an "update on 'The Twilight Zone' for a Digital Age" (2014), and, like its predecessor, philosophy in the show is buried in each story. Each of these two shows extrapolates ideas of the contemporary present into the near future and invites the audience to consider the implications of their own actions, addictions, and use of media, as well as drawing on the nature of rationality, morality, and social consciousness. In this edited collection, our contributors consider this presentation of a relatively unified philosophy, albeit projected into the future.

The series is written primarily by Charlie Brooker, with the writer also taking an executive producer role with Annabel Jones on all of the episodes to date, initially through the production company Zeppotron—a subsidiary of the Endemol Shine Group—and latterly through House of Tomorrow. The pair left House of Tomorrow to found a new company Broke and Bones in January 2020, leaving the rights with Endemol and future seasons in question. Although each of the twenty-two episodes and the feature film *Black Mirror: Bandersnatch* (Slade 2018) contains its own discreet story, the *Black Mirror* universe is unified and often self-referential, connecting iconography, production design, and narrative ideas. Brooker had described each episode as occupying a "psychologically shared universe" (Brooker in Daly 2017) and in "Black Museum" (McCarthy 2017) made these connections with previous episodes explicit through exhibits that made a direct reference to earlier shows. As such, the series can present a powerfully cogent singular worldview and, in the tradition of the very best science fiction, use the philosophical and sociological implications of the future to reflect upon the dystopia of the immediate present.

Brooker's background is in comedy, Zeppotron's output predominantly consisting of scripted and unscripted shows with Brooker having contributed his TV critique *Screenwipe* (2006–8) and current affairs platform *Newswipe* (2009–10). The production of *Dead Set* (Demange 2008), a five-part miniseries where a zombie apocalypse reaches the inhabitants of a Reality TV show during an eviction episode, can be seen as the seed of *Black Mirror*. The series drew upon the existing lore of zombie films and series, genre conventions that occupy a long tradition in film, television, and literature and serve as a lens through which a critique of philosophical questions is presented—with *Dead Set* exploring the conflation of private and public spaces, of the objectification of life played out as the performance of mediated and real-life identities, and questions of gender and masculinity.

These notions of a television series as parable were initially made manifest in the first season of *Black Mirror*, broadcast in 2011. The themes of each of the three episodes were centered on satire—musing on the impact of social media on news media reporting, the conflation of personal and national politics, and the consumption of reality television. The original treatment alluded to the significance of technology to the series, as Brooker explained: "Just as The Twilight Zone would talk about McCarthyism, we're going to talk about Apple" (Brooker, Jones, and Arnopp 2018). There was an immediacy to these episodes that responded to the conflation of politics and media in "The National Anthem" (Bathurst 2011), the fascination of audiences with the persecution of television talent show contestants in "Fifteen Million

Merits" (Lyn 2011), and ongoing concerns around privacy and online identity, extrapolated to a nightmarish level in "The Entire History of You" (Welsh 2011)—this final episode of that opening season was also the first episode to extend its articulation of the impact of technology from the *representation* of the self to subjective notions of identity and memory in the *construction* of the self. Over the course of this short season, and particularly this last episode, *Black Mirror* began to mine a seam of the fundamental nature of existence and explicitly connect with larger ideas of philosophy.

BBC Channel 4 had been seeking a coproduction partner to fund longer and more ambitious episodes proposed by Brooker and Jones, though challenges to the writer's story ideas—and subsequently to the budget of each episode—created an ongoing tension between the broadcaster and the writers. Netflix had licensed and distributed the first two series in the previous year, and, after negotiations ran their course at Channel 4, Brooker and Jones took the series to the streaming service. Netflix initially commissioned twelve episodes and committed to the higher budgets that sated Brooker and Jones' greater ambition for the show. The release of each season on a global platform set the bar for a worldwide television event, and Brooker responded with stories set at an appropriate scale. "San Junipero" (Harris 2016) was the first episode to be set outside of the UK and was followed by episodes shot in Iceland and Canada. Following the move, the show became increasingly sophisticated in both its social critique and its playful use of form—most apparent in the stand-alone feature-length film *Black Mirror: Bandersnatch* in 2018—where users were able to select their path through the narrative by making binary choices on their remote control to navigate the branching story structure. This first interactive story for adult audiences at Netflix allowed for some experimentation with a rudimentary form of nonlinear, rhizomic modes of storytelling that echoed the video game setting of the story. Though the film received a mixed reception, there is little doubt that this interactive device drew the audience further into the wider conceptual determinism of characters and the choices available to them in the narrative.

There is a logical progression to the order and grouping of sections of this book. In Section One, our contributors consider the philosophical implications and central metaphor of the series as a whole. Section Two examines the formation of identity and the self through the prism of technology. Finally, Section Three considers the relationship between a technologically augmented self and dystopic worlds.

In Chapter 1, Robert Sinnerbrink takes a step back from specific episodes and examines the implications of the central metaphor behind the series. Beginning with Charlie Brooker's observation that "The 'black mirror' of the title is the one you'll find on every wall, on every desk, in the palm of every hand: the cold, shiny screen of a TV, a monitor, a smartphone," it seeks to broaden the scope of our appreciation of the metaphor by examining the use of mirrors (and mirrorlike objects) in paramount filmic cases (such as the (black) mirrorlike monolith, the centerpiece of "the dawn of man" scene in Stanley Kubrick's *2001: A Space Odyssey* (1968)) and by discussing the strikingly self-referential "act of mirroring" in its current phase of binge-viewing television and internet streaming, the modus operandi of Brooker's series.

In Chapter 2, Lorraine K. C. Yeung and Kong-Ngai Pei suggest that the fourth episode of season three, "San Junipero," philosophizes immortality, technology, and human nature. The episode appears to have a singularly upbeat ending in that its protagonists get to enjoy life together forever in a virtual reality that preserves the life of their consciousness. The chapter demonstrates that the immortal lives in San Junipero illustrate Bernard Williams and Kagan's worry about the inevitability of boredom in an immortal life and shows how San Junipero adds another dimension to the philosophical debate over the desirability of immortality. Yeung argues that the *Black Mirror* world depicted by several other episodes of the series points to a gloomy view of the technology depicted in San Junipero. The gloominess, however, has less to do with the problem of tedium than with human malevolence and with our inherent vulnerabilities in the face of technology. In Chapter 3, Laura di Summa considers the manner in which *Black Mirror* can both exemplify postmodern and poststructuralist criticism, and prompts the audience to question what is described as the tyranny of technology and its transformative impact on the formation of the self.

Closing this section is Dan Shaw, who presents "The Entire History of You" as an archetypal example of the dystopic vision that is to dominate the series. Shaw argues that the inherently philosophical nature and value of dystopia is to serve as nightmarish visions of the future designed as cautionary tales to warn us about present trends in our society. He notes the striking similarities between its condemnation of the prospect of being able to recall and replay any moment in your life and Friedrich Nietzsche's case for the importance of forgetting, throwing light on both the episode and Nietzsche's philosophy.

In so doing, the episode is philosophical, whether or not Charlie Brooker intended to reflect this aspect of Nietzsche's philosophy.

Section Two considers versions of the self in *Black Mirror*. Starting in Chapter 5, Sander Lee considers the implications of viewers being presented with a "Choose Your Own Adventure" style drama in the stand-alone drama *Black Mirror: Bandersnatch*, in which a young programmer named Stefan Butler—along with the audience of the film—is faced with a series of choices. Supposedly, viewers can alter the trajectory and ending of the tale by the choices they make. However, many viewers complained that no matter what choices they made, the story took a pessimistic turn, leading to a depressing ending. The only control that viewers (and Stefan) seemed to have is over the degree of the horror in that, in virtually all versions of the story, Stefan murdered his father. The only way Stefan can avoid parricide is by committing suicide, and indeed, Stefan himself complains at one point that he feels that he is not in control of his choices. This chapter argues that the element of apparent determinism is not a failure on the part of its creators but is, indeed, precisely the point they wish to make. The philosophy underlying *Black Mirror: Bandersnatch* can be fruitfully compared with that of Arthur Schopenhauer, who believed that everything that exists is a manifestation of an irrational force he calls "the Will." There is only one Will, and it pervades all reality while determining every action. Free will is no more than an illusion, and life is primarily characterized by suffering and despair. Whether knowingly or not, the worldview of Charlie Brooker mirrors Schopenhauer's black philosophy.

In Chapter 6, Diana Stypinska and Andrea Rossi focus on the questions that the episode "White Christmas" (Tibbetts 2014) poses concerning the use of digital technologies as instruments for individual self-enhancement, as well as the management, control, and "optimization" of interpersonal and affective relationships. Building on the work of Pierre Hadot, Michel Foucault, Peter Sloterdijk, and Bernard Stiegler, Stypinska and Rossi demonstrate how the episode explores the ethical and political consequences of employing digital implements as technologies of the self—tools employed to transform the relationship that the subject entertains with itself (its desires, needs, and skills) and the others (friends, family, colleagues, society). The chapter asks how and under what conditions the enhanced performativity, sense of security, self-mastery, and self-contentment that the "digital technologies of the self" are designed to provide may bring about diametrically opposite outcomes (i.e., loss of selfhood, privacy, empathy, political freedom, and, ultimately, death).

Closing this section, Kingsley Marshall considers the representation of AI technologies in *Black Mirror*, focusing on "Be Right Back" (Harris 2013). In the episode, the recently bereaved Martha reconstructs a version of her deceased boyfriend through a machine-based entity, or AI, drawn initially from public data created from his lifetime of digital activity. Martha's eventual realization that the technological expression of her partner has corrupted her real-world memories of him and their relationship extends her bereavement rather than her intention of somehow resolving her grief.

In the third and final section, our contributors consider how these presentations of the individual relate to others. In Chapter 8, Clara Nisley considers how, in "Crocodile" (Hillcoat 2017), the moral character of the protagonist Mia Nolan is uncovered. After a night of partying with her friend Rob, Mia finds herself an accomplice to cover up an accident when Rob, driving the car on an isolated road, hits and kills a cyclist. Mia takes out her phone to call the police, but Rob begs her not to make the call. After a moment, she acquiesces to Rob's pleas, and Mia helps Rob throw the body over a cliff into a lake. Several years pass before Rob comes to Mia, announcing his intention to turn himself in to the authorities. Mia kills him; the first of a series of ever more appalling crimes she commits to conceal her guilt. The chapter explores what this episode says about human nature by comparing Immanuel Kant and Aristotle's notions of moral character. It uses Mia as a case study to explore whether moral character requires self-control by practical reason or whether it is an extraordinary force of will that is the foundation for a morally good character.

In Chapter 9, Leigh Rich focuses on "Men Against Fire" (Verbruggen 2016), an episode that depicts a dystopic society whose warriors have brain implants that cause them to see their opponents as monsters and not humans. This makes it easier to kill them, and the episode's title alludes to a 1947 book by S.L.A. Marshall that highlights how many combatants are hesitant to kill their fellow human beings and discusses ways to overcome this resistance. The chapter examines how the dehumanizing propaganda of Second World War sought to achieve precisely the effect of the brain implants: the "Othering" of one's opponents that would enable one to slay them more effectively.

Shai Biderman returns to the idea at the center of the series in Chapter 10, with a consideration of how the *Black Mirror* can only mirror those looking at, or attempting to look, through it. Where the pursuit of pleasure presents a challenge to a representation of the self, the mirror represents the confliction of an idea of the self—a voyage described in the chapter as familiar, but one that causes a questioning of the real.

Mona Rocha and James Rocha close the book with the most recent episode, examining selfhood and stardom in "Rachel, Jack and Ashley Too" (Sewitsky 2019). The pair argue that the story offers a critique of patriarchy through an entertainer whose consciousness is exploited as a digital copy but who is eventually able to extricate from the structures of capitalism in the search to regain her own identity.

Black Mirror offers a compelling case study for the idea of "television as philosophy." This collection explores this idea via three aspects: *Black Mirror* (1) as a thought experiment, (2) as reflecting a critique of modern technology, and (3) as engaged in critical self-reflection on audiovisual media and its own status as episodic television. The episodes of *Black Mirror* pose sophisticated thought experiments concerning the ethical implications of modern technology and digital screen culture. *Black Mirror* reveals precisely the kind of ambivalent potentiality of modern technology that Martin Heidegger warned against: it both threatens the imposition of a totalizing reduction of human beings to a stock of manipulable resources and harbors the promise of opening up a transformed way of inhabiting the technological world more thoughtfully.

Charlie Brooker has always been decidedly uncomfortable with having the overall worldview of the series being described as simply dystopic, as it often is in the popular media. This collection presents an argument that *Black Mirror* delivers a coherent and epistemically novel philosophical viewpoint through means that are specific to motion pictures. It does so by exploring how technology is depicted in the series and how such depictions may reveal something counterintuitive. The technology we encounter in the series is not always as bleak as it first appears. Contrary to the more typical portrayal of technology we encounter in most science fiction, technology in the series is not alien but familiar. Its devices are stunningly designed and are often like games that need to be mastered. Learning how to use a given technological device is a central plot point in many of the episodes, a familiar process. Furthermore, the speed with which we "consume" *Black Mirror* is a product of the present status of technology. The series exploits, in this sense, the very environment in which it creates and depicts technology in attractive pastel colors, making it seem so user-friendly.

References

Bathurst, Otto. (2011), "The National Anthem," *Black Mirror*, Channel 4. Season 1, Episode 1, Broadcast December 4, 2011.

Brooker, Charlie, Annabel Jones, and Jason Arnopp. (2018), *Inside Black Mirror*, London: Ebury.

Daly, Helen. (2017), "Black Mirror season 4 spoilers: Charlie Brooker CONFIRMS Enormous Fan Theory," in *The Daily Express*, December 21, 2017. Express.co.uk/showbiz/tv-radio/895234/Black-Mirror-season-4-spoilers-Charlie-Brooker-CONFIRMS-theory-Black-Museum-Netflix-return

Demange, Yann. (2008), *Dead Set*. E4, Broadcast October 27–31, 2008. [TV Series].

Harris, Owen. (2013), "Be Right Back," *Black Mirror*, Channel 4. Season 2, Episode 1, Broadcast February 11, 2013. [TV Series].

Harris, Owen. (2016), "San Junipero," *Black Mirror*, Netflix. Season 3, Episode 4. Release Date October 21, 2016. [TV Series].

Hillcoat, John. (2017), "Crocodile." *Black Mirror*, Netflix. Season 4, Episode 3. Release Date December 29, 2017. [TV Series].

Kubrick, Stanley. (1968), *2001: A Space Odyssey*. MGM. [Film].

Lyn, Euros. (2011), "Fifteen Million Merits," *Black Mirror*, Channel 4. Season 1, Episode 2, Broadcast December 11, 2011. [TV Series].

McCarthy, Colm. (2017), "Black Museum," *Black Mirror*, Netflix. Season 4, Episode 6. Release Date December 29, 2017. [TV Series].

Newswipe (2009–2010), BBC Four. [TV Series].

Screenwipe (2006–2008), BBC Four. [TV Series].

Sewitsky, Anne. (2019), "Rachel, Jack and Ashley Too," *Black Mirror*, Netflix. Season 5, Episode 3. Release Date June 5, 2019. [TV Series].

Slade, David. (2018), *Black Mirror: Bandersnatch*, Netflix. [Film].

Serling, Rod. (1959), *The Twilight Zone*. (1959–1964, 1985–1989, 2002–2003, 2019), CBS. [TV Series].

Tibbetts, Carl. (2014), "White Christmas," *Black Mirror*, Channel 4. Christmas Special. Broadcast December 16, 2014. [TV Series].

Verbruggen, Jakob. (2016), "Men Against Fire," *Black Mirror*, Netflix. Season 3, Episode 5. Release Date October 21, 2016. [TV Series].

Welsh, Brian. (2011), "The Entire History of You," *Black Mirror*, Channel 4. Season 1, Episode 3. Broadcast December 18, 2011. [TV Series].

Section One

Is *Black Mirror* Philosophy?

1

Through a Screen Darkly

Black Mirror, Thought Experiments, and Televisual Philosophy

Robert Sinnerbrink

The award-winning television show *Black Mirror* (Brooker, 2011–19) has attracted widespread praise and critical acclaim. Recalling the episodic anthology format of *The Twilight Zone*, *Black Mirror* presents compelling depictions of near-future scenarios exploring the dark side of contemporary digital technology and audiovisual culture. Although most belong to the genre of dystopian science fiction, the episodes of *Black Mirror* could also be described as works of speculative cinematic fiction, deploying a variety of genres such as psychological horror, science fantasy, and the sociopolitical thriller. The stand-alone episodes of the five series of *Black Mirror* explore the uncanny, the fantastic, and the marvelous, but always with specific reference to our technologically mediated sense of social reality. With its focus on the ethical implications of current and future technological possibilities, *Black Mirror* offers a compelling case for the idea of "televisual philosophy." In what follows I shall develop this thesis by exploring three related ways of approaching it: *Black Mirror* (1) as thought experiment, (2) as reflecting a critique of modern technology, and (3) as engaged in critical self-reflection on audiovisual media and on its own status as episodic television.

The episodes of *Black Mirror* concern the ethical implications of modern technology and digital screen culture. If long-form TV serials like *The Sopranos* (Chase 1999–2007), *The Wire* (Simon 2002–8), *Breaking Bad* (Gilligan 2008–13), and Netflix's *House of Cards* (Willimon 2013–18) adopt an extended narrative structure, character development, and complex world-building familiar from nineteenth- and twentieth-century (realist) novels, then the episodic anthology format of *Black Mirror*, focusing on particular situations, specific characters, and well-defined ideas, is more akin to the short story. They offer powerful cinematic thought experiments that engage in philosophical thinking. The idea of film as thought experiment, familiar from debates concerning "film as philosophy" (Wartenberg 2007; Sinnerbrink 2011, 2014), was further developed by Thomas Elsaesser in an essay on "mind-game films" (2009). His approach offers a productive way of conceptualizing *Black Mirror* episodes within the more compressed format of episodic serial television. In addition to testing our moral intuitions, framing alternative realities, and exploring possible outcomes in hypothetical fictional scenarios, cinematic thought experiments can also provide distinctive contributions to our ethical understanding.

Black Mirror offers critical reflections on the ethical implications of modern technology, which recall, but also extend, the speculations of philosophers of technology from Heidegger to Debord and Baudrillard. In a related vein, *Black Mirror* allows us to revisit the debate concerning "film in the condition of philosophy" (Wartenberg 2007, Mulhall 2008, Smuts 2009, Sinnerbrink 2011: 120–35) thanks to its self-reflexive engagement with contemporary media technologies. The episodes of *Black Mirror* reflect on their own status as audiovisual media and comment on the role of television and social and digital media as aspects of an integrated audiovisual system with disturbing ethical and political implications. By reflecting upon its own conditions, complicity, and critical potentials, *Black Mirror* displays the kind of aesthetic and cinematic self-reflexivity that Mulhall (2008: 1–11) claims is one way that cinema—or in this case episodic television—can exist in the "condition of philosophy."

What Is *Black Mirror*?

Written by Charlie Brooker, *Black Mirror* comprises five series spanning twenty-two episodes, which range between forty and ninety minutes long. Brooker worked in television as a presenter, comic scriptwriter, and online satirist, becoming infamous for his biting satirical website TVGoHome his critical commentary on news media (*Newswipe* Brooker 2009-10), and for writing and presenting the documentary series *How TV Ruined Your*

Life (Brooker 2011). He contributed scripts for the television horror serial *Dead Set* (Demange 2008), where zombies threaten to invade a Big Brother television set. He lampooned the media in the TVGoHome website that featured the fake Reality TV show *Daily Mail Island*, where the only source of news and information is the titular British tabloid that transforms the island's inhabitants into conservative bigots, and in satires such as *Nathan Barley* (Morris and Brooker 2005), based on a vapid and narcissistic would-be media/fashion "influencer." Many of these themes would be treated in more depth and with more seriousness in *Black Mirror*. The first two series, comprising three episodes each and a Special "White Christmas" (Tibbets 2014), were commissioned by Channel 4 in the UK (2011–13), while the next three seasons (six, six, and three episodes, respectively) were made for Netflix (2014–19). As I discuss later, Netflix also features in the interactive "television film" *Black Mirror: Bandersnatch* (Slade 2018).

All are stand-alone episodes with different characters, settings, and time frames (generally set in the United Kingdom and the United States, from the 1980s to the near future). Yet various episodes also allude to each other in implicit ways, including a number of "Easter Eggs" (implicit references, recurring symbols, or sundry connecting details) left for fans of the series to enjoy. Beyond adding "texture" (as Brooker puts it), cross-referenced features appearing in different episodes provide an intersecting network or "enfoldment" that could be described as comprising an interactive Black Mirror mediaverse (an idea explicitly articulated in *Black Mirror: Bandersnatch*).

The title of the series is telling, referring to the black appearance of a device's screen when switched off, a dark "mirror" in which the user can only see his or her face dimly. The title is also a metaphor for holding a mirror up to our fascination with digital media and social media culture. It alludes to the "dark side" of the technological possibilities afforded by modern media technologies and the social and cultural effects of their ubiquitous uses. As Circucci and Vacker (2018) point out, the opening credit sequence develops this idea in visual form. The black screen appears with a familiar graphic—the rotating circular figure of the device starting up, otherwise known as a "throbber"—suggesting obscure digital operations occurring behind the screen, which then disintegrates and reconstitutes itself as the title, "Black Mirror," accompanied by an ominous electronic sound as the screen glass suddenly cracks. Circucci and Vacker draw parallels with the opening sequence of *The Twilight Zone*, another series which, as creator Rod Serling remarked, allowed contemporary moral and political themes to be explored by transposing them into science-fiction or speculative genres. Brooker has taken up Serling's strategy and developed it into a highly self-reflexive engagement with the ethics and politics of contemporary digital culture. As Circucci and Vacker remark, *Black Mirror* is "*The Twilight Zone* of the twentieth first century," a "philosophical classic that echoes the angst of an era" (2018: vii); as Stephen King tweeted, *Black Mirror* is "like *The Twilight Zone*, only Rated R" (quoted in Harvey 2016). It also offers a fascinating case study of televisual philosophy.

As many commentators have noted, the series is best described as focusing on the "near future," or an "alternative present," extrapolating from social phenomena and technological possibilities that already exist and amplifying and examining their potential effects and social implications now and in the future (Martin 2018, Circucci and Vacker 2018). This generates an uncanny "anticipatory" effect, and/or *déjà là* (preemptive or premonitory) effect, that combines both recognizable features of the present and disturbing yet plausible amplifications of existing technologies in order to explore their future social and ethical consequences. The "allegorical" dimension of the 1950s *Twilight Zone* episodes—using science-fiction and speculative fiction scenarios to comment on contemporary cultural and political issues such as racism and Cold War politics—has shifted in *Black Mirror*. It adopts a reverse strategy to that of allegory: its episodes offer uncanny simulations, involving slight displacements and amplifications of the familiar present, which is rendered as both strange and threatening. Like the term "Kafkaesque," "Black Mirror" has itself become a byword to describe disturbing developments involving technological media and their social implications. Alexandria Ocasio-Cortez, for example, recently described the secret use of facial recognition technology as a "Black Mirror"–type situation: "This is some real-life 'Black Mirror' stuff that we're seeing here, and I think it's really important that everyone really understand what's happening because . . . this is happening secretly, as well" (Quoted in Houser 2020).

Black Mirror is also indebted to various television and film genres, such as psychological and social horror in "Shut up and Dance" (Watkins 2016), "Metalhead" (Slade 2016), and "Black Museum" (McCarthy 2017); the sociopolitical thriller through "The National Anthem" (Bathurst 2011) and "Hated in the Nation" (Hawes 2016); as well as domestic social drama in

"Be Right Back" (Harris 2013), elements of the police procedural by way of "Crocodile" (Hillcoat 2017), and romance in "San Junipero" (Harris 2016) and "Hang the DJ" (Van Patten 2017). Computer gaming technologies and formats are also featured explicitly in some episodes, including "Playtest" (Trachtenberg 2016) and "Striking Vipers" (Harris 2019), and the aforementioned feature *Black Mirror: Bandersnatch*. The cross-medial character of many episodes, combining cinematic, social media, and gaming styles and techniques, makes them difficult to classify and is a distinctive feature of the series' televisual style (which mirrors or mimics its objects). The episodes in general are characterized by tight scripting and high production values, using new directors (along with occasional veterans such as John Hillcoat and Jodie Foster) and lesser-known actors playing discrete characters who do not reappear across the different episodes.

"Fifteen Million Merits" (Lyn 2011), for example, combines a luridly colorful "gaming" style coupled with drab gray clothing and interiors that blend into the fictional world of the protagonists, who live as virtual prisoners in a digital environment as they earn "merits" by using stationary bike equipment. Their only hope of escape is via auditioning for a brutally exploitative Reality TV talent show *Hotshot*. In another case, "Nosedive" (Wright 2016), as I discuss later, adopts a smooth, slick, pastel-colored style to reflect the "Instagrammatization" of everyday life that defines the socially mediatized world of Lacey, who is desperately trying to boost her social media ranking in order to get a new apartment and thereby elevate her social status and economic prospects.

It is also worth noting how well the short-form episodic format fits with the series' focus on digital media culture. As opposed to the long-form television serial, with its multiple narrative lines, extended character development arcs, and complex world-building, the short-form episodic format focuses on particular characters situated within briefly sketched but well-defined contexts. Characters are rapidly delineated, depicted as rather "generic," and represent a particular social type or recognizable kind of subjectivity. Viewers have fewer opportunities for complex emotional engagement, compared with the long-form television serial. Dramatic narrative development is elliptical, often structured by a conceptual scenario or hypothetical situation, and swiftly articulated in narrative terms within a tightly defined temporal frame. The role of technology is foregrounded: not only are the relationships between characters mediated via various social media technologies but their very sense of self is essentially dependent on the technologies that shape and structure their shared world. In short, the deliberately "flat" presentation of character, sharply delineated situations, technologically mediated relationships and identities, and strongly conceptual or idea-driven narratives make this kind of short-form episodic series the ideal medium for staging complex film-philosophical thought experiments.

The series is distinguished by its "dark" vision of technology, exploring the ethical implications of digital technological culture and the ubiquitous power of social media to shape subjectivity under conditions that could be described as those of "surveillance capitalism" (Zuboff 2019). Techniques of surveillance are applied to the tracking and harvesting of information designed to shape consumer choices and social conduct, colonize personal identities, manipulate culture, and control political decision-making. Unlike long-form television serials, which compose complex fictional worlds populated by densely drawn characters, *Black Mirror* constructs its broader "global" perspective in a mosaic or fragmentary manner. It isolates problems or possibilities, exploring them within particular scenarios and allowing the accumulated perspectives to suggest a fragmentary constellation that does not constitute a uniform whole. One way of elaborating this thesis is to identify thematic clusters that recur across the various episodes, with particular episodes not only foregrounding particular themes but also allowing for intersecting, overlapping, and corresponding themes to be explored from different perspectives within particular narrative situations. In what follows I outline a range of such thematic clusters, which represent groupings of cognate themes and ideas that coalesce and recur over different episodes and seasons.

Black Mirror Thematic Clusters

There are a number of thematic clusters that recur within and across the stylistically and generically distinct episodes of *Black Mirror*, which lends the series both coherence and diversity. The most obvious thematic cluster concerns *digital media thought experiments*: film-philosophical fictional situations that extrapolate from, and explore further, the possible uses, abuses, and ethical implications of existing among slightly amplified forms of digital technology and audiovisual media. What if "wearable" technologies capable of "recording" our experiences, and thereby rendering memories available in digital formats to be reviewed by the "user" were devised? What might be some of the personal and social uses to which such a technology might be put? What kind of effect would it have on our sense of personal identity and on our personal and social relationships? "The Entire History of You" (Welsh 2011) stages just such a scenario as a film-philosophical digital media thought experiment, showing how individuals would be likely to adopt the new technology, outsource their personal memories, and share their experiences with others (in "redo" sessions with friends).

Companies could use this information in the selection and management of employees (as we see when protagonist Liam (Toby Kebbell) pores over the "redo" of his workplace performance management meeting), while government and security agencies could use it to monitor, check, and surveil members of the public (as we see during an airport security check scene in which Liam is asked to produce his memories of the previous days). It could also wreak havoc on personal relationships by eliminating the unreliability of memory or discretionary freedom afforded by forgetting, depicting a Nietzschean nightmare of objective veridical memory being available for forensic scrutiny at any time (as we see when Liam obsessively reviews the "redo" of his wife Ffion talking and laughing with what turns out to be an old flame, arousing Liam's soon-to-be-confirmed jealous suspicions).

Other episodes stage similar digital thought experiments: "Arkangel" (Foster 2017) envisions a parental surveillance device that allows overprotective parents to not only track their children but also edit unpleasant environmental stimuli by pixelating potential "stressful" perceptions or events. It even permits them to occupy their child's point of view (unbeknownst to the child), which becomes deeply invasive and morally unacceptable when Marie not only tracks her daughter Sara but inadvertently "tunes in" to her point of view while Sara is having sex with her boyfriend. In the fifth season, "Rachel, Jack and Ashley Too" (Sewitsky 2019) depicts a pop performer, Ashley O, whose consciousness is partially downloaded into a commercially available artificial intelligence (AI) doll. She also ends up being replaced by a holographic performer once she begins to assert her own artistic autonomy (after being rendered comatose by secretly administered drugs for refusing to comply with her record company's demands).

A related thematic cluster concerns "gamification" threats: which involve extrapolating from the increasing popularity of gaming as a paradigmatic form of audiovisual media and examining the potentially toxic effects that such immersive, distractive, and interactive formats could have, especially within the context of an exploitative neoliberal surveillance capitalism. These episodes also typically involve digital media thought experiments. "Playtest" focuses on the scenario of using a player as a live test subject in an experimental immersive "horror" gaming situation. The test player, Cooper, is an American traveler down on his luck who agrees to be a test subject to pay his way back home after losing his money. To his horror, he begins to lose his memories and suffer disruptions of consciousness, thanks to the augmented reality (AR) technology targeting the player's own personal deepest fears as key elements in constructing the immersive virtual reality (VR) game. In a final twist, we discover that the events we have seen were simulated; Cooper received a phone call from his mother during the gaming simulation, an unexpected interruption to the network linking his neural synapses with the VR simulation that results in his tragic death.

The question of interactive gaming, and the meaning of interactivity more generally (often cited as an affirmative counterpoint to the "passivity" of traditional film and television viewing) is subjected to critical scrutiny in *Black Mirror: Bandersnatch*. Set in the year 1984, it tells the choose-your-own-adventure story of a young programmer named Stefan. He is contracted by the gaming company Tuckersoft to work on a radical new game based on a cult interactive fantasy novel, written by a reclusive author, Jerome F. Davies (played by Jeff Minter, himself a prominent game designer), who went mad and murdered his wife. Stefan, under increasing pressure to finish the game in time for Christmas sales, finds his own grasp of reality beginning to slip the more immersed he becomes in creating the game. He is desperately trying to resolve problems, while suspecting something more sinister and inexplicable is happening behind the scenes.

There are multiple versions of the story, with different plot developments depending on the choices made by viewers. This feeds into the explicitly metafictional element reflecting on the nature of gaming, as well as the status of *Bandersnatch* itself as just such a commercial product (produced by Netflix, which itself features in the episode). There are intriguing reflections on free will and determinism within the context of fictional narrative and gaming culture, culminating in the enfoldment of the viewer/player into the intersecting fictional world of *Black Mirror*/Netflix itself. The viewer at home, controlling or directing events in the Netflix/*Black Mirror* story world, is the real source of Stefan's existential unease and of his intuition that he is subject to deterministic forces beyond his control. Stefan is a fictional character, not only created by a writer/director subjected to the demands of Netflix but also controlled, to some extent, by the consumer/user of this interactive narrative, who in turn is implicated in the manipulation of events, narrative meaning, and existential choice selected and organized for the viewer/player via *Bandersnatch*'s interactive narrative structure.

"Striking Vipers" explores a different aspect of gaming, the intersection between subjectivity, identity, and sexuality. It does so through the story of college buddies Danny and Karl, who renew their friendship in mature adult life, reestablishing their bond by playing the X-rated version of their favorite martial arts game "Striking Vipers." Not only do the men become more interested and immersed in the gaming world than in their real-life personal relationships, they also enter into an ambiguous VR fantasy sexual relationship, crossing gender and racial lines via their chosen gaming avatars (family man Danny and playboy Karl, both African-American men, adopting the avatars of a heterosexual "Eurasian" mixed-race martial arts couple). Here the focus of critical attention is the idea of technological prostheses (gaming avatars) becoming subjective supplements that might distort our real-world relationships (the characters' real-world relationships supplanted by hybrid identities enacting their sexual fantasies within a digital world). The "compromise" arrangement the men arrive at with their female partners (limiting their online sexual relationship and incorporating a real-world fantasy element) suggests an apt metaphor for the complex relationship between real-world and digital versions of our social subjectivities.

Another pervasive thematic cluster concerns *toxic social media effects* and *social-political hacking threats*, which together provide the focus for numerous episodes, which again could also be regarded as staging film-philosophical thought experiments. From *Black Mirror*'s first episode, "The National Anthem," to one of the fifth season episodes, "Smithereens" (Hawes 2019), the ubiquity of social media usage and its penetration of personal identity, shaping of subjectivity, distorting of social relations and potentially toxic cultural and political effects are recurring issues across the series. "The National Anthem," set in contemporary London, melds political thriller with contemporary anxieties over cyberterrorism, and the (social) media manipulation of politics and political opinion (see Ungureanu 2015). An unknown "terrorist" kidnaps "the people's Princess" and demands, by way of ransom, that the sitting prime minister perform a degrading sex act (with an animal) on live television. Apart from the recognizable references to contemporary political figures and plausibly realistic forms of (cyber)terrorist threat, the episode examines the toxic intertwining of prurient entertainment, pornographic degradation, shock art, and the manipulation of popular opinion and politics today.

The toxicity of social media–driven "pile-on" culture provides the premise for "Shut Up and Dance," where unknown hackers using toxic ransomware target individuals on morally questionable websites, blackmailing them to perform antisocial acts, including theft and, as it turns out, manslaughter. As with "The National Anthem" and numerous other episodes, "Shut Up and Dance" features a twist ending that plays on audience's sympathetic engagement with the tormented protagonist, who is an unassuming and somewhat bullied young man. Kenny, working as a kitchenhand, inadvertently downloads the malicious software and is forced into a harrowingly stressful sequence of actions culminating in a videoed fight "to the death" with another victim—whose status as victim is thrown into doubt by the revelation that he was caught browsing pedophilic websites. It becomes clear, by the episode's end, that the other individuals targeted by the malware ransom demands were all engaged in morally dubious uses of the Internet, whether for cheating, cyberbullying, trolling, or harassment.

"Nosedive" takes the pervasive influence of social media image curation, of "likes" and of social media "rankings," to its logical conclusion. It imagines a society in which individuals rate each other (on a scale of 1–5) for all of their social interactions, with one's media rating determining not only one's social status but also economic opportunities, career prospects, choice of real estate, travel options, and even membership in the social community. Like other *Black Mirror* episodes, it enacts a slight amplification of contemporary technological possibilities and social practices, magnifying their possibilities and drawing out their ethical implications. It explores what might happen if the "Instagrammatization of everyday life" were to become linked to social status, professional mobility, and economic success. It tells the story of Lacey, who seeks to boost her social rating score (4.2) in order to secure a new apartment;

she consults professionals, curates an online image, and accepts an invitation from a highly rated "influencer" friend to speak at her wedding.

After an altercation with airport staff, where Lacey becomes agitated following the unexplained cancellation of her flight, she is confronted by a security guard who penalizes her for antisocial behavior by deducting a whole 'social credit' point from her profile. After further unfortunate exchanges, Lacey's social rating "nosedives" as she struggles to make her way to the wedding in the cheapest, most outmoded hire car available, which breaks down and can't be recharged (all because of her lowered social rating). Her picaresque, nightmarish journey involves hitching a ride with a busload of sci-fi TV fans and a sobering encounter with a female trucker who opted out of the rating system after her husband died of cancer. Lacey finally makes it to the wedding, late, disheveled, and drunk; delivers a truth-telling rant to the bride and guests; and is arrested for assault. She is imprisoned, where she and a fellow inmate can express their anger and other emotions freely without fear of social punishment.

"Nosedive" offers a compelling critical reflection on social media image curation and self-marketization, which not only threatens to undermine social relationships but also provides the technological and social means for an oppressive and manipulative "social credit system." A similar system, designed to track, monitor, influence, and control its citizens' behavior, currently exists in China (see Zhou and Xiao 2020). *Black Mirror* episodes such as "Nosedive" also *mimic* social media/digital culture's *aesthetic style*: "Nosedive" uses a beguilingly appealing aesthetic style that mirrors or reflects its critical object, an "Instagrammatizable" pastel-colored world of arresting social media images and alluring consumer pleasure—a point missed by some critics (see Murray 2013).

The technological devices that feature in different *Black Mirror* episodes faithfully mimic technological devices that also embody an appealing design (what we might call the "Apple effect"). The episodes deploy temporal compression and narrative ellipsis, coupled with a rapidly sketched, deliberately "thin" characterization, reproducing the rapid tempo of narrative presentation, or even "gaming" style, familiar from contemporary digital media and their accompanying viewing (and playing) practices. In this sense, it adds performative counterpoint to the more familiar moral and social-political critique of the alienating, dehumanizing, or socially exploitative aspects of contemporary digital culture.

This focus on toxic social media effects links up with another thematic cluster, which we could call the dangers of "surveillance/data harvesting culture." The harvesting of data and information concerning consumer choices, preferences, attention, and behavior as a way of influencing and manipulating the population has become a defining feature of what Zuboff (2019) described as "surveillance capitalism". In "Hated in the Nation," one narrative strand dealing with the introduction of "drone" insect swarms to replace extinct bees intersects with another dealing with the phenomenon of online trolling and denunciation culture. The latter takes a deadly turn in a "game of consequences" centered on the viral spread of the #deathto hashtag, which gathers data in order to identify the most popular media pariah of the day. This person, the most hated in the nation, is then targeted by anonymous hacktivists and killed via the weaponized drone bees. The drone bees depend on a vast informational surveillance network that the hacktivists take over and exploit, brutally demonstrating the "real-world" consequences of the vicious manipulation of public opinion made possible by the convergence of social media, news as infotainment, and political opinion management.

In another cluster, a number of episodes explore the *distortion of personal identity* that occurs, thanks to the unbridled adoption of reality augmentation technologies. "Be Right Back" explores the fascinating possibility of constructing a posthumous avatar based on a deceased person's digital footprint. Social media addict Ash is tragically killed in a traffic accident, leaving his pregnant girlfriend Martha in grief. She reluctantly takes up the advice of a friend to try the new avatar technology, which recreates a digital version of her deceased partner that is supposed to help her cope with her loss, but instead becomes a substitute for her grieving. The episode takes this idea a step further by depicting the possibility of a synthetic bioflesh version of the deceased partner being brought to life. The synthetic Ash, who lacks many personality features of the real Ash, shifts from being an uncanny substitute for her dead partner—and one that she cannot bring herself to terminate or kill—to an awkwardly maintained prisoner locked away in Martha's attic and visited weekly by their young daughter.

Many episodes explore the possibilities of *digitizing consciousness*, examining the possible social uses and ethical implications of such technological processing of consciousness. In addition to "The Entire History of You," "Crocodile," and "Playtest," which feature technological means of digitizing consciousness as part of augmented reality technology, there are other episodes that focus on the pernicious uses to which such technologies could be put. One is the idea of a VR form of immortality involving the uploading of a digitized form of artificial consciousness. "San Junipero," one of the rare optimistic episodes in *Black Mirror*, is a romance centered on the idea of uploading consciousness into a virtual format such that deceased people could be visited in a virtual world, spanning different time periods, by friends and relatives who remain behind in the real world.

In the episode, introverted Yorkie meets extroverted Kelly in a bar in the resort town of San Junipero in 1987, and they have a brief fling. Later, Yorkie can no longer find Kelly and follows a suggestion from a stranger that she look for her by returning to a different time, trying unsuccessfully to find her in 1980, and 1996, before finally locating her in 2002. In reality, Yorkie is dying, having spent her life paralyzed after a car accident following a clash with her parents over her coming out as a teenager, and wishes to upload her consciousness into the virtual world of San Junipero. Kelly marries her and authorizes the uploading of Yorkie's artificial consciousness. In failing health herself, Kelly decides to do the same, leaving the memories of her husband and child behind as she is reunited with Yorkie in a virtual afterlife. Much like "Be Right Back," this episode considers the desire for immortality and reunion with the dead that might be made possible via the digitizing of consciousness and construction of artificial avatars of the dead in VR. This idea has recently been taken up in reality, according to a recent Korean television documentary on the recreation of a VR avatar of a mother's deceased daughter (see Hayden 2020).

Taking a broader, more contextual perspective, as the episodes of *Black Mirror* implicitly do, we can cite a number of episodes that deal with the idea of a "control society." The latter refers to a form of modern society that deploys subtle mechanisms of societal control of citizens (rather than overt forms of disciplinary power or mechanisms of punishment), where such control mechanisms (such as extending practices of performance management to all areas of life, "social credit" models of directing and shaping conduct) become internalized and thereby self-regulating. These eliminate the need for more coercive, disciplinary systems of control (Deleuze 1992). Such mechanisms are then harnessed by the broader networks of surveillance and data harvesting that facilitate control in the workplace, schools, and other institutions, tracking consumer choices and behaviors in order to influence citizens' attitudes and behaviors (Zuboff 2019). Episodes such as "Hated in the Nation," "Fifteen Million Merits," "Nosedive," "Men Against Fire" (Verbruggen), "White Bear" (Tibbets 2013), "Crocodile," "Arkangel," and "Smithereens" focus on different aspects of these mechanisms, their capacity to penetrate and shape our subjectivity, and their potentially oppressive social, cultural, economic, and political uses.

This theme links up with the cluster concerning the militarization of everyday life/weaponizing biotechnology/technoterrorism. A number of episodes show how one of the manifestations of this system of informational-societal control involves "militarizing" aspects of everyday life, harnessing the power of information data harvesting via social media platforms and other forms of ubiquitous online activity. This is coupled with the disturbing social manifestations of aggression, resentment, anger, and voyeurism familiar from online trolling and the desensitizing effects of openly streamed images of violence coexisting with more banal forms of streamed infotainment. As mentioned, "Shut Up and Dance" explores this tendency within the context of hacking and manipulating online activity, whereas "White Bear" stages the spectacle of punishment in the form of a televised survivor Reality TV "game" perpetrated on a woman who wakes up one morning in an unfamiliar room without any memories of how she got there (see Sola and Martínez-Lucen 2016). Her television screen displays a mysterious symbol or glyph (resembling an inverted Y, but also a symbol of binary code, which reappears in *Black Mirror: Bandersnatch*). She heads outside into the deserted streets, noticing that she is being filmed by anonymous neighbors and passersby, who refuse to reply to any of her questions. She quickly realizes that she is in imminent danger from violent masked and armed attackers ("the hunters") who suddenly appear in a vehicle and chase her brandishing weapons. She takes shelter in a shop and meets a woman, Jem, who explains that the passersby have been affected by the televised glyph, which has turned them into passive voyeurs; the women's task is therefore to attack and neutralize a local transmission station ("White Bear") in order to knockout the toxic signal.

As they attempt to flee the hunters, the woman and Jem are then picked up by a man in a van who is also unaffected by the signal, but turns out to be a sadistic hunter; he drives them to a forest and attempts to torture them before being shot by Jem. The woman and Jem then escape, find the White Bear transmitter site, and attempt to destroy it before being confronted by two other hunters. As the tense, grueling fight for survival concludes (with the hunters' shotgun turning out to be fake), the walls fall away to reveal a stage set and live audience: the woman has been unwittingly participating in a staged "survival game," with all participants played by actors. More shockingly, it turns out that the woman, who is called Victoria Skillane, undergoes this ordeal, repeated daily, as a punishment for her role (with her partner) in the kidnapping and murder of a young girl. Spectators are placed in the same disturbing position of the terrified and tormented woman, fighting for survival against unknown enemies and trying to resolve the mystery of "White Bear" and accomplish the difficult task that she is called upon to perform (recalling the hacking/ransom scenario in "Shut Up and Dance"). The revelation that what we have been watching was actually a staged punishment for a woman we initially assume to be an innocent victim of inexplicable assailants is deeply disorienting and morally troubling. The convergence of gaming and surveillance culture, punishment staged as social spectacle, harnessing current practices of consuming images of violence and suffering online, offers a confronting commentary on the convergence of punishment, media manipulation, social passivity, and suffering as entertainment in our highly mediatized "society of control."

Finally, it is worth noting that not all episodes of *Black Mirror* focus on the "dark side" of modern technology. Some also explicitly examine the ethical possibilities of such technologies in addition to exploring the ethical implications of the manner in which digital and social media technologies have pervaded everyday life. Moreover, there are a number of episodes that focus on a thematic cluster that we could call the "ethics of VR/AI entities," extrapolating from some of the most recent technological developments and possibilities and exploring the ethical questions raised by such technologies ("White Christmas," "Playtest," "Black Museum," "USS Callister," "Striking Vipers," "Rachel, Jack and Ashley Too"). What kind of ethical issues arise from the emergence of VR/AI entities that may soon have levels of interactivity, self-directed decision-making, functional autonomy, even artificial consciousness to rival those of human beings? What are the ethics pertaining to the treatment of VR/AI entities themselves? Should they acquire levels of AI sufficient to warrant recognition as conscious entities in their own right? The idea of AI entities developing consciousness—explored in films such as *A.I.* (Spielberg 2001), *Her* (Jonze 2014), and *Ex Machina* (Garland 2014)—

is extended in *Black Mirror* to more domestic digital technologies (Alexa-style domestic "helpers," VR gaming avatars, synthetic digitized AI entities that offer simulacra of deceased individuals, etc.), typically presented, again, via the use of compelling televisual thought experiments.

"Black Museum" tells the story of Nish, who seemingly wanders on a whim into a decrepit museum of curio technologies and talks with the owner Rolo, who tells the stories behind the various technological curiosities on display (some of which refer to other *Black Mirror* episodes). In the museum's showcase attraction, a holographic image of the consciousness of convicted murderer Clayton Leigh, experiencing extreme pain while being executed in the electric chair, is exhibited as a VR experience, inviting visitors to enjoy the spectacle of inflicting the fatal punishment. Nish reveals that she is the daughter of Leigh, who was wrongly convicted and executed, and has come to take her revenge. After poisoning Rolo, she transfers his consciousness into Clayton Leigh's holographic image, forcing Rolo to undergo the torture of Leigh's last minutes before death, an experience that destroys both Leigh and Rolo's digital copies. Nish procures a souvenir key ring depicting Rolo's agony, burns down the museum, and leaves with her mother (whose consciousness also resides within Nish), saying that her father would have been proud of her.

The ethics of capital punishment, institutionalized racism, the commodification of suffering as consumable spectacle, and the ethics of VR/AI entities are all probed and questioned here in the guise of a novel revenge thriller. Such themes are also explored, however, in episodes using disparate genres, from satirical forms of sci-fi drama (such as "USS Callister") to domestic/teen drama ("Rachel, Jack and Ashley Too"). "Black Museum," "San Junipero," "Rachael, Jack, and Ashley Too," and "Smithereens," all *explore ambiguous forms of technological-ethical resistance*, which remain important, if fragile and uncertain, in the face of the seemingly inexorable convergence of technological, digital, and social-political forces defining contemporary societies of control.

Conclusion: *Black Mirror* as Televisual Philosophy

Defenders of the "film as philosophy" thesis—the idea that cinema not only has a pedagogical value but can also make significant contributions to philosophical understanding via cinematic means—have often pointed to narrative "thought experiments" as one way of demonstrating the philosophical potential of cinema. Wartenberg (2007), for example, argues that not only do thought experiments play a significant role in philosophy (from Plato's ring of Gyges, Descartes' "evil demon," to Foot's "trolley problem") but many films can be taken as staging complex thought experiments dealing with recognized philosophical problems (such as our knowledge of reality versus appearances, puzzles of personal identity, the question of free will versus determinism, or competing accounts of moral judgment). Standard philosophical thought experiments are abbreviated, schematic, and stylized in order to reduce variables and to render particular features of a situation as more salient. As many philosophers have argued, however, literary fiction provides complex, nuanced, and realistic kinds of thought experiments (Elgin 2014; Johnson 2016). As Mark Johnson observes: "It is the narrative depth, complexity, existential validity of literary fictions that situates moral perception appraisal in contexts that are psychologically more valid than those we typically encounter in most moral philosophy" (2016: 365).

With its short-form episodic narrative format, elliptical presentation of character, well-defined articulation of narrative situation, and dramatic unfolding of a key idea or concept, *Black Mirror* offers an ideal platform for the staging of televisual thought experiments. Expressed differently, *Black Mirror* episodes stage *performative audiovisual critiques* of the ethical implications of digital media culture via televisual thought experiments that are immersive and reflexive, critical and satirical, experiential and speculative. It is clear too that *Black Mirror* episodes deal with the question of technology, probing our digital technological engagement with the world. They explore the possibilities, both positive and negative, afforded by "implantable" AR technology and the prospect of a "digitization of experience" (the pervasive use of "consciousness tracking" devices, the digitizing of perception and memory). They also question and reflect upon the ethical and ideological-political implications of these ways of transforming both individual consciousness and social relationships more generally via digital technology, social media, and the conjunction of data/information harvesting and internalized forms of social control.

At the same time, *Black Mirror* episodes *self-critically reflect* upon their own status as products of the televisual medium and the inevitable complicity of the viewers/producers of such critiques of audiovisual culture. This is what we might call, extending the idea of film as philosophy (Mulhall), "television in the condition of philosophy": reflecting upon their status as audiovisual works, their capacity for critique, and their implication within the very systems of digital technological control in question. Finally, these works of televisual speculative fiction are seductive: they enact an *aesthetic mimicry* of the sensuous allure of digital social media as part of their performative critique of the pernicious social effects of such media. *Black Mirror* thus offers performative, critical, and reflexive modes of critique, using the very medium that it is scrutinizing. In this respect, it offers not so much a traditional critique of modern technology but more a televisual disclosure of our technological mode of "being-in-the-world"—a dark digital screen reflecting our ambivalently mediatized selves within our technologically manipulated reality.

References

Bathurst, Otto. (2011), "The National Anthem," *Black Mirror*, Channel 4. Season 1, Episode 1, Broadcast December 4, 2011.
Brooker, Charlie. *Newswipe*. (2009–2010), BBC Four. [TV Series].
Brooker, Charlie. *How TV Ruined Your Life* (2011), BBC Two [TV Series].
Brooker, Charlie. (2011–19), *Black Mirror*, Channel 4 and Netflix [TV Series].
Circucci, A. M. and Vacker, B. (2018), "Introduction," in A. M. Circucci and B. Vacker (eds), *Black Mirror and Critical Media Theory*, Lanham, MA: Lexington Books.
Chase, David. *The Sopranos* (1999–2007), HBO [TV Series].
Deleuze, G. (1992), "Postscript on the Societies of Control," October 59: 3–7.
Demange, Yann. (2008), *Dead Set*. E4, Broadcast October 27–31, 2008. [TV Series].
Elgin, C. Z. (2014), "Fiction as Thought Experiment," *Perspectives on Science* 22 (2): 221–41.
Elsaesser, T. (2009), "The Mind-Game Film," in W. Buckland (ed.), *Puzzle Films: Complex Storytelling in Contemporary Cinema*, 13–41, Chichester: Wiley-Blackwell.
Foster, Jodie. (2017), "Arkangel," *Black Mirror*, Netflix. Season 4, Episode 2. Release Date December 29, 2017. [TV Series].
Garland, Alex. (2014), *Ex Machina*, Universal Pictures. [Film].
Gilligan, Vince. *Breaking Bad* (2008–2013), AMC [TV Series].
Harris, Owen. (2013), "Be Right Back," *Black Mirror*, Channel 4. Season 2, Episode 1, Broadcast February 11, 2013. [TV Series].

Harris, Owen. (2016), "San Junipero," *Black Mirror*, Netflix. Season 3, Episode 4. Release Date October 21, 2016. [TV Series].

Harris, Owen. (2019), "Striking Vipers," *Black Mirror*, Netflix. Season 5, Episode 1. Release Date June 5, 2019. [TV Series].

Harvey, G. (2016), "The Speculative Dread of Black Mirror," *The New Yorker* (28 November): https://www.newyorker.com/magazine/2016/11/28/the-speculative-dread-of-black-mirror Accessed June 18, 2019.

Hawes, James. (2016), "Hated in the Nation," *Black Mirror*, Netflix. Season 3, Episode 6. Release Date October 21, 2016. [TV Series].

Hawes, James. (2019), "Smithereens," *Black Mirror*, Netflix. Season 5, Episode 2. Release Date June 5, 2019. [TV Series].

Hayden, S. (2020), "Mother Meets Recreation of her Deceased Child in VR," *Road to VR* (7 February): https://www.roadtovr.com/mother-meets-recreation-of-deceased-child-in-vr/?fbclid=IwAR0zXE0BW0FyPIeTeE3q2XIaCGs1cYub7QJxqTYdyHbA4WTZH1--KwSFrzA. Accessed February 7, 2020.

Haynes, Toby. (2017), "USS Callister," *Black Mirror*, Netflix. Season 4, Episode 1. December 29, 2017.

Hillcoat, John. (2017), "Crocodile," *Black Mirror*, Netflix. Season 4, Episode 3. Release Date December 29, 2017. [TV Series].

Houser, K. (2020), "AOC Warns that Facial Recognition Technology is Real Life 'Black Mirror,'" *Futurism* (16 January): https://futurism.com/the-byte/aoc-warns-facial-recognition-real-life-black-mirror. Accessed January 20, 2020.

Johnson, M. (2016), "Moral Imagination," in A. Kind (ed.), *The Routledge Handbook of Philosophy of Imagination*, 355–67. London and New York: Routledge.

Jonze, Spike. (2013), *Her*, Warner Bros. [Film]

Lyn, Euros. (2011), "Fifteen Million Merits," *Black Mirror*, Channel 4. Season 1, Episode 2, Broadcast December 11, 2011. [TV Series].

Martin, A. (2018), "Cautionary Reflections: Looking into *Black Mirror*," *Screen Education* 90 (September): 16–23.

McCarthy, Colm. (2017), "Black Museum". *Black Mirror*, Netflix. Season 4, Episode 6. Release Date December 29, 2017. [TV Series].

Mulhall, S. (2008), *On Film, Second Edition*, London and New York: Routledge.

Murray, T. (2013), "Black Mirror Reflections," *Philosophy Now* 97 (July/August): https://philosophynow.org/issues/97/Black_Mirror_Reflections. Accessed June 4, 2019.

Morris, Chris and Brooker, Charlie. *Nathan Barley*. (2005), Channel 4. [TV Series].

Sewitsky, Anne. (2019), "Rachel, Jack and Ashley Too," *Black Mirror*, Netflix. Season 5, Episode 3. Release Date June 5, 2019. [TV Series].

Simon, David. *The Wire* (2002–2008), HBO [TV Series].

Sinnerbrink, R. (2011), *New Philosophies of Film: Thinking Images*, London and New York: Continuum/Bloomsbury Academic.

Sinnerbrink, R. (2014), "Film-Philosophy," in E. Branigan and W. Buckland (eds), *The Routledge Encyclopedia of Film Theory*, 207–13, London and New York: Routledge.

Slade, David. (2016), "Metalhead'. *Black Mirror*, Netflix. Season 4, Episode 5. Release Date December 29, 2017. [TV Series].

Slade, David. (2018), *Black Mirror: Bandersnatch*, Netflix. [Film].

Smuts, A. (2009), "In Defence of a Bold Thesis," *Journal of Aesthetics and Art Criticism* 67 (4) (Fall): 409–20.

Sola, J. C. and Martínez-Lucen, J. (2016), "Screen technologies and the imaginary of punishment: A reading of *Black Mirror*'s 'White Bear," *Empedocles: European Journal for the Philosophy of Communication* 7 (1): 3–22.

Spielberg, Steven. (2001), *A.I.*, Warner Bros. [Film].

Tibbets, Carl. (2013), "White Bear," *Black Mirror*, Channel 4. Season 2, Episode 2, Broadcast February 18, 2013. [TV Series].

Tibbetts, Carl. (2014), "White Christmas," *Black Mirror*, Channel 4. Christmas Special. Broadcast December 16, 2014. [TV Series].

Trachtenberg, Dan. (2016), "Playtest," *Black Mirror*, Netflix. Season 3, Episode 2. Release Date October 21, 2016. [TV Series].

Ungureanu, C. (2015), "Aestheticization of Politics and Ambivalence of Self-Sacrifice in Charlie Brooker's The National Anthem," *Journal of European Studies* 45 (1): 21–30.

Van Patten, Tim. (2017), "Hang the DJ," *Black Mirror*, Netflix. Season 4, Episode 4. Release Date December 29, 2017. [TV Series].

Verbruggen, Jakob. (2016), "Men Against Fire," *Black Mirror*, Netflix. Season 3, Episode 5. Release Date October 21, 2016. [TV Series].

Wartenberg, T. A. (2007), *Thinking on Screen: Film as Philosophy*, New York and London: Routledge.

Watkins, James. (2016), "Shut Up and Dance," *Black Mirror*, Netflix. Season 3, Episode 3. Release Date October 21, 2016. [TV Series].

Welsh, Brian. (2011), "The Entire History of You," *Black Mirror*, Channel 4. Season 1, Episode 3. Broadcast December 18, 2011. [TV Series].

Willimon, Beau. *House of Cards* (2013–2018), Netflix [TV Series].

Wright, Joe. (2016), "Nosedive," *Black Mirror*, Netflix. Season 3, Episode 1. Release Date October 21, 2016. [TV Series].

Zhou, C. and B. Xiao. (2020), "China's Social Credit System is Pegged to be Fully Operational by 2020—But What Will It Look Like?' *ABC News* Online (2 January): https://www.abc.net.au/news/2020-01-02/china-social-credit-system-operational-by-2020/11764740. Accessed January 10, 2020.

Zuboff, S. (2019), *The Age of Surveillance Capitalism: The Fight for a Human Nature at the New Frontier of Power*. London: Profile Books.

2

Black Mirror as Philosophizing About Immortality, Technology, and Human Nature

Lorraine K.C. Yeung and Kong-Ngai Pei

The *Black Mirror* episode "San Junipero" (Harris 2016) considers the possibility of technology's triumph over human mortality. By uploading their minds to the virtual world known as San Junipero, the two protagonists—Kelly, a terminally ill, widowed elderly woman, and the quadriplegic Yorkie, who has spent over forty years in bed attached to life-sustaining tubes—can be rid of the bondage of their physical bodies and live forever in simulated reality.

Unlike other episodes in the *Black Mirror* series, some critics find "San Junipero" uplifting. While showing awareness of the sometimes-frightening consequences of the technologies depicted in *Black Mirror*, Laura T. Di Summa argues that *Black Mirror* is not merely a portrait of a dystopia, instancing the mind-uploading technology of this episode "as a clearly positive take on the potentials of technology" (2019: 110). It allows Kelly and Yorkie to live a second life after their bodily death. The executive producer Annabel Jones, however, remarks that although the ending of "San Junipero" is positively upbeat, "it's not exactly a happy ever after. It's more about being happy for now, and seeing how this goes" (2018: 190). It suggests what might have been downplayed, if not missed, in the positive reading of the episode: Kelly and Yorkie do not merely live a second life in San Junipero—they live immortally.

Why does immortality cast a shadow on the upbeat ending of "San Junipero"? Wouldn't it be a dream come true for Dmitry Itskov and Ray Kurzweil? Kelly's emotional speech to Yorkie provides a clue: "You want to spend forever somewhere nothing matters? End up like Wes[ley]; all those ... lost fucks at the Quagmire, trying anything just to feel something?" Interestingly, Kelly's speech is reminiscent of many fictional stories in which immortal life goes sour (e.g., Jonathan Swift's *Gulliver's Travels*, Jorge Luis Borges' "The Immortal," Mary Shelley's *The Mortal Immortal*, and Anne Rice's *Interview with the Vampire*), as well as various philosophical arguments saying that immortality is tedious. Adopting Stephen Mulhall's "film as philosophizing" thesis (2008), this chapter shows how the *Black Mirror* series contributes to philosophical debates over immortality and mind-uploading technology. In particular, "San Junipero" provides a thought experiment that enriches current philosophical reflection on the desirability of immortality. Inspired by other episodes in the series—namely, "White Christmas" (Tibbets 2014), "Black Museum" (McCarthy 2017), and "USS Callister" (Haynes 2017)—we use maximin decision-making to construct a dilemma against choosing immortality via mind-uploading technology. In doing so, we reveal the gloomy view of the technology implicit in the *Black Mirror* universe.

Stipulations

The philosophical debate over the desirability of immortality has involved different notions and conditions of immortality (see Bruckner 2012, Fischer 2013, Benatar 2017). Fortunately, "San Junipero" lays down most of the stipulations necessary for a philosophical reflection of the immortality in question—that is, what futurists call "digital immortality" or "cyber immortality." The locals in San Junipero live in a disembodied state as a result of uploading their consciousness to a virtual world. However, they do not possess "true immortality" in which "one cannot die from any cause whatsoever" (Benatar 2017: 148). At best, their immortality is one in which they live as long as the computer that runs the simulated reality functions properly in the real universe. The locals will not experience aging, as they are reembodied in the simulated body of their younger selves, thus retaining youth and vigor. They inhabit a world filled with "visitors" who occasionally connect to San Junipero as well as those who "pass over" to San Junipero permanently. However, it remains unclear if this is a reversible or punctuated immortality. "Punctuated immortality" is one in which the immortal can opt out of immortality, while "irreversible immortality" is one in which the immortal cannot opt out (Bruckner 2012: 626). Although Yorkie remarks to Kelly that "forever" means "however long you want . . . you can remove yourself like that [click fingers]," how it is technically possible for the locals to delete themselves remains untold.

The Philosophical Arguments Underlying Kelly's Big Speech

Many contemporary philosophers hold a grim view of immortality, among which Bernard Williams' boredom argument (1993: 71–92) is arguably the most prominent. Williams' argument is based on his conception of "categorical desire." For any categorical desire X, if I have X, then I have a reason to live on and resist death. Take, for example, a Jewish writer who, despite the hardships she experiences in a Nazi concentration camp, strives to survive and refuses to commit suicide because she still has an unfulfilled desire—to complete her manuscript on a long-standing writing project. This desire suffices to propel her forward, resolving her doubts surrounding the choice to commit suicide; in other words, it is a categorical desire. Williams distinguishes "categorical desires" from "contingent desires." A contingent desire is one that I desire on the condition that I am to live on. It does not give reason for me to live on and to resist death; it relies on the fact that I live on. If the aforementioned Jewish writer lives on, she may desire better nourishment and freedom from confinement. These are contingent desires conditioned on the fact that she lives on.

To Williams, categorical desires offer a solution to the Lucretian puzzle rejecting the badness of death: death is a misfortune because it frustrates one's categorical desires. Categorical desires also matter ethically. Such desires define an agent's character and are necessary for happiness. A life without or alienated from one's categorical desires is devoid of subjective integrity and meaning.

Williams' argument runs thus: if immortals retain their characters, as defined by sets of categorical desires, then given infinite time, all their categorical desires will be fulfilled and thus exhausted. The outright absence of categorical desires results in a profound boredom that is "not just a tiresome effect, but a reaction almost perceptual in character to the poverty of one's relation to the environment" (Williams 1993: 87). Therefore, if immortals retain their characters, then they will suffer from profound boredom. Williams illustrates this point with the fictional character EM, who has lived for 300 years at the age of forty-two. Her problem is "a boredom connected with the fact everything that could happen and make sense to one particular human being of 42" and "of certain character" "had already happened to her." Therefore, "she must be . . . detached and withdrawn" (Williams 1993: 82). Put differently, the longer an individual lives, "the less place there is for categorical desire to keep him going, and to resist the desire for death" (Williams 1993: 83).

Williams notes that there are ways for immortals to elude the exhaustion of categorical desires. To assess their worthiness, he adds two conditions necessary for immortality to "meet the basic anti-Lucretian hope for continuing life" (Williams 1993: 83). The first, dubbed the "identity condition," is that "it should be clearly *me* who lives forever" (Williams 1993: 83). The second is called "the attractiveness condition," meaning that the immortal's future life is adequately related to their present categorical desires. After all, it is the categorical desires that propel one forward.

To elude the exhaustion of categorical desires, one might suggest that immortals can survive "by means of an indefinite series of lives" defined by distinct sets of categorical desires. But Williams remarks that this is, somewhat like reincarnation, no different from "a rebirth and a new birth" (1993: 84). As such, there is no clear, continuous identity that lives forever, and so such a life does not satisfy the identity condition. And even if immortals retained the continuity necessary to minimally satisfy the identity condition—living a "series of psychologically disjointed lives" characterized by ever-changing categorical desires—it is not clear if such a life is attractive enough. Imagine that the Jewish writer is deciding whether to live immortally. If in her unending life she will gradually evolve in a way that writing ceases to be her categorical desire, then she fails to retain her subjective integrity. This prospect is not promising. Even if she currently has numerous categorical desires that are individually sufficient for propelling her forward, given infinite time, they will be exhausted and hence she will experience profound boredom. If she lives the "indefinite series of lives" or the "series of psychologically disjointed lives," then her existence does not meet either the identity condition or the attractiveness condition. The trilemma concludes that immortality is undesirable.

One may wonder if Williams' threshold for a life to be worth continuing is too high. Indeed, some people do not have any categorical desires but eagerly look forward to the satisfaction of their contingent desires. Rosati (2013: 361) raises a similar point. Consider Yorkie's decision to pass over to San Junipero.

This decision need not rest on categorical desires; her realization that a life in San Junipero is preferable to her prior irreversible quadriplegic condition suffices. She also happily looks forward to what San Junipero can offer her given that she lives on. It sounds too demanding to say that her life is not worth continuing.

What if we lower the threshold? Shelly Kagan envisions that immortals can fill their endless days with a mixture of enjoyable activities that do not necessarily stem from categorical desires: eating, doing crossword puzzles, meeting friends, traveling, and so on (2012: 240). John Fischer argues that repeatable pleasures, including "the pleasure of sex, of eating fine meals and drinking fine wines, of listening to beautiful music, of seeing great art, and so forth," when enjoyed at intervals, is likely to stave off boredom (1994: 263). As such, he suggests that immortality is not as bad as Williams thinks. Their descriptions of an immortal life are similar to the one experienced by the locals in San Junipero. They can repeatedly enjoy the pleasures of sex, driving, music, clubbing, video games, and movies. This is especially so for Yorkie, for whom the simple joy of feeling the warmth of the sun and the sensation of walking on the beach are already immensely satisfying.

However, Kagan deems that an immortal life filled with a mixture of enjoyable activities is not endurable. The problem is, given infinite time, things will not feel "new in a way that can still engage you afresh." Yorkie would eventually reach the point where she feels like "there's really nothing new under the sun" (Kagan 2012: 240–3). A possible retort is that perhaps some people would not be easily bored with life, or even would actively want to live forever and enjoy an eternal existence. Kagan considers the possibility that, by giving the immortals a pleasure-making machine that guarantees intense bursts of pleasure via electrode stimulation, they would enjoy eternal existence. A comparable idea in "San Junipero" is the Quagmire, where inhabitants can enjoy intense pleasures from a hyperstimulating club that houses orgy parties, alcohol and other drugs, sadomasochism, and violence.

However, Kagan rejects this option altogether. For one thing, increasing familiarity with the pleasures depletes their value. Given unlimited time, one will eventually be bored with the repeatable pleasures, no matter how one spaces them out and however diversified and intense they are. For another, it is not likely that a human being who can engage in self-reflection would enjoy such an existence for eternity. Sooner or later, immortals will be troubled with the question, "Is this all that there is to life?" (Kagan 2012: 242). Perhaps, in order to continue enjoying a pleasurable existence, immortals could remove their ability to self-reflect. Even so, Kagan deems that such a life is unattractive. It reminds him of rats in a behavioral psychologist's electrode experiment. By spending their lives pressing a lever that emits electric shocks that stimulate the pleasure center of their brains, they are forever caught up in the moment. The immortals would be, in Kelly's words, "those lost fucks at the Quagmire, trying anything just to feel something."

According to the boredom arguments, immortals will eventually run out of desires that can keep them going or engage them afresh. Worse still, there are other reasons for immortality to be motivationally devastating. It has been argued that immortality depletes the weight, significance, value, and urgency of many of our life decisions and actions that fuel our motivation. Samuel Scheffler suggests that assignments of human value are "a response to the limits of time"; without "temporal scarcity," it becomes difficult to see how there could be a place for human values (2013: 99). Martha Nussbaum likewise remarks that "the intensity and dedication with which very many human activities are pursued cannot be explained without reference to the awareness that our opportunities are finite, that we cannot choose those activities indefinitely many times" (1994: 229). Inspired by Jorge Luis Borges' short story "The Immortal," Aaron Smuts argues that immortality would bring with it a loss of significance (2011: 134–40). For example, achievements of which we are proud as mortals would lose their significance in immortality. This is because immortals would know that they "could achieve almost anything by sheer perseverance" and that success in one project does not incur an opportunity cost of giving up other projects, for they can always return to them later. As a result, any achievements "would likely either be only mildly satisfying and boring or the hollow victory of diligence" (Smuts 2011: 139). Translating this point into Williams' language, this means that any fulfillment of desires, be they categorical or contingent desires, would leave immortals asking themselves, "So what?" Eventually, immortals would not care about anything; their lives would be imparted with "an unbearable lightness of existence" (Smuts 2011: 139). San Junipero further provides favorable conditions for this unbearable lightness. There Yorkie can get her wedding dress just by thinking about it, and Kelly can smash a mirror and even crash her car without significant repercussions. So, Kelly is right: San Junipero is a place where "nothing matters."

The foregoing predicament seems to be premised on the condition of irreversible immortality. But what about a punctuated immortality, in which immortal individuals can choose to opt out? We believe that there are some complications specific to the case of San Junipero. As already noted, how it is technically possible for the locals to delete themselves remains untold. Even if we grant that the locals can delete themselves voluntarily, San Junipero would make the choice of eliminating oneself far more difficult than Yorkie thinks. Unlike life on earth, where a continuous existence could be cost-incurring and toilsome, San Junipero is heavenlike: residents are free of risk and responsibility, and living requires little effort. Even if one becomes profoundly bored with this heaven, easy access to unlimited stimulation would make one feel like there might be something to hold onto for tomorrow, however illusionary and brittle it is, or that it is not utterly unmanageable to pass a few more moments in Tucker's or the Quagmire. Consider Wesley. He is bored with the locals of San Junipero and says that "they're like dead people." Occasionally meeting a truly lively visitor like Kelly restores him from this mind-numbing existence, giving him hope for a romance that does not make him feel like he is "in the retirement home." When things do not work out, he simply returns to the Quagmire to get drunk. A life like this might be tedious, but it is too effortless and convenient to be given up. It approximates a "chicken rib"—a metaphor used in a Chinese saying to refer to something tasteless that one is nevertheless reluctant to throw away.

But It Is Digital Immortality We Are Talking About

Charlie Brooker remarks that "across season three, film by film, we go, 'Bittersweet, nasty, bloody nasty, happy . . . and then nasty, nasty.'" "San Junipero," as the fourth episode in Season 3, is intended to be "happy" (Brooker, Jones, and Arnopp 2018: 190). As a tribute to "San Junipero," in this section our philosophical reflection turns from the "bloody nasty" to the "happy." Some critics have noted that the arguments against immortality seem to rest on several assumptions (see Temkin 2008, Bruckner 2012, Scheffler 2013, Benatar 2017, and Felder 2018). First, there is the assumption that an immortal would be, in Williams' words, "living as an embodied person in the world *rather as it is*" (1993: 81); second, their memories accumulate indefinitely; and third, they would maintain the psychology of mortals. However, as Benatar remarks, "given the conglomeration of far-fetched hypotheticals we are considering," these assumptions can be justifiably discarded (2017: 155). With this in mind, we put forward two technological solutions to rescue the locals in San Junipero from the problems of immortality discussed in the previous section.

In response to the second assumption, some critics advance what is called "the forgetting argument" to solve the problem of boredom. Donald Bruckner argues that our memory naturally decays (2012). We lose skills and forget facts and even what experiences were like. Memory decay would help mitigate the problem of boredom, rendering repetitive experiences fresh again. If there are cases in which Williams' identity condition is not satisfied, then so be it. After all, such a life is still worthwhile "from the perspective of the person living it" (Bruckner 2012: 640). Kagan likewise ponders a special kind of amnesia that allows immortals to forget what they were doing, or who they were, say, 200 years ago (2012). But he dismisses it, for it is not likely to meet the identity condition and the attractiveness condition. Ryan Felder has recently proposed the solution of "partial forgetting" to meet the two conditions (2018). In "partial forgetting," "certain important memories stay available to the immortal person throughout the entirety of their lives," and she just loses memories "that are non-essential to her self-conception" (Felder 2018: 847). Recall the Jewish writer. Partial forgetting means that she would lack many specific memories of things she has written, but she would remember that she has always been a writer. As such, she retains her character and personal integrity and at the same time is eternally refreshed with respect to the experience of writing every time she returns to the task.

Or we can consider a more dramatic form of partial forgetting adopted in the television series *The Good Place* (2016–20). There the immortal demon Michael has to trick the protagonists Eleanor, Chidi, Tahini, and Jason into believing that they have been sent to the heavenlike "Good Place" after their earthly death. Every time the group sees through Michael's trick, Michael erases their memories of the Good Place, then reboots them, making them feel like they are waking up in the afterlife for the first time. Each time they are awakened, the four get to know each other again as if they were meeting new people, and they are put into new scenarios in which they have different roles. Their lives in the Good Place always remain fresh to them. In this form of partial forgetting, the memories that are lost are just those they have acquired after they have woken up in the Good Place. This allows the protagonists to retain the characters and memories of their earthly life. The philosophy professor, Chidi, for example, completely preserves his character as a die-hard Kantian and his seemingly categorical desire to do philosophy. Also, he can indeed live as a philosopher in the Good Place. Putting aside Michael's trick, Chidi's immortal afterlife arguably satisfies Williams' two conditions. Regardless of what form it takes, then, partial forgetting might be a saving grace for the locals of San Junipero.

Furthermore, in cases where immortals prefer to retain all their memories, they can look to technological interventions to change their psychology. In his paper "Qualia Surfing," Richard Loosemore brings up the possibility for the uploads to change their motivation system so that they will take pleasure in a wider range of simulated experiences than their characters allow (2014: 231-9). Thrill seekers can modify their motivation system to make gardening feel enjoyable rather than boring. To adapt this solution to meet Williams' two conditions, let us imagine this psychological tweaking is done in a way that it makes, say, the Jewish writer find writing to be a deeply rewarding activity for all eternity. Even though she has unlimited time at her disposal, she treasures every opportunity to write and sincerely cares about her undertakings. Going further, if she resided in San Junipero, she may even delegate the visitors to help her to publish her books in the physical world. Knowing that her works could have an impact beyond the virtual world would provide a "natural" boost to her motivation to write. Similar modifications can be devised to make Yorkie and Kelly be forever newly in love, while Wesley could enthusiastically pursue new romances forever.

We are aware that the solutions just considered open up some potential worries. The intervention on memory, especially the one adopted in *The Good Place*, may remind some of Nietzsche's idea of "eternal recurrence" (though with some crucial differences). In evaluating another similar forgetting argument, Stephen Hicks cautions that knowing that what one enjoys now seemingly for the first time might have happened millions of times before would limit its worth (1992). Moreover, the solutions may sound more like cheats. Larry Temkin concedes that he cannot rule out the possibility of developing "freshness, rejuvenation, or selective memory pills or enhancements" to solve the problems of immortality (2008). But he has some worries "akin to Robert Nozick's worries about the experience machine": it is not clear if the altered mind is still "in contact with reality" (Temkin 2008: 204). We do not have space for fully worked out responses to these worries. However, when we weigh it against the alternative of death as annihilation, is this modified digital immortality clearly an unworthy choice? The answer does not seem to be a straightforward "no." That being said, we do have some grave worries that sufficiently outweigh the promises of mind-uploading technology. In the following we argue that it is irrational or immoral to upload a digital mind. Establishing this claim, however, requires us to go deeper into the very idea of mind uploading.

An Argument Against Digital Immortality

Basically, mind uploading is the process of attempting to transfer one's conscious self from one's biological brain to a physical computational device, say a computer (in the *Black Mirror* series, such devices are called "cookies"). This process can be done in various ways. One way to do it may be called "instant mind uploading" in which your brain is stabilized and its structure is studied layer by layer in detail. The scanning device records the configuration of neurons and synapses of each layer, along with their interconnections. Once this is done, all the recorded information of the neural patterns and dynamics is implemented and then activated in a computer.

If you decide to undergo instant mind uploading, there are two options available to you. One is non-destructive mind uploading, where you can press the "upload" button while at the same time keeping your biological brain intact. As a result, you will be duplicated: both your biological original and your upload will believe that they are you. The other is destructive mind uploading that destroys your brain simultaneously with the upload being activated in the computer. Choosing this option will result in only one conscious being claiming to be you.

There are two prominent presuppositions underlying mind-uploading technology. The first is the "functional theory of consciousness," according to which conscious experiences are merely grounded in certain functional organizations or networks, independent of what physical bases these networks are implemented in. Consequently, provided that a system realizes the right kind of functional organizations, even if the system is silicon-based rather than carbon-based, it can also be fully conscious. The second presupposition is the "principle of organizational invariance," which holds that "given any system that has conscious experiences, then any system that has the same fine-grained functional organization will have qualitatively identical experiences" (Chalmers 1996: 249).

As previously mentioned, the ultimate goal of mind uploading is to transfer a conscious self from a biological brain to another physical system. However, as David Chalmers rightly points out, "personal identity is not an organizational invariant": even if the upload is fully conscious and has the same conscious contents as the original brain, this does not entail that the upload and the original brain are the same person with the same conscious self (2014: 108). If Derek Parfit's psychological theory is right, according to which a person at a later time ($t2$) is identical to a person at an earlier time ($t1$) if and only if there is exactly one person at $t2$ who shares the same neural patterns as the person at $t1$, then in the case of destructive uploading, the original mind can survive in the new hardware. But in the case of non-destructive uploading, the original mind will die simultaneously with two conscious individuals possessing her personalities and false memories being emerged. If personal identity is essentially manifested in biological networks (despite conscious experiences being functional phenomena), then whichever form of uploading one chooses, the person in the cookie is one's mind-clone. And if Robert Nozick's "closest continuer" theory of personal identity is correct (1981), then the upload resulting from non-destructive uploading is only the mind-clone of the original person, since compared with the intact biological original (whose brain and mind are not destroyed), the upload is just perfectly like the original with respect to the functional organizations. As a result, the biological person after uploading remains the closest continuer of the original. According to this theory, the upload will be the original person only in destructive uploading, since in this situation the biological original is killed and so the closest continuer is the upload.

Although the problem of personal identity has long been debated, there is still no consensus as to what theory is correct. In the absence of an adequate theory, it remains possible that in some situations (destructive or non-destructive uploading), the person who awakens in the cookie is not you but your replica, a new conscious being possessing all your personal traits and harboring false memories. We will return to a situation like this shortly.

Meanwhile, let us assume, as "San Junipero" seemingly does, that destructive mind uploading preserves personal identity. If this is the case, should we choose to upload? Some may be quick to say "yes." For, if we refuse to upload, we will soon biologically die; all goods we value in our earthly lives will then vanish eternally. But if we choose to upload, we can immortally live in a heavenlike digital world. Is this not a perfect workaround for avoiding nothingness?

Unfortunately, there are some problems with this line of reasoning. It assumes that it is certain that digital heavens can be maintained as long as the system functions properly; consequently, the locals can enjoy extremely wonderful afterlives for as long as the age of the universe. However, we contend that the assumption is false.

As mentioned, the digital world in which the uploads live is not run in a vacuum but in the real world. This being so, what happens in the real world may affect the lives of the inhabitants of the virtual world. Joe Strout cautions that uploads would have no access to the computer facilitating the virtual world and little control over it. It is possible that "[w]hen the computer crashes or goes down for any reason, from the point of view of its inhabitants, the whole universe ceases to exist, taking them with it into oblivion" (2014: 210).

But abrupt termination of a digital afterlife is not the most horrible thing imaginable. More troubling is the possibility of a cyberattack, which becomes increasingly probable as the technology becomes more prevalent. A cyberattacker may, in order to take revenge or to achieve other gains, disrupt the well-being of the inhabitants in the virtual world by altering the simulation machine or making changes to the programs that sustain the simulation. Imagine that some politically or religiously fanatic cyberattackers want to punish dissidents for some perceived transgressions. Abhorred by, for example, Yorkie and Kelly's interracial homosexual relationship, the cyberattackers may decide to transfer them from San Junipero to another system in which their afterlife is entirely undesirable, or even absolutely unbearable. After disabling their control over their pain slider and psychological modifications, they may choose to lock the couple in a cabin and force them to listen to an annoying song for one million years, as what happens to Joe's cookie in "White Christmas," or have them burnt for eternity. It is highly likely that the companies responsible for the technology (such as the Silicon Valley–based TCKR Systems in "San Junipero") would launch some security initiatives to combat this type of threat. But it seems safe to predict that such threats will never be completely eradicated.

Another possible threat is the dual use of the technology. It is not implausible that tech companies, in order to maximize profits, would allow the cookies in their virtual worlds to be harvested by third parties. For instance, they could sell them to (mad) scientists who want to replicate society *in silico* (see Christopher Wylie, *Mind F*ck: Inside Cambridge Analytica's Plot to Break the World*, London: Profile Books, 2019). In these replications, some experimenters might want to test, for example, people's reactions to ethnic tension; an even more problematic scientist might want to see how long it takes for the uploads to go mad by putting them into a blank room, like what Trent does to Greta's digital incarnation in "White Christmas." They could also rent the cookies out to be used privately by abusive gamers like Daly in "USS Callister" or commercially by perverted minds like Haynes in "Black Museum," who makes money by creating a hell for the holographic Leigh, in which Leigh is repeatedly electrocuted. The list of malevolent uses of the technology can go on. Let us not forget that technology empowers those who can control it. If we consider the disturbing (mis)uses of technologies that are already occurring—such as disruptive psychological warfare enabled by social media and state and corporate surveillance—Lord Acton's 1887 warning that "power tends to corrupt and absolute power corrupts absolutely" looms large. It thus appears to us that even if the original goals of the technology were noble, the risk that inhabitants in a digital heaven might eventually live in a hellish world is not negligible.

This is why we think that the assumption that the digital heaven can be maintained is untenable. Table 2.1 summarizes the possibilities pointed out thus far that a decision-maker has to face when pondering over whether she should upload herself to a digital "heaven" or not.

This is what theorists call "a decision problem under ignorance," a problem facing a rational agent making a choice when she has no, or at most an insecure, basis on which she can assess the probabilities of states (of affairs) of a partition. Although we should not underestimate the chance that any of the four states that constitute the partition may come about, it seems safe to say that the probabilities of their arising cannot be assessed on a firm basis. So how should we rationally decide whether or not to upload ourselves to a digital afterlife?

Table 2.1 Should we upload to the digital heaven?

	The digital heaven lasts till the end of the universe	The digital heaven is terminated	The digital heaven is changed to a digital hell	The digital heaven is changed to a world that is neither a hell nor a heaven
Choosing to upload	Agent experiences an extremely wonderful afterlife (modified digital immortality)	Agent eventually ceases to exist (the system shuts down)	Agent experiences an extremely terrible afterlife (cyberattacks; dual use by mad scientists, abusive gamers or disturbed minds)	Agent experiences an afterlife that is better than those in hells and worse than those in heavens (dual use by scientists)
Choosing not to upload	Agent undergoes a biological death	Agent undergoes a biological death	Agent undergoes a biological death	Agent undergoes a biological death

In normative decision theory, there are a number of rules or strategies that can be applied in situations like this. One such rule is called "the maximin principle" (hereafter "maximin" for short), according to which we should play it safe, focusing on the worst possible outcome of each act, and "[i]f the worst possible outcome of one [act] is better than that of another, then the former should be chosen" (Peterson 2017: 44).

Maximin is not a rule that can be appropriately applied to all decision problems under ignorance. To properly use this rule, two further conditions need to be satisfied: (1) the worst possible outcome(s) of the rejected act(s) is (are) unacceptable and (2) the worst possible outcome of the act we choose by following maximin is acceptable and not just barely better than the outcome of the rejected act (Rawls 1990: 134). The rationale for the first condition is intuitive enough. If an act has some outcome so catastrophic that we cannot accept or live with it, then of course we should avoid it; this choice ensures that the disastrous outcome can never befall us. The reason for the second condition is also evident: "There's little point in choosing conservatively if it results in an *un*acceptable worst outcome that is only marginally better than some other possible worst outcome" (Freeman 2007: 177). In what follows, we will argue that the two conditions are satisfied in our "to upload or not to upload" situation and thus we should follow maximin to choose the latter rather than the former.

To establish this conclusion, we first need to evaluate the possible outcome(s) of each act. As can be seen in the matrix, there are four possible states that could occur if we choose to upload. Of all these, surely the best one is that the digital heaven permanently functions properly, since if that happens, the uploads can enjoy extremely wonderful afterlives until they are annihilated with the universe. The worst state is no doubt that the digital heaven is maliciously (or for other reasons) changed to a digital hell, for if that occurs, the uploads' afterlives will become unimaginable nightmares. On the other hand, if you refuse to upload, none of these states will affect you. As a result, the best, worst, and indeed the only outcome of refusing to upload is that you will die when your brain ceases to function.

Condition (1) is met easily in this scenario, since no one can tolerate living in hell. In response to this, believers in the fantastic container theory (to borrow a phrase from Kagan)—who hold that being alive is so valuable that the grand total value of well-being will always be positive, regardless of how terrible the contents of our lives are—may insist that life is still good even in this state. However, this view strikes most of us as completely implausible or even ridiculous, and we suspect that few people truly believe in it.

Is the outcome of the act of choosing not to upload acceptable? This amounts to the question, "Is death (understood as annihilation) acceptable when you are presented with a heavenlike wonderful life?" To be sure, this outcome is bad since it deprives you of the future goods you would otherwise have were you to upload; and if you also value your existence, it is even more regrettable since it deprives you of your conscious self as well. However, although death may be a very bad thing for many of us, if we also recognize that it is much better than being tortured in a digital hell, the badness of death is alleviated, or even becomes acceptable. Since the two conditions for the proper use of maximin are met, we suggest that not uploading is the most rational choice; in other words, it is irrational to upload ourselves to a digital afterlife.

Thus far we have assumed that the mind-uploading technology preserves personal identity. But what if mind-uploading machines fail to be life-extending technologies but just conscious mind duplicators? Again, our answer is definitely "no"—however, this time for a moral reason.

If the upload is not you but your digital copy, at the outset a newly emerged conscious individual will enjoy a very high quality of life. However, the unneglectable chance of an immortal being trapped in a digital hell is still there, which means that that individual has to (involuntarily) bear a grave risk that can be entirely avoided if you choose not to upload in the first place. While admitting that imposing risks on unknown individuals is sometimes morally justifiable (e.g., we will not condemn someone who drives very carefully, even though she inevitably puts pedestrians into risk), we believe that it is wrong to create an individual who bears an unbearable but avoidable risk. If you choose to upload, you blatantly violate this rule, since you expose your replica to the disastrous but entirely avoidable possibility of living in a digital hell.

We are now in a position to clearly see the gloomy view of the technology implicit in the *Black Mirror* universe, even in "San Junipero." Assuming that the upload has the same conscious experiences as you, there are only two possibilities: (1) the upload is you, or (2) the upload is not you but someone else perfectly like you. If (1) holds, then it is irrational to upload, since due to the possibilities of cyberattack and malignant dual use that would see you tortured in a digital hell, you will bear an unbearable risk. But if (2) holds, then it is immoral to upload, since you would be performing the morally condemnable action of exposing your replica to the same grave risk. Either way, you cannot be both a rational and moral person, as you either put yourself or your replica into a grave risk. For those who desire not to bring about any unnecessary risk, the only reasonable choice is to face their death outright, even if they have the chance to live in a heaven. For, as pointed out earlier, there is no generally accepted answer to the problem of personal identity. Consequently, we do not know for sure whether (1) or (2) is more likely to be true. Under this uncertainty, choosing not to upload dominates: in all states, no outcome of this choice is worse than that of the alternative; but there is at least one outcome that is better than those of the alternative. The outcome in which it is certain that neither you nor your replica will be harmed is definitely not worse than—and is indeed better than—the outcome that either one of you will be harmed. This is the gloomy view of digital immortality advanced by *Black Mirror*. The gloominess lies not in the tedium of immortality but in the malevolent side of human nature. Our mind is susceptible to corruption in the face of technology that empowers us.

References

Benatar, D. (2017), *The Human Predicament: A Candid Guide to Life's Biggest Questions*, New York: Oxford University Press.

Brooker, C., A. Jones, and I. Arnopp. (2018), *Inside Black Mirror*, London: Ebury Digital.

Bruckner, D. (2012), "Against the Tedium of Immortality," *International Journal of Philosophical Studies*, 20: 623–44.

Chalmers, D. (1996), *The Conscious Mind: In Search of a Fundamental Theory*, Oxford University Press.

Chalmers, D. (2014), "Uploading: A Philosophical Analysis," in *Intelligence Unbound: The Future of Uploaded and Machine Minds*, 102–18, R. Blackford and D. Broderick (eds), Chichester, West Sussex: Wiley Blackwell.

Di Summa, L. (2019), "Black Mirror: The Not So Fearful Consequences of Technology," *Film and Philosophy*, 23: 95–113.

Felder, R. (2018), "Forgetting in Immortality," *Journal of Applied Philosophy*, 35 (4), 844–53.

Fischer, J. M. (1994), "Why Immortality is Not So Bad," *International Journal of Philosophical Studies* 2: 257–70.

Fischer, J. M. (2013), "Immortality," in B. Bradley, F. Feldman and J. Johansson (eds), *The Oxford Handbook of Philosophy of Death*, 336–54, New York: Oxford University Press.

Freeman, S. (2007), *Rawls*, London; New York; Routledge.

Harris, Owen. (2016), "San Junipero," *Black Mirror*, Netflix. Season 3, Episode 4. October 21, 2016.

Haynes, Toby. (2017). "U.S.S. Callister," *Black Mirror*, Netflix. Season 4, Episode 1. December 29, 2017.

Hicks, S. (1992), "Would Immortality Be Worth It?' *Objectivity* 1 (4), 81–96.

Kagan, S. (2012), *Death*, New Haven: Yale University Press.

Loosemore, R. (2014), "Qualia Surfing," in R. Blackford and D. Broderick (eds.), *Intelligence Unbound: The Future of Uploaded and Machine Minds*, 231–9, Chichester, West Sussex: Wiley Blackwell.

McCarthy, Colm. (2017). 'Black Museum'. *Black Mirror*, Netflix. Season 4, Episode 6. December 29, 2017.

Muhall, S. (2008), *On Film*, New York: Routledge.

Nozick, R. (1981), *Philosophica Explanations*, Cambridge, MA: The Belknap Press of Harvard University Press.

Nussbaum, M. (1994), *The Therapy of Desire: Theory and Practice in Hellenistic Ethics*, Princeton, NJ: Princeton University Press.

Peterson, M. (2017), *An Introduction to Decision Theory* (2nd Edition), Cambridge: Cambridge University Press.
Rawls, J. (1990), *A Theory of Justice* (Revised Edition), Oxford: Oxford University Press.
Rosati, C. (2013), "The Makropulos Case Revisited: Reflection on Immortality and Agency," in Ben Bradley, Fred Feldman, and Jens Johansson (eds.), *The Oxford Handbook of Philosophy of Death*, 355–90, New York: Oxford University Press.
Scheffler, S. (2013), *Death and the Afterlife*, Oxford: Oxford University Press.
Smuts, A. (2011), "Immortality and Significance," *Philosophy and Literature* 35 (1): 134–40.
Strout, J. (2014), "Practical Implication of Uploading," in in R. Blackford and D. Broderick (eds.), *Intelligence Unbound: The Future of Uploaded and Machine Minds*, 201–11, Chichester, West Sussex: Wiley Blackwell.
Temkin, L. (2008), "Is Living Longer Better?" *Journal of Applied Philosophy* 25 (3): 193–210.
Tibbetts, Carl. (2014), "White Christmas," *Black Mirror*, Channel 4. Season 2, Episode 4. Broadcast December 16, 2014.
The Good Place (2016–2020) NBC Universal. [TV Series].
Williams, B. (1993), "The Makropulos Case: Reflections on the Tedium of Immortality," in J. M. Fischer (ed), *The Metaphysics of Death*, 71–92, Stanford, CA: Stanford University.

3

Technology in Pastel Colors

An Alternative Take on *Black Mirror*

Laura T. Di Summa

The world of motion pictures, of images that *move*, is very different from what it used to be ten years ago. So are its audiences, and the ways in which such moving images are experienced. Among numerous changes, I am here interested in the growing number of TV series, YouTube channels, Web series, and so on that are today available through platforms that are enlarging, if not trumping, the world of cable television. Such products have long attracted the attention of both film and philosophy scholars (e.g., Nannicelli 2017), and have allowed, in some instances, for the reopening, and reassessment, of some of the most well-known debates within both fields.

My thesis in this chapter is that some TV series are capable of doing philosophy in the strong sense of the term, namely by making a significant contribution to the philosophical discussion of important issues through means that are specific to the genre in question. Stellar instances of such philosophizing can be found in *Black Mirror*. Created by Charlie Brooker—well-known provocateur and exploiter of media (Harvey 2016)—the show has been a success first in Britain, and then globally, where Netflix began its distribution in 2016.

In what senses does *Black Mirror* do philosophy? There are at least two answers to this question. The first, which I will only briefly consider, is that the show has been able to replicate, and exemplify, postmodern and poststructuralist criticism in tandem with a reflection—sharp, sardonic, and, to the point—on the world of social media and, more broadly, on the kind of technology that, like smartphones and tablets, typically travels in our pockets.

However well this analysis fits a first viewing of the show, I believe *Black Mirror* does more than simply articulate, or "spell out," existing philosophical theories. It can also challenge these theories, thus broadening the philosophical debate.

My primary intent here is to argue that the philosophical significance of *Black Mirror* should not be seen exclusively in its ability to exemplify existing political and philosophical theories and their critique of the so-called dominant ideology. For the display, through moving images, of such theories is coupled with a sense of pragmatic disillusionment which undermines their critical impact. *Black Mirror* is about accepting technology, a technology whose consequences we may fear, but that offers us a spectacle, where fear can be subdued by a sort of dark enjoyment.

In the first section of this chapter, I briefly consider science fiction's typical portrayal of technology and highlight how *Black Mirror* has modified, and sometimes even reversed, such treatment. After assessing the extent to which science fiction lends itself to philosophical analysis, I will articulate in some detail what I take to be *Black Mirror*'s philosophical contribution, paying particular attention to the cinematic means through which it is delivered.

Science Fiction, Technology, and Philosophical Discussion

Science fiction is a popular genre; it captures the imagination of many, thanks to its use of relatively simple structures and captivating topics. Yet, despite its popularity, it is not, as a genre, easy to define. Damon Knight has famously summarized this difficulty by saying that science fiction is "what we point to when we see it" (Knight 1956), a definition that has been further elaborated by scholars such as John Rieder, who has claimed that science fiction may best be identified as an evolving mix of genres, which does not follow excessively reified conditions (2010: 191–209).

It is nonetheless possible to specify at least some distinguishing features which, while not to be taken as necessary conditions, are readily observable across a large variety of works. More narrowly, commonalities can be seen in how technology—which is a central theme of many science-fiction works—is most often portrayed. Technology is typically seen as alien, and as menacing. In fact, the emphasis on the dangers of technology finds a close parallel in the way in which monsters have been depicted in the horror genre.

Noël Carroll has characterized monsters as "categorical violations" (they can be dead and yet alive, their body both human and animal-like, etc.) that remain fundamentally "unknown," and, for these reasons, they are bound to excite our curiosity (Carroll 1987: 51–9). The way technology is portrayed in science fiction is similarly monstrous. Think, for example, of Samantha, the heroine of Spike Jonze's *Her* (2013), or of Ava, the dangerously seductive android of *Ex Machina* (Alex Garland 2015), or of the characters of *Westworld* (Jonathan Nolan, Lisa Joy, Halley Wegryn Gross 2016–). They are amalgams of physical bodies and computers, perhaps capable of love, but also potentially unable to feel anything. They exude strong sexuality, and yet they are also divorced from it. They combine contrary features, which make them interesting and captivating but hard to define or fully understand.

Seeing technology as a categorical violation, as an exemplification of something unknown and mysterious does not, however, as in the case of horror, uniquely serve the purpose of eliciting the audience's curiosity. For the categorical violations embodied by characters in science fiction can also point to a profound conflict between the world of technology and our society. On the one hand, we have the domain of technological efficiency, an efficiency gained at the expense of feelings, values, and individual aspirations. On the other hand, there is us. Humans in science fiction are often prisoners who must fight against technology to regain their values and a sense of truth. Fighting technology is seen as a fight against evil and deception, against something that is ambiguous, alien.

Furthermore, by making the audience reflect on such categorical violations, on a sense of alterity, and ultimately on our relationship with technology itself, science fiction proves to be a conceptually challenging genre. For, as I aim to show in this chapter, the way in which technology is portrayed also invites critical and philosophical reflection. Differently put, and adopting a term first introduced by Darko Suvin, technology can function as the *novum* (1972: 372–82).

The *novum* is, literally, the addition of a novel component; unlike regular fictions, which are more typically based on reality and on the rules by which reality abides, science fiction is a "fiction of the imagination," with rules that are for this reason unique and designed specifically for a given work. The *novum* in *Solaris* (Tarkovsky 1972), for example, is the mysterious force that allows thoughts and memories—such as Kris Kelvin's memory of Khari, his dead wife—to materialize. But in addition to being novel, and inventive, the *novum* has two other important functions.

First, it exercises a "rationalizing force" over the story; its workings explain the progression of the story, making the somewhat implausible—or at least unrealistic—scenarios of science fiction seem plausible and engaging. Strange things happen in science fiction. Technology has multiple powers; the understanding of (and consequent acceptance of) its capabilities is essential to our comprehension of the story. *Total Recall* (Verhoeven 1990), for example, makes sense only if we believe in machines being capable of providing us with convincing memories of a virtual vacation; in *The Matrix* (Lana and Lilly Wachowski 1999), we need to accept the possibility that a computer mastermind could simulate and recreate an entire world. It does not matter how absurd these scenarios may be; their acceptance is essential to understanding, and appreciating, the work.

Second, the *novum* can be seen as having a profound theoretical and philosophical function: it is an epistemic tool. By acting as a commentary on our society, or, as in Tarkovsky's case, as a way of reflecting on the intricate web of identity and memory, the *novum* is capable of delivering novel insights on our world. It is capable, I'd like to argue, of doing philosophy. To begin with, in a surprisingly large number of cases, academics have used science fiction as an inspiration for their theories—as in David Chalmers' "The Matrix as Metaphysics" (2005: 132)—and as a vehicle for the exemplification of preexisting philosophical positions. Numerous publications on science fiction and philosophy demonstrate their natural affinity, which is further confirmed by how often introductory philosophy courses make fruitful use of examples taken from the world of science fiction. But science fiction—and this is a capacity that I will attribute to *Black Mirror* in the next section—can do philosophy in a stronger sense.

The debate on the ability of the movies to do philosophy is an open and ongoing one. Among those who defend the notion are Thomas Wartenberg (2006: 19–32) and, more recently, Aaron Smuts (2009: 409–20), who has supported the plausibility of the so-called bold thesis, a phrase first introduced by Paisley Livingston (2006: 11–18). Broadly speaking, the bold thesis identifies two conditions for films to effectively do philosophy. The first, which is epistemic, specifies that to do philosophy, movies should be able to provide novel, or at least innovative, philosophical viewpoints. The second (which can be called the artistic criterion) is that films must deliver this contribution through means that are exclusive to the cinema. I believe *Black Mirror* meets these two criteria and hence should be considered to be doing philosophy in several of its episodes.

On *Black Mirror* and Philosophy

The *novum*, in *Black Mirror*, revolves around how technology is portrayed and how it affects both our identity and our daily lives. Importantly, this is done not by singling out an overarching characterization of technology but through the introduction, in each episode, of new features. In an episode such as "Nosedive" (Wright 2016), for example, the *novum* is the ability, reminiscent of Instagram, of rating each other as we proceed in our daily interactions and of using that rating as a standard for who we are ultimately taken to be by society. In "Be Right Back" (Harris 2013), it is the ability to resurrect a computerized version of the deceased that is novel and that structures the development of the narrative; in "The Entire History of You" (Welsh 2017), it is an implant that records every minute of our lives, allowing us to recollect anything that has occurred. Each of these scenarios presents us with questions that can easily be linked to existing philosophical theories which may, or may not, hold their own against the particular kind of sardonic criticism that *Black Mirror* routinely delivers.

Black Mirror has generated a frenzy of critical attention, which spans from prominent magazines reviewing each episode to a plethora of blogs that not only review and comment on each episode but also attempt to dig deeply into what is believed to be its quintessential philosophical message. It is there to be shared: it begins with technology, it depends on it, and it continues to live through and thanks to it. It is interesting to observe, in this respect, that while *Black Mirror* is being reviewed on websites such as Rotten Tomatoes—which owns a virtual monopoly on criticism of film content—it is also a common topic of discussion on Reddit. Reddit, unlike Rotten Tomatoes, focuses less on reviews and more on "problem solving"—viewers launch questions and problems that are then solved collaboratively in chat. It is, for this reason, a natural appendix to the show, as several episodes are open to multiple interpretations and can be analyzed in several different ways, according to how technology and its workings are interpreted and assessed. Streaming platforms, smartphones, laptops, tablets, and the Internet are both the essence and the medium of the show, so much so, in fact, that it would not be outrageous to claim that it may have contributed to recent technological innovations: the inspiration for a future (and often a present) that takes the fiction out of science fiction.

But let's return to the philosophical content of the series. A first thread of analysis focuses on scenarios that are dear to the hearts of philosophers of mind and metaphysicians. The nature of personal identity and the distinction (if there is one) between human and artificial consciousness, for example, are central to "Be Right Back," where a virtual replica of the protagonist's boyfriend is introduced as a substitute for the actual beloved individual, who is presently deceased. Memory and how memories can shape our present and who we are are the subjects of "The Entire History of You" and are further analyzed in the popular episode "White Christmas" (Tibbetts 2014). This is undoubtedly an interesting way of looking at *Black Mirror*, and it is ripe with possibilities that I will not, however, explore in this chapter.

Rather, I am proposing a reading of the series that focuses on its ability to make us question the ideological apparatus that characterizes our society and how our dependency on the tyranny of technology has transformed who we are. The title of the series does not, according to this reading, refer solely to the black mirror we see when our devices are off but also to a certain darkness of the soul we may be able to observe when looking at ourselves in that mirror. More formally, *Black Mirror* can be seen as the embodiment of (mostly) postmodern and poststructuralist theses on the interaction between technology, society, politics, and the "apparatus"—the ideological system that, as Althusser and Marcuse remarked, is capable of shaping our society and behavior "from the inside." It shapes us by making us endorse its aims and needs, and by making us conform to a reigning ideology, which is carefully masked as the most innocuous version of our everyday reality.

An account which aptly exemplifies this kind of reading of *Black Mirror* is Terry Murray's analysis of "Fifteen Million Merits" (Lyn 2011), the second episode of the first season of the series (2015). Murray's interpretation is in line with the ideological criticism introduced earlier, and it is certainly a praiseworthy example of the importance of analyzing *Black Mirror* from this perspective. However, I will argue in the next section of this chapter that

Murray's analysis is missing something. For, as I will demonstrate, *Black Mirror* does not simply illustrate the validity of theories proposed by Marcuse and Althusser, it also highlights their limitations, thus providing us with a more nuanced (and more original) standpoint on their philosophical underpinnings. It does so by providing us with a compelling take on the technology it depicts, one that is both epistemically and aesthetically interesting, challenging the boundaries of science fiction and making us reflect on our own relationship with it. First, allow me to summarize Murray's argument.

Denouncing Ideology: "Fifteen Million Merits"

In "Fifteen Million Merits" society has been turned into a sort of game, where the population is either relentlessly pedaling a stationary bike (their only way of acquiring the capital to buy the things they want) or being force-fed a barrage of advertising and pornography, which is screened on the walls of the futuristic cells where they are supposed to rest. Murray's essay relates the major tenets of Herbert Marcuse's *One Dimensional Man* (1964) and *Repressive Tolerance* (1965) to this horrifying scenario. In both works, Marcuse points to the tension between individual autonomy and the state, which underlie not only the state's power dynamics—which take the form of a totalitarian technology—but also the way in which such dynamics are incorporated and accepted by the people. Totalitarian societies do not simply embrace technology; they allow technology to permeate our consciousness, thus hindering the possibility of rebellion and freedom.

Virtually every aspect of the episode connects with some aspect of Marcuse's thought. Murray notices how pornography further fuels one's enslavement to the system, channeling frustrations into the intimate sphere, as opposed to spending those energies against the system. She dissects Abi and Bing's relationship in light of Marcuse's concept of mimesis. Abi, with her beautiful voice, becomes the system itself, and Bing, after proving himself to be unable to stage an effective protest against it, faces a similar fate.

Her analysis is detailed and largely on point. "Fifteen Million Merits" exemplifies Marcuse's fear of the power of technology as a tool for social control, a control that is totalitarian and enslaving, and which is so pervasive as to become the only accepted reality. It depicts a technocracy that transforms the people and that ultimately makes any revolt both impossible and implausible (as the citizens gradually conform to the needs imposed upon them). The result is bland homogeneity masked as tranquil control.

Relating central Marcusian tenets to the episode, Murray returns, at the end of the article, to the metaphor of the "black mirror," which

> fully reflects back to us the terrifying image of what we have become and how helpless we are against the totalitarian media manipulation of our needs and desires by vested interests. This is because the institutions he [Charlie Brooker] critiques have already assimilated his message. In fact, what is so remarkable (and depressing) about *Black Mirror* is that these hour-long television episodes constantly reference their own impotence and obsolescence: they are about how the system absorbs the very energies that oppose it, eviscerating and precluding any intelligent rejection, or even widespread recognition, of its mind-numbing, sense-deadening cycle of oppression. (Murray 2015)

These observations are in line with Marcuse's philosophy and, more broadly, with an overall criticism of the ideology that invests technology with hegemonic power over the society that lives by its rules.

Beyond Ideology

Now let me propose an alternative reading from the one that she offers. Specifically, I'd like to argue that, despite being an "entertaining, pleasant instrument of our systematic repression and pacification" (a claim I do not necessarily deny), *Black Mirror* is also capable of criticizing Marcuse's treatment of "the" ideology, thereby clarifying the difference between moving pictures acting as an exemplification of philosophical theories and their ability to do philosophy per se.

I am here advancing a different philosophical interpretation of "Fifteen Million Merits," and of *Black Mirror* in general, one that is neither concerned with its connections to topics within philosophy of mind nor politically and socially orientated toward the kind of technology-based ideology described by Murray—at least not in the same fashion. For while *Black Mirror* does show how the ideology functions (or malfunctions), and its all-pervasiveness, it never fully condemns it. I argue that the unique power of *Black Mirror* can be attributed to its combination of a certain pragmatic disillusionment with an undeniable dark enjoyment: pragmatic disillusionment, because we recognize the technology behind the show not only as familiar but also as what we use to satisfy our daily social and personal tasks, and dark enjoyment, because of the sharp irony with which the devastating effects of technology are portrayed.

Murray contends that *Black Mirror* exemplifies the kind of criticism of capitalist ideology championed by Marcuse. But I find this interpretation to be only partial. *Black Mirror* does more than just exemplify philosophical theories: it has the ability to challenge them and advance novel viewpoints. It exposes the ideology, and its dystopian features, without fully condemning it. To justify my position, it is crucial to observe how, besides being a work of science fiction, *Black Mirror* is also a satire. There is irony in disgrace, as shown in the episode "The National Anthem," where the Prime Minister of England is called upon to have sex with a pig on television to save the life of the Princess of Wales. I suspect that irony, to no small extent, facilitates our desire, as members of the audience, to think about the implications of *Black Mirror*, to reflect on its message, and to assess the show in light of our own experience. If *Black Mirror* merely showed the frightening consequences of the technology-based world we live in (or will live in soon enough), it would not resonate with us in the same way. But it also shows us its inevitability, an inevitability we are perhaps guilty of having created. We can smile at *Black Mirror* because we know that we went too far, but we also know that we are unwilling to go back. Perhaps, the trick with dystopic science fiction is to embrace it, to accept the future that it depicts as ours. To this extent, *Black Mirror*'s philosophical potential resides in its ability to make us both engage in the kind of criticism of ideology that philosophers such as Marcuse have developed and *temper* such criticism. More narrowly, *Black Mirror* seems to be pointing at a particular failure in postmodern and poststructuralist criticism.

Rather than merely exemplifying a specific theory, *Black Mirror* allows the audience to engage in the critical assessment of various philosophical positions. The audience of *Black Mirror* hardly shares the revolutionary aims that animated poststructural criticism. Nor does it share, importantly, the fear that technocracy will erase human values. *One Dimensional Man* was published in 1969. Fifty years later, society has changed and so has the attitude of the audience (and especially of the younger generations). We all spend a disproportionate amount of time in the company of technology:

we need it and we enjoy it. While one may become poignantly aware of its dangers, I suspect few are truly ready to abandon it. With a certain pragmatic disillusionment and a good dose of irony, both the characters of *Black Mirror* and the audience are made to realize that there is nothing we can do but embrace the technology we have—it makes us who we are, no rebellions are in sight and no revolution is needed. The series is epistemically interesting, but it is also artistically compelling, and some of its aesthetic solutions are essential for the delivery, understanding, and assessment of its philosophical import.

Satire and irony are not the only artistic means used by the series to convey its message, for they are not, by themselves, sufficient to deliver the kind of philosophical contribution I have outlined. Furthermore, they are the means that are not exclusively cinematic. It is for this reason important to look further into how the philosophical perspective of *Black Mirror* is expressed by the kind of aesthetic choices that characterize the series. At least two deserve to be mentioned. The first revolves around the *Black Mirror*'s use of narrative; the second is instead based on the look of technology. I will begin with the former.

Structurally, *Black Mirror* does not follow what in most shows is the standard narrative arc; there are few explicit connections among its episodes, with each of them featuring new characters and novel scenarios. The lack of an ongoing narrative is responsible for what ultimately amounts to a comparative detachment from the characters. Series like *The Sopranos* (1999–2007) or *Breaking Bad* (2008–2013) relies on the complexities of their central characters, on their ability to change, grow older, evolve, and so forth. They are liked, they are entertaining, and they are philosophically and aesthetically interesting precisely in virtue of the complex forms of empathetic and sympathetic identification we develop toward them.

Fans of characters such as Walter White, the chemist-turned-drug-dealer who is the protagonist of *Breaking Bad,* are often accused of virtually worshipping a character that is profoundly evil—his drug dealing, and the violence it involves, is obviously not commendable, and it is shown as such. The tight narrative, the engaging twists, and the way in which the audience gets to know the personality of such characters can be immensely effective in conditioning our assessment of the show. These factors can blur moral boundaries, with the result of making one cheer for the anti-hero. Philosophers such as Noël Carroll (2013: 371–6), A.W. Eaton (2011: 511–24), and Matthew

Kieran (1996: 337–51) have written copiously on the topic, providing different, though equally fascinating, responses to the issue.

The lack of such a form of identification in *Black Mirror* makes our interaction with the characters more disengaged, but such disengagement may, in turn, fine-tune our critical skills. Rather than focusing on the emotional states the characters are going through, we are more likely to analytically assess the situation and to relate it less to subjective experience than to general concerns about society, technology, and our interaction with it. Dispassionate viewers make better critics, and *Black Mirror* has, undoubtedly, led to a critical wave of responses. *Black Mirror* puts the audience in a privileged position to "philosophize," thus engaging in an active dialogue with present and past theories on the status of technology and on our relation to it.

But in what sense does *Black Mirror* make us reflect on our relation with technology and on its nature? This is an important question for two reasons. First, because if, as I want to claim, technology is not such a demonic force in the series, then the tempering of ideological criticism I have advocated in this section becomes appropriate. If its depiction of technology is not tremendously dystopian and frightening, then the ideology it discloses may seem less threatening. Second, *Black Mirror* can, at times, show us how technology is not just a dictatorial force that drives and conditions us. We recognize it as a part of ourselves and something we need to keep up with. It is about learning how to play with it, a form of play that has its risks but that is also enjoyable. We, in the end, live quite comfortably in the ideology created by technology; it is scary, at times, but it is also, like the show, a fantastic form of entertainment.

Not So Black: Technology in Black Mirror

I began this chapter by suggesting that technology is, in science fiction, generally seen as monstrous, as a categorical violation that closely resembles the one characterizing monsters in horror films. Technology, the reader will recall, is typically portrayed as alien, as devoid of moral values, as something that imprisons us and that should, for this reason, be feared and fled. But is this the way technology is portrayed in *Black Mirror*? My answer is "no" for a number of reasons.

There are, specifically, four characterizations of technology that I would like to highlight. To begin with, the kind of technology we see in *Black Mirror* is strikingly similar to the technology we use in our daily lives, a technology we are close to, a technology that is personal. In "Nosedive," for example, technology is sleek, portable, and delicate: it is in pastel colors. More than portable, it is sometimes wearable, a portion of us or an appendix that it is implanted, as in the case of "The Entire History of You" and "Playtest" (Trachtenberg 2016), or that is applied at one's convenience, as in "San Junipero." In all these cases the application of technology—the insertion of an implant or the activation of a device—is presented in a way that resembles the wearing of jewelry. It is elegant and precise, and it may even complement one's look. Everything appears as slick as the latest Apple gadget. It is virtually impossible to see the look of technology in *Black Mirror* as simply intimidating. It is also aesthetically pleasing, and fashionable. While the consequences of technology can be frightening, its appearance isn't.

In fact, it is interesting to notice how what is most frightening is usually the moment in which technology is abandoned. I will admit that the endings of episodes such as "The Entire History of You," "Playtest," and "Nosedive" are not pleasant to watch. But we also need to recognize how the last minutes of each of these episodes is about separating oneself from the life afforded through technology. A second look at *Black Mirror* reveals that there is always a fine line between the danger and the beauty of technology, an insight with which we are very familiar. Technology is everywhere in *Black Mirror*, just as it is everywhere in our lives: it is quotidian and occupies a good chunk of our time, with few exceptions. It does not involve a separate dimension: there are no more sharp distinctions between replicants, humans, and blade runners; technology is instead the only reality there is—one that is inescapable but can be mastered.

Indeed, the second point I would like to emphasize is precisely the relation between technology and the practices that allow us to master it. For, in watching *Black Mirror*, we become spectators of such mastery. To follow the progression of the story is similar to learning how to use a new device or to figuring out how to productively employ the latest app, which is what the characters in *Black Mirror* often seem to be doing. As I remarked earlier in the chapter, discussions of *Black Mirror* are very popular on Reddit, with extremely detailed threads speculating on how technology works in the series and on what it may be able to do. Importantly, there is little commentary on how dystopian such technology may be.

The thousands of people—and especially young audiences—contributing to such threads have very little interest in the (supposedly) dark and nefarious consequences of a technology-driven world. After all, it is the only one they have, and their main curiosity is learning how it works. In fact, there is a striking similarity between posts on Reddit discussing *Black Mirror* and posts that discuss videogames. There is a certain detachment, one that puts aside evaluative claims and instead focuses on strategy, on the workings of these products, on, once again, what to do in order to "play well." After all, even when characters do not appear to enjoy the technology they have in their hands (or, as seen, implanted in their bodies), the importance of mastering it, of learning how to use it, remains a key narrative component. For, as it is evident in "Fifteen Million Merits," they cannot escape it (or at least it is very hard to). And even if, in a way, they do rebel against it, their rebellion gives them no respite: they are not to find freedom, or joy, or a sense of value.

Mastering technology may then be what allows for a brighter future (and, in turn, a brighter look at it). In "Fifteen Million Merits," the cruelty that is associated with stationary bikes and cells invaded by pornographic images is tempered by a different vision of technology, which emerges only at the end of the episode. Here we see Bing, whose attempted rebellion against technology has made him, paradoxically, a star of the very world he was rejecting, alone in a quiet, beautiful suite. Finally at peace, he contemplates a beautiful landscape, one that appears natural but that is also obviously the product of the same kind of system that previously inundated his room with loud pornography. Technology is still the master, and while he is still, to no small extent, imprisoned, he seems to be enjoying it. Bing's relation to technology involved a series of failed attempts to free Abi. But he ultimately learns how to use it for his own purposes. It may be a prison, but it is a much better prison. Bing's individual needs appear to be finally satisfied.

The duality of the ending, which may or may not disclose a hint of hope in the episode, has also been noted by Ted Wilkes (2016). Wilkes observes that the image of Bing, in his stylish suite looking out of the window at a lush forest, may indeed be a way of revealing a gap between the world of technology and the real, natural world out there. It is yet another screen image, but, undoubtedly, a better one, or, at least, one that Bing wanted and has, at this point, learned how to obtain.

But if we endorse an understanding of technology in *Black Mirror* as something that belongs to and blends with daily life and routine, and as involving devices one needs to learn to use well, then there is something else that should be noted—namely, that it can be fun (or, better, both fun and frustrating). I am not here in the position to discuss our psychological relation—and attachment—to technology, but certain components of it can help us better understand our responses to the show. For a third connotation of technology we encounter in *Black Mirror* is the idea that technology is, in the end, a "life-hack." The kind of technology we are routinely in contact with is closely connected to our daily life (as is the case with most of the technology we see in *Black Mirror*); it improves it, it modifies our habits, and sometimes it even defines us, as appears to be the case with social media. Technology enhances our problem-solving skills, allowing us to develop new crafts, new masteries. It is mesmerizing to realize that, just this morning, on my way back from a run, I scheduled a walk for my dog, made a dinner reservation, did my grocery shopping, scheduled a pick up for dry cleaning, and took a short German class. It took me about fifteen minutes, and I only had to open a few applications on my iPhone. It is legitimate to stop and ask myself whether I would be an equally organized person without technology. I doubt it.

In *Black Mirror*, there is at least one episode that offers a clearly positive take on the potentials of technology as being able to effectively improve our lives: "San Junipero." San Junipero is a mix between a purgatory and a second life, a place that has no assigned time slot, as you can decide to visit it in different decades. It can become the next-life destination after one is "scheduled to pass"—when one decides that it is time to die. It is important to remark that technology does not appear until late in the episode, where we are introduced to TCKR. We will, in the last sequence, see the actual factory responsible for the technology, absolutely gorgeous and scintillating, with long sinuous corridors that appear, indeed, to be leading to heaven. What we have specifically are the lives of the two protagonists: Yorkie and Kelly. They are both searching for a way to extend their lives. As we come to learn, the two are not the young women we meet in the beginning. They are, instead, old and frail, living, respectively, in a hospital and a retirement home. To prepare for their future (and death) they plug into the reality of San Junipero (here too, the look of the technology is particularly attractive), every week for five hours, to experience life, as it was (or could have been, or will potentially be, once they pass). Technology makes that experience possible and is also, importantly, what will make their lives virtually eternal.

More positive connotations of technology can be inferred from the story. First of all, the two fall in love, and the artificial reality of San Junipero is the only setting in which that could have happened. Second, San Junipero represents a future they have chosen. It is not something that is forced upon them but something one may or may not decide to use. At the cost of cheapening a rather beautiful romantic story, it is possible to see San Junipero as what I have previously referred to as a life-hack. It can make life better, but only if we want it. Just as I am free to delete one of the apps on my phone, people are free not to opt for the eternal life that technology can afford. Technology is overwhelming, but it can be helpful, and there still exists a degree of separation between us and the inventions of technology.

Finally, it is important to look at *Black Mirror*, in itself, as something resembling a technological gadget. *Black Mirror* depends on the distribution system championed by Netflix. An entire season is released at the same time, and it is likely to be watched on an array of devices, from smartphones to laptops, to virtually anything that can afford an internet connection. The speed with which we "consume" *Black Mirror* is a product of present-day technology. *Black Mirror* exploits, in this sense, the very environment in which it was created. But while it exploits, it also makes us aware of how much we need it. We need it because without it entertainment would not be the same. In this sense, *Black Mirror* makes us aware of the necessity of technology, of how useful it can be, and of how its use is fundamentally linked to our entertainment. Such a strong connection between technology and entertainment is crucial when assessing the philosophical value of the series, for it contributes to us being able to take *Black Mirror*, and the way it portrays technology, more lightly. To enjoy *Black Mirror* we need the technology, and while our level of technological dependency may not be exactly the one we see in the series, it is unmistakably close to it. It is familiar, it is ours, and it is our main source of entertainment, of quotidian joy.

Conclusions

I have argued that *Black Mirror* can contribute to the philosophical discussion about technology by both exemplifying and critically assessing existing philosophical theories. By making the audience assess philosophical positions, the series does more than merely show the importance, and veracity, of such approaches. Much of its philosophical potential resides in its ability to engage us in dialectical thinking, of making us reconsider previous theses and conclusions. It does so by presenting us with a view of technology that is both novel and aesthetically captivating.

The philosophical value of the series is epistemically interesting because it challenges the standard understanding of technology as alien and monstrous. It makes technology instead an essential part of daily life, a tool, but also something that, much like the technology we have in our own apartments, is sleek, portable, fascinating, and fashionable. It is almost too easy to see the episodes of *Black Mirror* as simply portraying dystopic scenarios. While I can agree with those who find it frightening, and see it as foreshadowing a future we rightfully fear (while pretty much being forced to accept it), I maintain an independent perspective, one that calls for a more nuanced view of the show. I'd like, provocatively, to describe it as a closer, more intimate version of our own lives. *Black Mirror* is never too far from us and that black mirror is quite pristine: it's not too different from my phone, from the social media platforms I regularly use and from the screen that is reflecting back to me the very words I am writing. But at the same time, it is a lot more engaging, and its underlying irony keeps its dedicated viewers yearning for more. It's a fun show, and it is too close to us to be that scary. It's up for binge-watching, and there is nothing more addictive, or more satisfying.

Acknowledgment

This article was previously published in *Film and Philosophy* [Laura T. Di Summa, "Black Mirror: The Not So Fearful Consequences of Technology," *Film and Philosophy*, Volume 23, 2019, pp. 95–113, https://doi.org/10.5840/filmphil2019236], and is reprinted here with the kind permission of the

Philosophy Documentation Center and the Society for the Philosophic Study of the Contemporary Visual Arts (SPSCVA).

References

Breaking Bad (2008–2013), AMC [TV Series].
Carroll, N. (1987), "The Nature of Horror," *The Journal of Aesthetics and Art Criticism* 46 (1): 51–9.
Caroll, N. (Fall 2013), "Rough Heroes: A Response to A.W. Eaton," *Journal of Aesthetics and Art Criticism* 71 (4): 371–6.
Chalmers, D. (2005), "The Matrix as Metaphysics," in Christopher Grau (ed.), *Philosophers Explore the Matrix*, 132, Oxford: Oxford University Press.
Eaton, A. W. (2011), "Rough Heroes of the New Hollywood," *Revue Internationale de Philosophie* 258 (4): 511–24.
Garland, Alex. (2014), *Ex Machina*, Universal Pictures. [Film].
Harris, Owen. (2013), "Be Right Back," *Black Mirror*, Channel 4. Season 2, Episode 1. Broadcast February 11, 2013.
Harris, Owen. (2016), "San Junipero," *Black Mirror*, Netflix. Season 3, Episode 4. Release Date October 21, 2016. [TV Series].
Harvey, G. (2016), "The Speculative Dread of Black Mirror," *The New Yorker*, 28 November. https://www.newyorker.com/magazine/2016/11/28/the-speculative-dread-of-black-mirror Accessed online on January 22, 2020.
Jonze, Spike. (2013), *Her*, Warner Bros. [Film].
Kieran, M. (Autumn 1996), "Art, Imagination, and the Cultivation of Morals," *The Journal of Aesthetics and Art Criticism* 54 (4): 337–51.
Knight, D. (1956), *In Search of Wonder: Essays on Modern Science Fiction*, Chicago: Advent Publishers.
Livingston, P. (2006), "Theses on Cinema as Philosophy," *The Journal of Aesthetics and Art Criticism* 64 (1): 11–18.
Lyn, Euros. (2011), "Fifteen Million Merits," *Black Mirror*, Channel 4. Season 1, Episode 2, Broadcast December 11, 2011. [TV Series].
Murray, T. (2015), "Black Mirror Reflections," *Philosophy Now*, Issue 97. https://philosophynow.org/issues/97/Black_Mirror_Reflections Accessed online on January 22, 2020.
Nannicelli, T. (2017), *Appreciating the Art of Television: A Philosophical Perspective*, London: Routledge.
Nolan, Jonathan, Lisa Joy, Halley Wegryn Gross. (2016-), *Westworld*. [TV Series].

Rieder, J. (2010), "On Defining SF, or Not: Genre Theory, SF, and History," *Science Fiction Studies* 37 (2): 191–209.

Smuts, A. (2009), "Film as Philosophy: In Defense of a Bold Thesis," *The Journal of Aesthetics and Art Criticism* 67 (4): 409–20.

Tarkovsky, Andrei (1972), *Solaris*, MosFilm. [Film].

Suvin, D. (1972), "On the Poetics of the Science Fiction Genre," *College English* 34 (3): 372–82.

The Sopranos (1999–2007). HBO. [TV Series].

Tibbetts, Carl. (2014), "White Christmas," *Black Mirror*, Channel 4. Christmas Special. Broadcast 16 December 2014. [TV Series].

Trachtenberg, Dan. (2016), "Playtest," *Black Mirror*, Netflix. Season 3, Episode 2. Release Date October 21, 2016. [TV Series].

Verhoeven, Paul. (1990), *Total Recall*, TriStar Pictures. [Film].

Wachowski, Lana and Lilly. (1999), *The Matrix*, Warner Bros. [Film].

Wartenberg, T. (2006), "Beyond Mere Illustration: How Films Can Be Philosophy," *The Journal of Aesthetics and Art Criticism* 64 (1): 19–32.

Tarkovsky, Andrei. (1972), *Solaris*. Mosfilm. [Film].

Welsh, Brian. (2017), "The Entire History of You," *Black Mirror*, Channel 4. Season 1, Episode 3. Broadcast December 18, 2011. [TV Series].

Wilkes, T. (2016), "Beyond Black Mirror: Fifteen Million Merits" http://methodsunsound.com/black-mirror-fifteen-million-merits-episode-review/ (October 19, 2016).

Wright, Joe. 2016. "Nosedive," *Black Mirror*, Netflix. Season 3, Episode 1. Release Date October 21, 2016. [TV Series].

4

The Virtue of Forgetting in Nietzsche's Philosophy and *Black Mirror*

Dan Shaw

Black Mirror considers the implications of developments in present-day technology for the near future in a manner reminiscent of the cult hit *Her* (Jonze 2013). Like that melancholy masterpiece, the best episodes of the show explore the saddest implications of plausible future technological developments. Episode 3 of Season 1 is entitled "The Entire History of You" (Welsh 2011) and is set in a near future where people have so-called Grains implanted in their heads. A Grain is an electronic monitor and recording system that films every moment of your life, storing the data for easy access and viewing. Given the notorious unreliability of the persistence of memory (which often melts away like Dali's drooping watches), that may sound like a desirable arrangement. But, for the protagonist of this episode, it turns out to be disastrous.

Like the most memorable installments of Rod Serling's *The Twilight Zone*, "The Entire History of You" is an allegory about the future with a message for the present. That message, to put it bluntly, is that sometimes it is better to forget the past for the sake of the present and the future. As I first watched the episode, I was reminded of Friedrich Nietzsche's strikingly similar take on the importance of forgetting. This chapter will highlight a series of parallels and show that, by either intention or coincidence, the conduct and fate of the episode's protagonist illustrate Nietzsche's contentions in remarkable detail, throwing light on both the philosophy and the film.

The dystopic episodes of *Black Mirror* can be considered to be doing philosophy. They are thought experiments that examine popular trends in modern-day society and offer "arguments" that those trends are potentially destructive. The depictions of the disastrous consequences of these trends extrapolated into the near future are compelling, forcing the viewer to look at them with a critical eye. In so doing, these dystopias fulfill one of the essential tasks of the philosopher, according to Nietzsche:

> their hard, unsought for, inescapable task—but finally the greatness of their work—was for them to be the bad consciences of their age. By applying the knife of vivisection to the chest of the virtues of the day, they revealed what their own secret was—to know a new greatness for man, to know a new untrodden path to increasing his greatness. (*Beyond Good and Evil* 1882, Aphorism 212)

The River of *Lethe*

anyone who acts . . . forgets most things in order to do one thing, he is unjust to whatever lies behind him and recognizes only one right, the right of what is to be. (Nietzsche 1874, 129)

One of five that flowed in the Greek mythological underworld, Lethe was the river of forgetfulness and oblivion. Once having drunk from its waters, those who crossed over the river Styx to the Underworld had no memories with which to torment themselves for all eternity. Friedrich Nietzsche believed that it was much healthier to forget many of the details of our past, rather than seeking to recall them with total clarity. He develops his case for forgetfulness as a virtue (in Aristotle's sense of the term, i.e., a habit that can help us to realize our full potential) throughout his philosophical career.

In an early essay, "On the Utility and Liability of History," Nietzsche cautioned the German people of his era against becoming too obsessed with studying their past. Contrasting the human being to the animal (the latter of which he considered to be "healthier" in some important respects), Nietzsche remarked:

> Then the human being says "I Remember" and he envies the animal that immediately forgets and that sees how every moment actually dies, sinks back into fog and night, and is extinguished forever. Thus the animal . . . disappears entirely into the present . . . the human being, by contrast, braces

himself against the great and ever greater burden of the past. (Nietzsche 1874, 126)

Nietzsche consistently stresses that we should jettison that burden, the better to fulfill our future potentials.

He then poses a convincing argument in favor of forgetting: "All action requires forgetting . . . it is possible to live almost without memory, indeed, to live happily, as the animals show us; but without forgetting it is utterly impossible to live at all" (Nietzsche 1874, 127). Consider a couple of commonplace examples. Someone who has been consistently unlucky in love cannot dwell on that dismal past if she is ever to risk loving anyone again. If she focuses solely on her memories of failure, she will never change her luck and will simply circle the wagons and retreat into emotional invulnerability. Similarly, members of a sports team that has met with consistent failure in recent years must put their past behind them in order to have the resilience necessary to rewrite history and turn their fortunes around.

Nietzsche's defense of forgetfulness deepens in his mature central works (*The Gay Science, Thus Spoke Zarathustra,* and *Beyond Good and Evil*), where it is a pivotal virtue in his vision of what is noble and of the next progressive stage in human evolution (which he eventually dubs the Overman). It was in the first of these books that Nietzsche has "the madman" declare that God is Dead and that "we have killed him" (Nietzsche 1882, 224). Later, in a section called "*The greatest weight,*" he introduced his notion of "The Eternal Recurrence" in a dramatic fashion: what if some demon came to you and posed the following possibility:

> This life as you now live it and have lived it, you will have to live it once more and innumerable times more; and that there will nothing new in it, but every pain and every joy and every thought and sigh and everything unutterably small or great in your life will have to return to you, all in the same succession and sequence? (Nietzsche 1882, 236)

He asks whether the prospect of such a repetitive recurrence would be crushing or exhilarating. Nietzsche concludes the section with a suggestive question: "how well disposed would you have to become to yourself and your life *to crave nothing more fervently* than this ultimate eternal confirmation and seal?" (Nietzsche 1882, 236)).

When Julius Irving ("Dr. J") retired in 1987, four years after winning his only NBA championship, a commentator asked him what he would change if he had to do it over again. The questioner probably had in mind Irving's decision to play in the American Basketball Association for the first several years of his career, before joining the premiere league when the ABA collapsed. Dr. J, in his own inimitable fashion, claimed that he wouldn't change a thing. Despite having missed out on the chance to capture multiple NBA championships (instead of just one), he still had no regrets. This perfectly illustrates Nietzsche's point: to affirm your life wholeheartedly, you must accept your entire history, while refusing to dwell on it. Putting the past behind you (when it threatens to hinder your future progress) is a prerequisite to becoming who you are.

Nietzsche's vision of the Overman is a complex archetype, most of the details of which need not concern us here. He believed that contributing to the progress of the species is what makes life worth living, and his vision of the type most able to do so is what he designated as the Overman. In his elucidation of the concept in *Thus Spoke Zarathustra*, Nietzsche claims that one of the major indicators of *Übermenschlichkeit* (literally, what it is to be an Overman) is freedom from regret, guilt, and the desire for revenge. As he saw it, the bridge to the *Übermensch* can only be crossed by overcoming our obsessive focus on the past.

In a section entitled "Of Redemption," Nietzsche rejects the Christian notion of salvation and contends that only the individual can save him- or herself: "To redeem the past and transform every 'it was' into a 'thus I will it so!' —that alone do I call redemption" (Nietzsche 1883–84, 275). To live without regret, or vengeful desires, is a mark of the Overman, who would gladly do it all over again, secure in the realization that the sum total of his life up to that point has resulted in the person he is now. Adopting this self-affirming attitude promotes the attainment of what Nietzsche calls "the great health," which allows the *Übermensch* "to give birth to a dancing star."

Overcoming regret, guilt, and the desire for revenge enables the noble soul to possess the self-confidence to act with steely conviction. As Nietzsche subsequently observed (in *Beyond Good and Evil*): "It is not works, it is *faith* that is decisive here and establishes a hierarchy . . . some fundamental certainty about itself . . . the noble soul has reverence for itself" (Nietzsche 1886, 359). Achieving that sense of reverence means putting aside vengeful thoughts or personal regrets, refusing to hold the past against others or against oneself. It means letting go of all past disappointments and slights, whether real or imagined. I can learn from the past without dwelling on it by remaining focused on the future and its possibilities. The Will cannot will backward, and the past is unchangeable. The future is mine to fashion as I like (within reason), but only if I wholeheartedly adopt the attitude that "I wouldn't have it any other way" toward everything that has occurred thus far.

So, as Nietzsche summarized his case in *On the Genealogy of Morality*:

> Forgetfulness is not just inertia, as superficial people believe, but it is rather an active ability to suppress, positive in the strongest sense of the word, to which we owe the fact that we simply live through, experience, take in. . . . To shut the doors and windows of consciousness for a while . . . a little peace, a little *tabula rasa* of consciousness to make room for something new, above all for the nobler functions and functionaries, for ruling, predicting, predetermining . . . that, as I said, is the benefit of active forgetfulness. (Nietzsche 1887, 408)

Nietzsche promises that the individual who achieves this active virtue will obtain more power over himself, his surroundings and his inferiors. The episode of *Black Mirror* that I will now discuss shows how powerless a person can become if they obsess about the past to the detriment of the future.

The third episode of the first season of *Black Mirror* (written by Jesse Armstrong, and the only episode not penned by showrunner Charlie Brooker) offers a scary vision of the near future, where most people have had recording devices implanted in their skulls, enabling them to access every moment in their past since implantation. The "Grain" permits the wearers to have total recall; they can "redo" past moments by replaying them in their head or even projecting them onto a screen for the delectation of others. This revolutionary technological development raises some serious questions, especially given its plausibility. Like so many other quality works of science fiction, "The Entire History of You" is a thought experiment that tests whether its premise is a good idea or not.

At first, we see that it could definitely have potential. The episode opens with our protagonist, a lawyer named Liam, facing a high-pressure job interview. Wondering whether it went well as he is walking out of the building, it occurs to him that the main interviewer used a strange locution to end the session. He is able to call up the moment and review it, discovering that his potential boss said the following: "We really hope to look forward to seeing you again." This confirms Liam's fears that the interview went poorly, as the more straightforward way to say it (if the interviewer felt positively toward him) would simply be "We really look forward to seeing you again." In short, Liam caught the man in a Freudian slip, with the circumlocution revealing his true feelings.

The first sequence is intriguing, for who among us hasn't wanted to replay some key scene from the past to confirm what went on. Memory is notoriously unreliable, influenced by our individual perspective on, and personal interests in, the matter at hand. Memory fades rather quickly, and as it does, wishful thinking often takes over. Initially, then, the device seems to have legitimate uses, as when the parents replay their little child's Grain recordings to see whether the nanny did a responsible job (she did). It offers the ultimate sitter cam, from the child's perspective.

Having access to such a complete library of recordings is soon shown to have its downsides, however. For one thing, security men at travel hubs can insist you rewind through the last forty-eight hours, or even the last week, of your life to confirm you do not pose a terrorist threat. But the focus of this story is not on the "Big Brother" implications of such devices, which are explored to a shattering effect in "White Christmas" (Tibbets 2014).

One of the greatest drawbacks of being able to access "The Entire History of You" is that it facilitates the unhealthy human tendency to be nostalgic. With such a resource at their disposal, it is unsurprising that people tend to redo the best moments of their life. Some go to troubling extremes, however, like replaying earlier encounters while engaging in sex with someone who is actually present. One fellow even admits that he will sit downstairs reliving his best orgasms, while keeping his present girlfriend waiting for him to come upstairs and make love to her.

It is that remark, made at a party Liam attended after his return, which sets him off on a self-destructive vendetta. He went directly from his interview to the party, where he unexpectedly interrupted his wife Ffion and a friend named Jonas engaged in an intimate conversation. We soon learn that Liam and Ffion are a married couple with a very young child, and their love for one another seems evident. But, with the help of their personal Grain devices, Liam's jealousy is about to ruin their marriage and their lives.

The couple invited Jonas over to their house after the party, though Liam insists Ffion was the one who really got behind the idea. Liam has since had second thoughts, so, when Jonas arrives, the couple begs off and does not receive him. While enjoying a nightcap after his departure, Ffion admits to having had a brief fling with Jonas, long before she knew Liam. Since he considers Jonas to be a lothario "searching for an orifice," Liam does not welcome this news. He tells her that she should be embarrassed by her revelation. When she recognizes that this threatens to get blown out of proportion, she insists that it wasn't significant and goes up to bed. After some minutes elapse, he follows her up and apologizes, and they have make-up sex. But both of them choose to simultaneously redo a prior passionate encounter (one wonders if it is even the same one), which, along with the tensions between them, renders their actual intercourse unfulfilling.

Liam is totally cranked up by now. He drinks all night, sleeps not at all, and keeps replaying sequences from the party. In a passage that particularly disturbs him, Jonas tells an unfunny joke, and Ffion is the only one within earshot to laugh at it (another indication of intimacy and flirtation). The nanny comes in for the morning, and he insists she watch the sequence where they invited Jonas to come back to their home and tell him who she thinks is extending the more enthusiastic invitation. In the face of his evident and continued hostility, Ffion blurts out that she had a six-month relationship with Jonas and walks away. He then replays Jonas' speech about preferring redoes to sex with actual women and jumps to the (prophetic) conclusion that Jonas was redoing scenes with his wife.

Outraged, and falling down drunk, the husband storms over to Jonas' house. He bitterly levels his accusations and then hits the poor man over the head with a vodka bottle. Finally, Liam breaks it and holds the jagged glass at Jonas' throat, demanding that he delete all the recordings of his encounters with Ffion (to which, as Liam suspected, he would return from time to time). Jonas does so; Liam stalks out before the cops come and wakes up behind the wheel of his totaled car, which he has crushed against a tree.

When he returns home, he confronts Ffion viciously, triggering even more painful revelations. We learn that the couple had experienced marital problems in the period right before they conceived their child (perhaps because they were having difficulty doing so). Ffion admits that she had an affair with Jonas when they were separated (a matter of only a few days). Liam asks if Jonas wore a condom, and she claims that he did, at her insistence. But her personal recording of the event puts the lie to her contention, and Liam forces her to watch the replay, in all its damaging detail. The questions this raises, both about whether she loves him and about the paternity of his child, devastate him completely.

Predictably, the episode concludes with Liam alone and his house, a mess. He replays several of his favorite moments of life with Ffion over and over again, in most of which she is gazing at him lovingly. It is clear that he now realizes what he has lost, and he is struggling to accept the fact that his wife and child are gone forever. In order, I assume, to stop tormenting himself with these poignant redoes, Liam cuts the Grain out from behind his ear, and the episode ends.

Nietzsche was no stranger to jealousy, considering that Lou Andreas Salomé, the love of his life, ran off with his best friend Paul Rée. But he warned against its corrosive effects: "He whom the flame of jealousy encompasses will at last, like the scorpion, turn the poisoned sting against himself" (Nietzsche 1883–4, 270). Liam fulfills Nietzsche's sobering prediction to the letter, though it must be admitted he had good grounds for being jealous.

Ffion had always lied about the length and significance of her relationship with Jonas, whom she initially dismissed as "the Marrakesh Man" with whom she admittedly had a fling in that exotic part of the world. She also subsequently failed to disclose the renewed affair during their estrangement, no doubt because she had thoughtlessly engaged in unprotected sex during a period when the married couple was trying to conceive a child within wedlock. From the point of view of social convention, Liam had every right to do what he did, *but it ruined their marriage and left him alone and bereft*. In the end, I suspect that he wished he had cut the Grain out a good deal sooner.

The initial resentment that Liam felt was inappropriate, since it concerned Ffion's comparatively distant past. Since most of *us* have old flames, expecting our beloved *not* to have *any* past loves is clearly unreasonable. So, to begin with, Liam's jealousy is on shaky ground. But Liam has ample reason to be deeply hurt by the revelation of her recent infidelity and is understandably livid at discovering that he might not be the biological father of their child. Liam has at least two alternatives at this point: he can decide to be moralistic, assume the role of the superior accuser, and judge her harshly, or he can forgive her. Liam chooses to adopt the former attitude, which spells the end of his marriage. Nietzsche consistently condemned all moralizers and would have diagnosed Liam's judgmental attitude as resulting from his own personal sense of insecurity.

That insecurity is made evident in the situation with which our story began. The interviewer informs Liam that they intend to have him litigate

"Retrospective Parenting" cases, where one sues one's parents, on such shaky grounds as "insufficient attention leading to damaging of confidence." Though he initially registers surprise at such a prospect (revealing his true disdainful attitude), he denies having any qualms about pursuing such cases when asked directly.

Having recognized a mutual attraction between his wife and Jonas, Liam should simply have looked the other way. But he felt particularly vulnerable after the ambivalent job interview, and, as Nietzsche often observed, moralizing is one way for the powerless to feel powerful, albeit in an illusory manner. It is clear that the existence of the personal recording device is pivotal to how events unfold here. While it is common for married folks to envision their unfaithful spouses engaging in adulterous sex, they are unable to replay such events for detailed examination. The trauma of Liam insisting that they watch her unprotected sexual fling was, no doubt, the last straw. He had torched their relationship, and no matter how much he regretted having done so, there are no literal redos in life.

So, like the best *Twilight Zone* episodes, "The Entire History of You" is a cautionary tale. The Grain is *not* seen as a promising social development; on the contrary, it is depicted in a decidedly negative light. Unfortunately, it facilitates two of the worst vices of the species, our tendencies to lose ourselves in nostalgia for the past and to define ourselves as superior by judging others as morally deficient.

Simply put, Liam would have been better served by putting what had happened in Ffion's romantic past behind them. Obsessing over her former relationship (and more recent infidelity) hindered his enjoyment of the present and shattered his prospects for the future. Liam's forlorn replays at the end confirm our suspicion that they were a genuinely loving couple, at least until he launched his jealous vendetta. He forgot what he had, and their potential future together, and allowed his obsession with past indiscretions to destroy it all and himself in the process.

Rather than seek vengeance against Ffion and Jonas, Liam would have been better off to drop the whole issue. His wife admitted to feeling affection for Jonas in the past but claimed that it was over and that now she only cared for her husband and their child. As is often the case, her infidelity did not mean that she no longer loved Liam. Both Liam and Ffion failed to respect one another, and their marriage collapsed as a result.

Most people are inclined to withhold embarrassing details about their past lives in the early stages of a new romantic relationship. We want to put our best foot forward, so to speak, and that is both understandable and appropriate. But, by this stage in their marriage, respect for Liam and trust in his love should have prompted Ffion to reveal both the earlier relationship and the more recent infidelity. True friends are frank with one another and protective of each other's feelings. That the truth only comes out as the result of Liam's ruthless interrogation makes the disclosure all the more devastating.

For his part, Liam deals with the revelations in a completely childish manner. From early on in the evening, he suspects the worst, refusing to extend the benefit of the doubt to his wife, someone he should consider his best friend. Then, rather than confronting the situation sensibly, he gets blind drunk (an apt phrase). While severely under the influence, he terrorizes Jonas and Ffion into admitting the affair, while nearly killing himself in an auto accident in the process. The link between drunkenness and domestic violence is well established, and Liam must be blamed for choosing to put himself in that state at such a time.

Realizing that no friend is perfect, true friends forgive each other for the occasional disappointments that must result from their fallibility. The old cliché is "forgive and forget," and with good reason. Forgiveness requires active forgetfulness—that is, refusing to dwell on the infraction. Ffion should have shared her painful confidences much earlier and given Liam a chance to forgive her. Liam should have stopped to recognize how much she meant to him before choosing the path of righteous indignation.

Having the "Grain" implanted in our heads would make putting the past behind us far more difficult, as a veridical replay of controversial past events would always be just a redo away. Like Liam, we in the audience are intended to conclude that the thing to do if we had such an implant would be to cut it out as soon as possible, ending our capacity for total recall. But Brooker told *The Guardian* that he believes that such a gadget would be irresistible: It is "probably inevitable," he says, that people will soon wear face cameras to record their every interaction. "It's creepy and eerie [but] you'd only need to find it useful five times to adopt it as an everyday thing, and you'd just put up with the fact that it was ruining your life in all sorts of other ways."

References

Jonze, Spike. (2013), *Her*, Warner Bros. [Film].

Nietzsche, Friedrich. (1874), "On the Utility and Liability of History for Life," in Taylor Carman. (ed.) (2019), *On Truth and Untruth: Selected Readings*, 124–41. Malden, MA: Blackwell Pub.

Nietzsche, Friedrich. (1873), "On Truth and Lies in the Nonmoral Sense," in Taylor Carman. (ed.) (2019), *On Truth and Untruth: Selected Readings*. London: HarperCollins

Nietzsche, Friedrich. (1882), "The Gay Science," in Keith Ansell-Pearson and Duncan Large. (eds.) (2006), *The Nietzsche Reader*, 362–84, Malden, MA: Blackwell Pub.

Nietzsche, Friedrich. (1883–84), "Thus Spake Zarathustra," in Tom Griffith (1997) *Nietzsche: Thus Spake Zarathustra*. Ware: Wordsworth Editions.

Nietzsche, Friedrich. (1886), "Beyond Good and Evil," in Taylor Carman. (ed.) (2019). *On Truth and Untruth: Selected Readings*, London: HarperCollins

Nietzsche, Friedrich. (1887), "On the Genealogy of Morality," in Keith Ansell-Pearson and Duncan Large. (eds.) (2006), *The Nietzsche Reader*, 390–436, Malden, MA: Blackwell Pub.

The Twilight Zone. (1959–1964, 1985–1989, 2002–2003, 2019–2020). CBS. [TV Series].

Tibbetts, Carl. (2014), "White Christmas," *Black Mirror*, Channel 4. Christmas Special. Broadcast December 16, 2014. [TV Series].

Welsh, Brian. (2011), "The Entire History of You," *Black Mirror*, Channel 4. Season 1, Episode 3. Broadcast December 18, 2011. [TV Series].

Section Two

Versions of the Self in *Black Mirror*

5

Free Will in *Black Mirror*

Bandersnatch

Sander Lee

In the film *Black Mirror: Bandersnatch* (Slade, 2018) viewers are presented with a *Choose Your Own Adventure* style drama in which a young programmer named Stefan Butler is faced with a series of choices. Supposedly, viewers can alter the trajectory and ending of the tale by the choices they make. However, a number of viewers have complained that no matter what choices they make, the story takes a pessimistic turn leading to a depressing ending (Harris, Lyons, and Ryan 2019).

In this chapter, I will argue that the element of apparent determinism in what is advertised as a *Choose Your Own Adventure* is not a failure on the part of its creator Charlie Brooker but is, indeed, precisely the point he wishes to make. To do this, I will compare the philosophy underlying *Black Mirror: Bandersnatch* with that of Arthur Schopenhauer (1788–1860). Schopenhauer believed that everything that exists is a manifestation of a force he calls "the Will." This Will is fundamentally spontaneous and irrational. Free will is no more than an illusion, and life is primarily characterized by suffering and despair. I will contrast Schopenhauer's determinism with the existential philosophy of Jean-Paul Sartre. Sartre defends a belief in free will and responsibility. I will examine the consequences of attempting to analyze *Bandersnatch* from Sartre's perspective and the reasons why I believe this interpretation is ultimately the most important.

In *Black Mirror: Bandersnatch*, I contend that Brooker tells us that our feeble attempts to pretend that rationality and order can be successfully imposed on computer games and ourselves are doomed to failure. Those who hold these beliefs, such as Stefan at the story's beginning, are portrayed as living in a world of fantasy. Sadly, even the best of us are irresistibly drawn down into the degrading, the brutal, and the violent. No matter what choices viewers make, in the world of *Black Mirror: Bandersnatch*, the story is always the same.

Schopenhauer's Determinism

Arthur Schopenhauer (1788–1860) believed that everything that exists is a manifestation of an irrational force he calls *the Will*. There is only one Will, and it pervades all reality while determining every action. In making these claims, Schopenhauer is opposing his philosophy to those of Immanuel Kant (1724–1804) and G.W.F. Hegel (1770–1831), the most influential German thinkers of his time. For Kant, this inner Will is rational. By following our common intuition of duty (which derives from the Will), all of us are freely able to act morally. In Hegel, this force becomes an all-encompassing Absolute Spirit that drives human history progressively toward a better, more moral future.

Schopenhauer reacts negatively to such optimism. Turning these ideas upside down, Schopenhauer's Will is made up of our worst impulses, the irresistible violent and sexual drives that most of us try to hide behind a veneer of civility. These impulses are evil and overpowering.

While we like to pretend that we are strong enough to overcome these instincts through rational action, the sad truth is that we can never escape their grip. The most we can do is lie to ourselves that all is well when we know in our hearts that it is not.

In fact, for Schopenhauer, human life, like all animal life, is best characterized by a senseless brutality, by nature's seemingly uncaring processes of violence, illness, and death.

Humans try to hide these sordid truths through happy fantasies of religion and love, but, in fact, we are powerless to control the savage forces of nature, forces that exist not only outside of us but also in our very essence as human animals. We pretend that human nature is fundamentally caring and good, but the reality is that we are secretly fascinated by the barbaric and the violent. Thus, our feeble attempts to impose rationality and order on the world are doomed to failure. The conspiracy to shield the "innocent" from life's harshness can never fully succeed because we are all too "curious." He states, "For the world is Hell, and men are on the one hand the tormented souls and on the other the devils in it" (Schopenhauer). Schopenhauer claims that the Will is composed of primal instincts that motivate all human behavior. In this belief, Schopenhauer prefigures Sigmund Freud's (1856–1939) later claim that all of us are driven by our most basic desires, especially our need for sexual gratification. Another philosopher, Friedrich Nietzsche (1844–1900), while a great admirer of Schopenhauer, believes our primal instincts, what he called the *will to power*, transcend morality altogether. Where Schopenhauer describes the desires of the Will as evil, Nietzsche famously celebrates what he calls the *Dionysian* virtues of a *master morality*. He actively encourages strong-willed individuals to transform themselves into superior people who will be untouched by the weapon of guilt used by those in the *slave morality*. Such individuals will overcome the self-deception practiced by those who accept traditional morality and religion. Schopenhauer was very interested in Eastern philosophy, especially Buddhism. The first two Noble Truths of Buddhism state that all life is suffering (*Dukkha*), and suffering is caused by desire (The Buddhist Centre). In Buddhism, it is common to associate this desire with the image of fire. Giving in to one's desires is like adding fuel to the fire, making it stronger and harder to quench. If no more fuel is added to the fire, it will eventually burn itself out and die. In the same way, to extinguish desire one must stop giving in to it. For example, I may love to eat chocolate. Yet, if I give in to my desire to eat chocolate whenever I want, my appreciation of the taste will diminish to the extent that I find myself eating more and more and enjoying it less. In addition, my overeating will eventually make me feel sick and bloated.

Thus, my desire for the pleasure of eating chocolate has instead led me to pain and suffering. For Buddhists, this is life's unavoidable pattern. We desire something, so we seek it. Yet when we get it, it is never everything we dreamed it to be, so we seek more. But we never get enough and the pursuit of pleasure always leads to suffering. Desires can never be fully fulfilled. The only way to escape suffering is to escape desire altogether A follower of Nietzsche might claim that these inner forces are necessary to drive the most talented and courageous of us to acts of great imaginative intensity. Schopenhauer, on the other hand, sees life as a cycle of pain and suffering in which each of us is determined by irresistible evil impulses we can hide but never escape.

Sartre's Existentialism

Let's compare Schopenhauer's determinism to the existential philosophy of Jean-Paul Sartre, a philosophy that emphasizes individual free will and responsibility. Sartre describes the human condition, that of the *for-itself* (consciousness), as one of emptiness and nihilation in the face of the *in-itself* (the world), which is both complete and meaningless. The for-itself has neither essence nor being, which is why it is able to comprehend the in-itself; for Sartre, only "what is not" is able to understand "what is." It is through this nihilating capacity that the for-itself is able to distinguish itself from the in-itself. The for-itself always retains the possibility of negating the in-itself. While the in-itself is always complete in its existence, the for-itself is always a lack due to its isolation and non-being. Condemned to this state by our self-awareness, we are what we are not (yet) and are not what we have been thus far. Because of the for-itself's lack of essence, one is also totally responsible for one's acts. One does what one does because one has chosen to do so. When a person comes to really understand and experience this total freedom and responsibility, one is filled with anguish (also called "nausea"). Anguish is the apprehension born of the realization that you must make choices, that not choosing is a choice in itself, and that there is nothing to guarantee the validity of the values that you choose to serve. Values must be chosen without reference to any ultimate guideline, since we are unable to establish that such guidelines exist. Persons create value by choosing to cherish those things that they see as desirable. Each seeks fulfillment in the sense that the in-itself is fulfilled. Thus, each person completely creates herself by the way she constitutes her values. Self-deception often arises out of anguish. This self-deception can take two forms, *bad faith* and *good faith*. Bad faith occurs when a person lies to herself and refuses to accept her freedom and the responsibility that goes with it. In bad faith, one blames one's failure on other people, or one's situation. Sartre himself distinguishes between good and bad faith as follows: "Good faith wishes to flee the 'not-believing-what-one-believes' by finding refuge in being. Bad faith flees being by taking refuge in 'not-believing-what-one-believes'" (Sartre 1993: 115). In his book *Bad Faith, Good Faith, and Authenticity in Sartre's Early Philosophy,* Ronald Santori explains good faith as follows:

> Good faith, like sincerity, initially aspires to be what it believes. But as Sartre points out earlier in *Being and Nothingness*—to which I have made mention above—the original structure of our "not being what we are" makes this movement impossible ("renders impossible in advance all movement towards Being-in-itself") and far from being "hidden from consciousness," this impossibility is "the very stuff of consciousness." (1995: 78)

Sartre gives the example of a *good* friend:

> I believe that my friend Pierre feels friendship for me. I believe it *in good faith*. I believe it but I do not have for it any self-evident intuition. I *believe it*; that is, I allow myself to give in to all impulses to trust it; I decide to believe in it, and to maintain myself in this decision; I conduct myself, finally, as if I were certain of it —and all this in the synthetic unity of one and the same attitude. (1993: 114)

I interpret good faith as another way of lying to oneself, in which a person objectifies herself and pretends she has to act the way she does because of her fundamental nature. In my view, Sartre sees good faith, like bad faith, as self-deception and as distinct from what he calls "authenticity." At the end of his section on bad faith in Part I of his book *Being and Nothingness*, in which he demonstrates the ontological identity of many aspects of good and bad faith, as well as the important differences between this distinction and that which opposes morality to immorality, Sartre presents a footnote containing an essential clue concerning his position on this issue:

> If it is indifferent whether one is in good or in bad faith, because bad faith reapprehends good faith and slides to the very origin of the project of good faith, that does not mean that we can not radically escape bad faith. But this supposes a self-recovery of being which was previously corrupted. This self-recovery we shall call authenticity, the description of which has no place here. (1993: 116)

One common form of self-deception discussed by Sartre derives from our desire to become simultaneously conscious (i.e., free) and complete. We want to control everything, especially the reactions of others to us, while maintaining the fiction that they choose to be with us, and admire us, of their own free will.

The Importance of Art

Despite their disagreement about free will, there is one topic on which Schopenhauer and Sartre agree. They both think that art plays a crucial role in human life. For Schopenhauer, art is the one activity that can create a momentary escape from life's endless suffering. Aesthetic experience does not add to the suffering in the world and even has the power to diminish that suffering (*Schopenhauer's Aesthetics*). While I am engaged in experiencing art, I am temporarily transported away from my individual suffering. While I may empathize with the pain of a character (e.g., Hamlet or Stefan), and may even be moved to tears by their plight, by the same token, I recognize that their suffering is not my suffering. Despite the sadness of a tragedy, I feel a form of aesthetic pleasure that eases my suffering until I am returned to my own life and remember my personal problems:

> All willing, according to Schopenhauer, involves suffering, insofar as it originates from need and deficiency. Satisfaction, when it is achieved affords a fleeting joy and yields fairly quickly to painful boredom, which is tantamount to a deficiency, and which starts the entire process anew. Given this grim account of willing, it is not surprising that Schopenhauer describes aesthetic experience in truly rapturous terms as "the painless state that Epicurus prized as the highest good and the state of the gods," and as "the Sabbath of the penal servitude of willing" when the "wheel of Ixion stands still." (*Schopenhauer's Aesthetics* 2018)

For Sartre, on the other hand, we live in a world that is meaningless and absurd. However, the very act of choosing creates values for which each of us is responsible. We all face the existential problem of choosing meaning without objective standards to guide us. Art is one area in which it is possible to overcome one's nausea and create meaning for one's life. In this sense, the creation of my personal identity is my greatest work of art:

> His first novel, *Nausea*, painstakingly chronicles this ontological disgust towards the strangeness of the world. A proffered hand becomes "a big white worm," a glass of beer a hostile partner whose "gaze" the hero attempts to avoid for half an hour; a pebble on the beach reveals the "nausea" that is communicated from the world "through the hands." Even here, however, aesthetic experiences trigger some exceptional moments in which the hero manages to escape ontological "nausea." This occurs, for example, when

the novel's main character suddenly hears a jazz song in a café, which, like a "band of steel," points to a different time beyond the drudgery of the everyday. (*Existentialist Aesthetics* 2019)

This song playing in a café at the end of Sartre's *Nausea* inspires the main character, Antoine Roquentin, to realize he can create meaning for his life by becoming an artist:

> Can you justify your existence then? Just a little? ... Couldn't I try.... Naturally, it wouldn't be a question of a tune ... but couldn't I, in another medium? ... It would have to be a book: I don't know how to do anything else. But not a history book: history talks about what has existed—an existant can never justify the existence of another existant. My error, I wanted to resuscitate the Marquis de Rollebon. Another type of book. I don't quite know which kind—but you would have to guess, behind the printed words, behind the pages, at something which would not exist, which would be above existence. A story, for example, something that could never happen, an adventure. It would have to be beautiful and hard as steel and make people ashamed of their existence. (Sartre 1969)

In fact, I would argue that the novel *Nausea* is Roquentin's own attempt to escape his anguish by channeling it into art.

Charlie Brooker clearly agrees with both Schopenhauer and Sartre concerning the power of art both to help understand human suffering and to create meaning for our lives. *Bandersnatch* demonstrates Stefan's attempt to escape the suffering of his mother's death and gain meaning for his otherwise humdrum life through the creation of his own aesthetic adventure, the game *Bandersnatch*.

Bandersnatch

With this philosophical background, let us now turn to an analysis of *Bandersnatch*. In July 1984, Stefan Butler prepares to meet with Mohan Thakur, the owner of the Tuckersoft software company. Stefan wants to turn the "choose your own adventure" novel *Bandersnatch*, written by Jerome F. Davies, into a video game. The name "Bandersnatch" was originally created by Lewis Carroll in the 1872 novel *Beyond the Looking Glass*. The Bandersnatch is a fictional animal that exists only in imagination. Other authors have borrowed the term for their own purposes, although Davies' novel exists only in the fictional *Black Mirror* universe. It is appropriate that *Beyond the Looking Glass* and *Black Mirror* both refer to fictional worlds that exist on the other side of mirrors. In addition, there really was an unfinished video game from the 1980s with this title (*Bandersnatch: All Endings Explained*).

Stefan initially believes in his own capacity to control the events of his own life and in the video game he is creating. An ongoing symbol of his struggle to maintain his freedom is the question of whether he should take the meds prescribed by his therapist Dr. Haynes. At one point we can see a scenario in which he takes his meds and his game receives a terrible review, implying that his psychological suffering is the cost he must endure so he can maintain his creativity and produce a successful game. Of course, Stefan himself doesn't initially know that he is a character in the film *Bandersnatch*, a "choose your own adventure" episode of the series *Black Mirror* presented on the streaming service Netflix in the year 2018. Because *Bandersnatch* is a "choose your own adventure" in which the viewer can make choices for Stefan, we become active participants in Stefan's story. Because of this, from this point on I will refer to *Bandersnatch* as a "game," rather than a "film," and ourselves as "players," rather than "viewers."

As the game progresses, Stefan's belief in his own free will is repeatedly undercut as he comes to realize his actions are not under his own control. This fact doesn't necessarily support Schopenhauer's determinism over Sartre's belief in free will as we are the actual players of the game *Bandersnatch*. Stefan's growing realization of his role as the game progresses is both amusing and upsetting to us, but it does not address the most important question—namely, whether we, the players, have free will.

Initially, the choices we are offered seem trivial, which cereal to have for breakfast or what music to listen to on the bus. In fact, the choices do affect the possible scenarios available in the game, so much so that many players replay the game repeatedly to find all the possible scenarios. The first apparently major choice takes place when Thakur asks Stefan whether he wishes to make his game in the Tuckersoft offices with the help of other designers or on his own at home. If he chooses the first option, his game is a critical failure and our game is over.

To continue, one must go back and choose to work on the game alone. This sequence of events, which recurs often, gives us the first indication that our choices are not as free as we have been led to believe. While giving us the Sartrean appearance of freedom, the game really seems to be masking a Schopenhauerian determinism in which our choices are preordained.

This scenario occurs again if Stefan accompanies his idol Colin Ritman, a famous game designer, to his home. Stefan is apparently given the choice of whether to take LSD (Lysergic acid diethylamide). However, even if he chooses not to take it, Colin puts it in his tea anyway. Once they are both high, Colin explains his theory that the world they inhabit is only one possible timeline and that jumping from the balcony won't actually kill them. Colin asks Stefan to choose which of them will jump to test his theory. We must choose one of them to jump; we can't choose no jump at all. If Stefan jumps, he dies and we must go back and choose Colin or end the game. If we choose Colin, he dies and leaves the game.

This makes it seem as though Colin's theory is wrong and the actions of the characters do have real consequences, a Sartrean position. However, in reality, Colin's theory is vindicated in that the game allows us to undo either characters' death and endlessly return to the point of choice. Of course, this is one of the major differences between the lives of characters in video games and those of real life. In video games, characters are resurrected again and again with no memories of their deaths. Because of this, our choices for these characters have no real consequences, so, there can be no existential anguish in the face of own freedom and no responsibility for the impact of our choices as players.

This point is made most definitively in the events surrounding Stefan's murder of his father Peter. Unless you choose to stop playing the game, there is no way to avoid murdering Peter and disposing of his body in a grotesque manner (only chopping up the body allows the game to proceed without the dog digging it up). Patricide is one of the most despicable crimes, yet we must choose to make Stefan a murderer for the game to continue. In this way, *Bandersnatch* forces us to give up our free will as the price for playing.

This reinforces the overall themes of *Black Mirror* as a series. Again and again, the series tells us that our desire to use technology to make our lives better actually results in giving up control to an inhuman technology that degrades us. In the episode "Hated in the Nation," well-intentioned scientists create thousands of artificial bees to save the environment, only to find that they have inadvertently given a crazed fanatic a weapon for mass murder. This is an appropriate point to momentarily step away briefly from our examination of *Bandersnatch* in order to better place it in the context of *Black Mirror* universe as a whole.

The series *Black Mirror* is the creation of showrunner Charlie Brooker. It is often compared to the classic science-fiction anthology show *The Twilight Zone*. However, *Black Mirror* differs from *The Twilight Zone* in some important ways. As many have pointed out, a common theme seems to permeate the series, namely the dangers posed by technology to the possibility of authentic human life. The title *Black Mirror* refers to turned-off screens (TVs, phones, tablets, etc.). The implication is that we as a society would live better if we simply turned off all the screens. While each of the episodes tells a different story with different characters, it is clear that all the episodes take place in the same universe, albeit at different points of time. References to other episodes are littered throughout the series. For example, in *Bandersnatch*, Stefen works for Tuckersoft, a company referenced in other episodes like "San Junipero." At Tucker's offices there are posters advertising 1980s video games with the same titles as other episodes, including "Metalhead" (Slade 2017). While some of the episodes take place in the very near future, such as "The National Anthem" (Bathurst 2011) and "The Waldo Moment" (Higgins 2013), some take place in a future with technological changes that are plausible but currently unattainable such as "Be Right Back" (Harris 2013), "Hated in the Nation" (Hawes 2016), and "San Junipero" (Harris 2016). A few seem to take place in a far-off future, including "Fifteen Million Merits" (Lyn 2011), and "Metalhead" (Slade 2017). *Black Mirror: Bandersnatch* (Slade 2018) is unusual in that it takes place in the past; however, that past is 1984, a year made famous by George Orwell as a dystopian era that will forever seem to be in the future.

It has often been remarked that all episodes of *Black Mirror* have unhappy endings, although some endings are unhappier than others. "Hated in the Nation" ends in mass murder, and in "Fifteen Million Merits," the protagonist's anger at an unjust system is co-opted to support that system. In contrast, "San Junipero" appears to have a happy ending in which the lovers Yorkie and Kelly are reunited after death in a virtual reality that conforms to their every wish. However, the happiness of this ending is undercut by Kelly's passionate speech in which she insists on an actual death as a way to honor her dead husband and daughter. We are given no explanation for her apparent change of mind as we see her joining Yorkie in San Junipero during the end credits. One possibility, however, is that Kelly did really die and her presence in the virtual world is an artificial one created by the Tucker software program to please Yorkie. The other indication that all is not well in San Junipero is the existence of the nightclub called "The Quagmire," where the dead inhabitants do horrible things to each other to elicit feelings of any kind, even the most unpleasant.

Another episode with an apparently happy ending is "Hang the DJ" (Van Patten 2017). We root for Amy and Frank as they apparently defy the "system" in the name of true love. However, in the end we learn that the Amy and Frank we have been rooting for are nothing more than computer simulations. Their supposed "rebellion" is just part of the game. So, in the end, when the real Amy and Frank are set up by a dating app that gives them a 99.8 percent chance of compatibility, they are actually relinquishing their free will (and the responsibility for the consequences for their choices) in exchange for following the easy path, a path that avoids the painful emotional growth required to find love on one's own.

Given *Black Mirror*'s aversion to using technology to substitute for genuine human emotion, perhaps the episode "Be Right Back" presents one of the most positive outcomes. After the death of her lover Ash, Martha turns to a service that provides an android resembling Ash in appearance. Eventually, Martha comes to realize that no technological duplicate can fully replace the complex emotional relationship she had with an actual human being. To truly move on with her life she must experience genuine grief, no matter how painful that may be. Accordingly, she banishes the android to the attic, only allowing her young daughter to visit him briefly on special occasions like her birthday. This ending captures the thematic thrust of the entire series. While Brooker is not a complete Luddite, he does forcefully argue that interactions with technology should not be allowed to replace human relationships and values.

Before returning specifically to *Bandersnatch*, I think it is instructive to compare the themes in *Black Mirror* to those often found in *Film Noir*. In his classic essay "Notes on *Film Noir*" (1972) Paul Schrader contends:

> The *noir* hero dreads to look ahead but instead tries to survive the day and, if unsuccessful at that, he retreats to the past. Thus *film noir*'s techniques emphasize loss, nostalgia, lack of clear priorities, insecurities, then submerge these self-doubts into mannerism and style. In such a world style becomes paramount, it is all that separates one from meaninglessness, (Schrader 1972: 58)

These themes also permeate *Black Mirror*. Schrader describes the film *Kiss Me Deadly* (Aldrich 1955) as the "masterpiece of *film noir*" in that its protagonist "overturns the underworld" in search of "the great whatsits," and when he finally finds it, it turns out to be—joke of jokes—an exploding nuclear bomb. The inhumanity and meaningless of the hero are small matters in a world in which the bomb has the final say. *Kiss Me Deadly* shares *Black Mirror*'s concern with the tendency of advanced technology to exaggerate humanity's worst instincts. Such technological advances, despite their initial appeal, plant the seeds of our degradation and eventual destruction. *Kiss Me Deadly*'s protagonist, the seedy private eye Mike Hammer, thinks he is smarter than everyone else. He believes he can find the suitcase containing a nuclear bomb and sell it for personal profit. Instead, the film ends with a nuclear explosion. The characters in *Black Mirror* also think they are smart enough to exploit technology for their own ends, but, in all too many episodes, they are unable to foresee the negative impact the technology will have on their lives.

In *Black Mirror: Bandersnatch*, Stefan's most traumatic memory occurred before the episode ever began. When he was a child, his mother tried to take him on a train that left at 8:45 a.m. When Stefan can't find his beloved stuffed rabbit, his mother leaves him behind. She takes the train alone and is killed when the train crashes. In one possible scenario, Stefan inputs the password TOY into a safe which opens to reveal his rabbit. He is then able to transport himself back in time by going through a mirror (another *Alice in Wonderland* reference). He returns to the moment when his mother comes to get him to go on the train. As he now has his rabbit, he accompanies her on the train and dies with her. We simultaneously see him die in his therapist's office, although, as he now dies as a child, this timeline, and his game, never exists. In a way, this is the happiest possible ending to the story. We, as players, are able to make an existential free choice that has real consequences, consequences that resolve Stefan's greatest personal dilemma. There is no doubt than Stefan would prefer dying with his mother over living an unhappy life filled with guilt.

On the other hand, entering the password PAC into the safe reveals that Stefan has spent his entire life as a subject in a "Program and Control Experiment" in which he has been conditioned and controlled by Peter and his therapist. His whole life is a lie. His mother didn't die and Peter isn't really his father. He watches a video of the staging of his last moments with his mother described as a process of "trauma inception." We even see Peter hiding Stefan's beloved rabbit. This revelation leads Stefan to confront Peter and kill him. The scenario ends with Stefan in prison watching on TV as his game gets a bad review. With its Schopenhauerian determinism, this is perhaps the darkest ending possible, and it ties in with the fate of Jerome F. Davies, the author of the fictional novel *Bandersnatch*, who also believed in grand conspiracies, eventually going mad and murdering his wife.

In another scenario, Stefan comes to realize that all of his actions are being controlled by some mysterious force. We can choose to tell Stefan that he is being controlled by Netflix, a twenty-first-century entertainment streaming service, "like TV but online." This sends Stefan to his therapist, who tries to persuade him that this must be a fantasy because his life is so boring that no one would watch it as entertainment. This reassurance is immediately invalidated when we are given the opportunity to pit Stefan in a bloody death match against both his therapist and his father.

If, on the other hand, we choose to have Stefan jump out the window, the fourth wall is broken and Stefan discovers to his horror that he is actually an actor playing a scene on a set and that his "memories" come from a script written by someone else. This ending appears to be a homage to the Season 1 *The Twilight Zone* episode "A World of Difference" in which the same thing happens to businessman Ted Post. However, in *The Twilight Zone* episode, Ted is eventually able to return to his life while Stefan's revelation ends the game in yet another deterministic manner. As to the fate of Stefan's game *Bandersnatch*, our choices result in a variety of possibilities. In some scenarios Stefan never finishes the game. In others, the final game gets review ratings ranging from terrible to average to outstanding. While this last result would initially seem to be the happiest (i.e., the game is a success and Stefan is free), the fact remains that to achieve this ending, Stefan must murder his father and chop up his body. Thus, in this ending, Stefan achieves professional success only by playing a pivotal role in the deaths of *both* of his parents. Furthermore, in the post-credits to this ending, we learn that Stefan is sent to jail for murdering his father and his game has been pulled from the shelves.

This ending also leads to a flash-forward in which we see Colin's daughter in the present. In her attempt to reboot the game, we see her begin to experience the same madness previously suffered by both Davies and Stefan. No matter when one plays this game, who plays it, or what level of technology is available, the pessimistic results remain the same.

Conclusion

Bandersnatch reinforces the themes underlying *Black Mirror* as a series. The more we choose to live our lives inauthentically, the more dehumanized and unhappy we become. While *Black Mirror* is often portrayed as claiming that this degradation is being forced upon us by advanced technology, it is not the technology which is at fault. Jerome F. Davies, like the real science-fiction writer Philip K. Dick, voluntarily drives himself mad by choosing fantasy over reality (with its often-difficult human relationships). He does this in a time, the 1970s, before the easy availability of personal computers or video games. Stefan does the same thing using the primitive video game technology of the 1980s. *Black Mirror* may not be critiquing technology at all. Its real target is our choice to avoid the hard work of human intimacy for the sake of fantasy.

In Sartrean terms, blaming contemporary problems on our ongoing overreliance on technological advances is a form of bad faith (self-deception) in which we attempt unsuccessfully to escape our own responsibility by shifting it to external conditions. On the other hand, if we claim that our intrinsic human nature coerces us into pursuing greater and greater technological distractions, we choose to fall into Sartre's other form of self-deception, good faith. In good faith, one objectifies oneself to escape responsibility. The slogan of Sartrean existentialism is "existence precedes essence," meaning that we each create who we are by the choices we make. Again, you are the artist who creates yourself as your most important work of art.

Thus, our only real choice is whether to obsessively play games that distract us away from our freedom and responsibilities toward others. If we do play, we are deterministically locked into choices made by the games' designers. Stefan does indeed seem to be a victim of Schopenhauer's determinism. His fate is mandated by a Will that contrives to force him into a life of suffering and at least one indisputable evil act, killing Peter. On the other hand, as a fictional character in a fantasy universe created by Charlie Brooker, Stefan's situation is not necessarily ours.

We can choose whether to play *Bandersnatch* and when to stop playing it. It is only while playing it that our choices have so little effect that they are virtually irrelevant to the game's pessimistic outcome. However, if we play games responsibly, or don't play at all, we are free to make our own choices,

choices which do have real consequences and offer us the possibility of an authentic life. So, in the end, I argue that Brooker's purpose is to advocate Sartrean freedom over Schopenhauer's determinism. We each have the freedom to decide how much control over our actions we allow our technology to have over us. If Brooker really believed that we have no freedom, then he wouldn't have created *Black Mirror* in the first place. While the series is certainly entertaining, it is very clear that Brooker's main purpose is to warn us of the dangers of choosing to hand over our freedom to dehumanizing technologies. There would be no point to issuing such a warning if he didn't think we have the freedom to heed it.

References

Aldrich, Robert. (1955), *Kiss Me Deadly*. United Artists [Film].

Bandersnatch (2018), ALL Endings Explained (Including 'Secret'). Available online: https://www.youtube.com/watch?v=FxYkSR5jJF8&t=29s. (accessed December, 28, 2019).

Bathurst, Otto. (2011), "The National Anthem," *Black Mirror*, Channel 4. Season 1, Episode 1, Broadcast December 4, 2011.

Black Mirror Timeline Explained | Seasons 1–5 & *Bandersnatch*. Available online: https://www.youtube.com/watch?v=Hz6yLg9MGu4 Accessed 12/23/19.

Existentialist Aesthetics. Available online: https://plato.stanford.edu/entries/aesthetics-existentialist/#ArtAbs (accessed December 23, 2019).

Harris, A., M. Lyons and M. Ryan. (2019), "'Bandersnatch' Has Many Paths, but Do Any of Them Add Up to Anything?" *The New York Times*, 4 January. Available online: https://www.nytimes.com/2019/01/04/arts/television/bandersnatch-black-mirror-netflix.html. (accessed June 28, 2019).

Harris, Owen. (2013), "Be Right Back," *Black Mirror*, Channel 4. Season 2, Episode 1, Broadcast February 11, 2013. [TV Series].

Harris, Owen. (2016), "San Junipero," *Black Mirror*, Netflix. Season 3, Episode 4. Release Date October 21, 2016. [TV Series].

Hawes, James. (2016), "Hated in the Nation," *Black Mirror*, Netflix. Season 3, Episode 6. Release Date October 21, 2016. [TV Series].

Higgins, Bryn. (2013), "The Waldo Moment," *Black Mirror,* Netflix. Season 2, Episode 3. Release Date February 23, 2013. [TV Series].

Lyn, Euros. (2011), "Fifteen Million Merits," *Black Mirror*, Channel 4. Season 1, Episode 2, Broadcast December 11, 2011. [TV Series].

Van Patten, Tim. (2017), "Hang the DJ," *Black Mirror*, Netflix. Season 4, Episode 4. Release Date December 29, 2017. [TV Series].

Sartre, J. (1993), *Being and Nothingness*, trans. H. Barnes, New York: Washington Square Press.

Sartre, J. (1969), Nausea, trans. L. Alexander, New York: New Directions. Available online: http://users.telenet.be/sterf/texts/phil/Sartre-Nausea.pdf (accessed December 20, 2019).

Santoni, R. (1995), *Bad Faith, Good Faith, and Authenticity in Sartre's Early Philosophy*, Philadelphia: Temple University Press.

Schopenhauer's Aesthetics. Available online: https://plato.stanford.edu/entries/schopenhauer-aesthetics/ (accessed December 23, 2019).

Schopenhauer, A., *Quotes*. Available online: https://www.goodreads.com/author/quotes/11682.Arthur_Schopenhauer?page=4 (accessed June 28, 2019).

Schrader, P. (1972), "Notes on *Film Noir*," in A. Silver and J. Ursini (eds), *Film Noir Reader*, 53–63, New York: Limelight.

Slade, David. (2018), *Black Mirror: Bandersnatch*. Netflix. [Film].

Slade, David. (2017), "Metalhead," *Black Mirror*, Netflix. Season 4, Episode 5. Release Date December 29, 2017 [TV Series].

The Buddhist Centre: Buddhism for Today Available online: https://thebuddhistcentre.com/text/four-noble-truths (accessed December 20, 2019).

The Twilight Zone. (1959–1964, 1985–1989, 2002–2003, 2019). CBS. [TV Series].

6

"White Christmas"

Technologies of the Self in the Digital Age

Diana Stypinska and Andrea Rossi

A luminous, aseptically white hospital room. This year Christmas sales, the screen announces, have dropped due to high snow. The patient, Greta—a young, well-off woman—is visibly anxious. The sounds of the TV give way to her nervous thoughts: the poor sales will wreck her portfolio; too many unread messages in the inbox; the toast the nurse brings is burnt—should she ask for another one? As the anesthetist comes in, Greta's mind naturally drifts back to the surgery, the pain, and what might go wrong—until, that is, the drugs take effect and she passes out. Yet, curiously, in a matter of seconds Greta's thoughts reawaken, while the operation has only just begun. She rises up, leaving her body behind. Greta can now see herself lying on the hospital bed, though, evidently, she is not dead. Quite to the contrary, *she is just reborn as a digital duplicate of herself.* The inner dialogue of Greta now seamlessly continues through the bodiless, cybernetic copy of her mind—which we will hereafter refer to as Greta 2.0. The latter is a data double, a "cookie," as surgeons call her, ready to be installed into an electronic device shaped like an egg—symbol of birth, fecundity, and beginning. Greta 2.0 has been created to attend to Greta's private and social needs. She will switch on the lights in her apartment, cook to her tastes, play her favorite music, regulate the temperature of her house, and manage her appointments—all this without Greta 2.0 having to be instructed, for, as an exact copy of Greta's brain, she already knows what the "original" needs and desires. Perhaps, she already feels and desires as the other does.

Greta 2.0—the main character of one of three stories of *Black Mirror*'s Christmas Special "White Christmas" (Tibbetts 2014)—appears as a futuristic rendition of cybernetic "data doubles" (Lyon 2003, 2007), as currently formed, in our "primitive" digital age, by the cookies that record the traces of our online activities. She is at the same time a filmic representation of the transhumanist dream—shared also, in passing, by many neuroscientists—of copying and downloading, perhaps in the near future, our minds into electronic supports. Greta 2.0 is a cookie that no longer operates through the mediation of screens and algorithms but directly translates our synaptic connections into the language of artificial intelligence.

That such a possibility could ever come true—or, for that matter, that machines could ever develop anything like consciousness, feelings, morality, or, in a word, intelligence—is a question that we will deliberately leave aside here. Our concern is not with whether we could effectively be cloned by digital means but rather with how our subjectivity and sense of self-identity are filtered, mediated, transformed, and rearranged by technology—something that is, at least partially, already at play with certain existing digital features.

Yet this will not only involve an interrogation of the ways in which our thoughts, desires, and, more generally, psychology are being transformed by new technologies. Our focus will be on the slightly different—and in a sense, as we shall argue, more basic—question of *how digital technologies modify the way we constitute ourselves as ethical subjects and* therefore *the way we experience, come to know, and relate to ourselves, to others, and to the world.*

It is from this perspective that we will read the different technologies portrayed in the episode as *technologies of the self*, in the way that authors such as Pierre Hadot, Michel Foucault, and Peter Sloterdijk, among others, have understood this phrase (see Section "Technologies of the Self").

By examining the central themes of the three stories of "White Christmas," we will ask who *we* become as we enter into a relation with intelligent machines that, to different degrees, substitute, replace, or supplement parts of our "selves." To be more precise, we will inquire into how, in the name of individual self-enhancement, digital technologies (and especially those based on the externalization and automatization of intellectual, relational, and emotional faculties) may alter the conditions under which we encounter both others and the world. By doing so, we will demonstrate that these interventions tend to produce what we will concernedly call a "subjective stasis" (see Section

"Digital Technologies of the Self"). In conclusion, we shall show how the loss of the care of self, others, and the world that this entails exposes us to ubiquitous programs of governmental control.

Technologies of the Self

The expression "technologies of the self"—along with similar ones such as the "care of the self" and the "practices of the self"—originates in Michel Foucault's writings, and, more specifically, in his late work on ancient philosophy (Foucault 1985, 1988, 2005). One of Foucault's intuitions—primarily inspired by Pierre Hadot's seminal studies on the subject (1995)—was that Western philosophy did not exclusively, or even primarily, emerge out of a desire to attain a purely rational understanding of man, the world, and their ultimate principles. The complex speculative systems elaborated by ancient philosophers and theologians might better be understood as part of an attempt to fundamentally (re)form modes of being and ways of thinking. It is in this sense that Foucault interpreted ancient philosophy through the notion of the technologies of the self: as a practice that entailed the acquisition of a *techne*—an art, a set of attitudes and skills—through which the knowing subject could give itself a new and different *form*.

The notion of "form" is in every sense central to this way of interpreting subjectivity, not only within the domain of philosophical knowledge but, more generally, in so far as the definition of who we are—and of our self-understanding—is concerned. The subject, Foucault asserts, "is a form, and this form is not primarily or always identical to itself" (1997: 290). Among other things, this means that the self is never "already there" as an essence or a substance but is the product of the "technologies" through which humans—like sculptors working on themselves—shape their own dispositions, attitudes, and modes of thought. As a "form," subjectivity is not defined by some objective or preexisting truth—be it the truth of our drives (as psychoanalysis generally holds) or that of our social or economic conditions (as in Marxist perspectives). Subjectivity coincides with the *modalities* whereby we relate to ourselves—our needs, desires, preferences, as well as social and economic context—with a view to better understanding and transforming *how* we are. In this sense, the history of not only philosophical but all Western subjectivity might be seen as the collection of diverse practices through which individuals and groups have sought to reform their attitudes toward, and experience of, both themselves and their existence as a whole (see Sloterdijk 2013).

Focusing on the relation between "oneself and oneself" as the referent object of the technologies of the self should not be taken, however, as indicative of an egoistic or self-absorbed attitude, where the "I" would only figure as an autonomous and perfectly self-sufficient entity. After all, to reject the existence of a substance underlying identity is precisely to deny that we could ever come to fully realize "who" or "what" we are, compelling us to recognize the impossibility of identifying an individual sphere—or some "inner" qualities—existing independently of the web of relationships and experiences that define human existence. To conceive of subjectivity as a form is to envision it as a point of tension between us and what surrounds us—that is, that which is heterogeneous and cannot be reduced to our individuality, expectations, and desires. As Foucault made clear, the care of the self—especially in its pre-Christian forms—was aimed at establishing a fitting relation between *itself*, the *others*, and the *world*, where the latter would not only refer to a physical or metaphysical entity—the *kosmos* and its divine or rational essence—but, more generally, to the complex of meanings, values, norms, rituals, and practices defining the life of a community.

The *form* of the subject emerges through the triangulation of this set of relationships. It is therefore "a relational mode of knowledge, because when we now consider the gods, other men, the *kosmos*, the world, etcetera, this involves considering the relation between the gods, men, the world and things of the world on the one hand, and ourselves on the other" (Foucault 2005: 235). It is only through the modulation of our knowledge and attitudes toward these different spheres of life—rather than through the mere optimization of some supposedly individual faculties—that "a full, perfect, and complete relationship of oneself to oneself" could be established (Foucault 2005: 320). This, in turn, would entail "an open and an orientated preparation of the individual for the events of life" (2005: 320). There could be no (trans) formation of the self without, at the same time, a (trans)formation of one's attitudes toward that which exceeds one's control (e.g., nature, the *kosmos*, social norms, the will and desires of other men, and unforeseeable events) and, therefore, without the ability to deal with the "open" nature of time and of existence, more generally. Subjectivity is formed in the process whereby we accustom ourselves—through education, training, and practice—to deal with, and position ourselves, vis-à-vis this crucible of relationships. Decisively, this presupposes an attentive specialization—a craftsmanship, as it were—rather than a "general attitude," for one cannot meaningfully relate to anything or anyone with "an unfocused attention" (Foucault 1988: 50). Care is always particular; it is always singular, and yet learning to care is never a solitary task.

For the ancients, undergoing a period of philosophical or spiritual training—in which the subject would unreservedly submit to the will and the instructions of a guide—was the basic condition of the acquisition of the skills and knowledge needed to tend to one's relations. The technologies of the self thus appear invariably embedded within preexisting social milieus and are largely a matter of cultural transmission, rather than individual invention (hence, the function of the philosophical schools, the religious orders, the monasteries, sects, etc.). That notwithstanding, they do not merely consist in the automatic reproduction of predetermined behaviors and forms of knowledge but require instead the establishment of a critical, independent, and thoughtful relation to oneself and others. The subject, as it were, is guided only in order to be able, at some point, *not to be guided anymore* and to take full *ethical responsibility* for its thoughts, actions, and modes of being (cf. Foucault 1997: 268–71).

To the extent that the subject is never "already there" but constitutes a point of tension between different forces ("inside" and "outside" of itself), its (trans)formation necessitates a critical dialogue between itself and the heterogeneous elements it encounters. Thus, the internalization of the norms and precepts that would allow the individual to *know itself*—that is, to enter into an autonomous relation with itself—requires at the same time the establishment of a critical distance toward its own habits, dispositions, and desires. While this critical reflexivity was explicitly central to the classical care of the self, it is nevertheless foundational, as we shall argue, to any practice aimed at the ethical constitution of subjectivity. This is what Foucault referred to as the "undefined work of freedom" (Foucault 1997: 316). To thrive, the subject needs knowledge, along with an ongoing questioning of its own form and possibilities.

Digital Technologies of the Self

The actual history of the practices of the self since Antiquity, as recounted by Foucault and others, is obviously too broad and varied for us to even begin relating it here. In an absolutely schematic way, one might say that, whereas the care of the self tends to disappear as a theme from modern philosophy, it reappears in many different domains, from athleticism, craftsmanship, and art (as virtuosity) to the economic realm, with labor becoming a way of producing and enhancing the self (see Sloterdijk 2013; Rossi 2015). Today, these preoccupations are resurfacing primarily in the sphere of the digital and biotechnological revolutions, for which the concern with the reengineering and enhancement of man is absolutely central—as attested, most notably, by the growing influence of post-humanist and transhumanist movements (see, for instance, Bostrom 2011; Kurtzweil 2005). Obviously, the old philosophical and spiritual tools of the ancient care of the self are here inflected in purely techno-scientific terms. And, yet, it appears increasingly evident that what is at stake are subjectivity itself and its ethical constitution (see Lemmens 2015). It is for this reason that—in spite of the dramatic difference between the classical and the contemporary care of the self—the theoretical framework outlined earlier seems especially pertinent to understanding the out-turns of the digitalization of the practices of the self-portrayal in "White Christmas." With this in mind, the chapter proceeds by accounting for these transformations in relation to three domains—economy, romance, and privacy—each corresponding to a substory of the episode.

Economy

The story of Greta, as introduced in the opening of the chapter, provides a clear example of a technology devised to enhance the life-experience of its owner through the creation of a digital double or a "cookie." Greta 2.0 is, in a sense, nothing but a tool of convenience for Greta. Through controlling the networked devices and appliances in her house, she performs a mix of traditional domestic and secretarial work ("See, this is your job now. You're in charge of everything here. The temperature, the lighting, what time the alarm clock goes off in the morning. If there's no food in the refrigerator. You're in charge of ordering it. ~ For who? ~ For the real you" (*Black Mirror*)). In this regard, Greta 2.0 functions like existing system software, such as Alexa or Siri. Yet there could be no doubt that she is at the same time more than a machine or a virtual assistant programmed to respond to the owner's requests. Greta 2.0 is not only a tool, external and subordinated to her user, but *the user herself*, or, at least a part of her, in as far as her neural make-up—and therefore her thoughts and intentions—is a precise copy of her owner's. It is in this sense that Greta 2.0 might be said to function as a "digital technology of the self," with her use literally transforming the way Greta "uses" and relates to herself too.

To be sure, Greta 2.0 may appear as only a technological "parody" of the classical care of the self. After all, in so far as she is meant to give Greta automatic control over her needs and tastes (and over the ways of satisfying them), she does not help her to learn to relate to her instincts and will in a different way—which, as seen, was something essential to the classical technologies of the self. Neither, in fact, does Greta 2.0 facilitate her owner's acquisition of new skills or a higher form of knowledge. In a way, Greta 2.0 could be simply viewed as an automated version of a domestic assistant. And yet, her very nature, we would suggest, makes her into something more than a mere servant to a master.

To explicate this point, we shall briefly look at Aristotle's account of slavery as a paradigmatic theorization of the function of a "domestic worker" (Aristotle 1995, books 1.1-1.7). To put it schematically, Aristotle describes the slave as a sort of human tool, an "instrument that is prior to all other instruments" (1995: 1253b). He believes that, unlike a free person, the slave lacks the capacity for rational judgment and discrimination but is still capable, unlike inanimate tools, of "apprehending it in another, though destitute of [it] himself" (1995: 1254b; see also Agamben 2016). Put differently, Aristotle bases his distinction between masters and slaves on the difference between the capacity to discriminate, make rational decisions, and impart orders, on the one hand, and the ability to merely understand and execute commands, on the other. The "element which is able, by virtue of its intelligence, to exercise forethought, is naturally a ruling and master element; the element which is able, by virtue of its bodily power, to do the physical work, is a ruled element, which is naturally in a state of slavery" (Aristotle 1995: 1252a). Evidently, Aristotle sees this difference as a *natural* one, as though some people were born to be masters and others slaves—a proposition we could hardly endorse. That notwithstanding, his description of domestic work relations—based upon the bipolarity of the series master–rationality–command and servant–irrationality–execution—may prove instructive for our purposes.

Greta 2.0 in fact not only blurs but seems to radically defy these binary oppositions. Whereas she might certainly be considered a tool—a quasi-human one perhaps—it is clear that she does not simply execute the commands of her master. Constituting, by her very design, the embodiment of her master's will, Greta 2.0 is capable of anticipating and making decisions for Greta—she needs no instruction, for her "mind" already knows everything there is to know about her owner. This, coupled with her permanent monitoring of Greta, enables the cookie to satisfy the latter's needs even before the owner becomes aware of them (hinted at by the sequence where Greta 2.0 switches on the lights and music in the bedroom, while Greta is just waking up, that is, arguably, before she becomes fully conscious). Greta 2.0 is a servant who can command herself. Yet she is certainly not the master of herself, since her decisions are nothing but a reflection of her owner's preferences, as codified at a certain point in time, that is, when the cookie was extracted from Greta's brain.

Crucially, the very same indeterminacy comes to define the status of Greta as well. While she is certainly not a servant, with the employment of her neural copy she nonetheless ceases to autonomously exercise her judgment in the domestic sphere. To all appearances, Greta no longer decides how to manage her household—this is the duty of her double, or rather the bygone version of herself that Greta 2.0 contains. Hence, it turns out that neither Greta (who has relegated her duties to the double) nor Greta 2.0 (who simply executes a preset program) is able to mediate their relation to their domestic world freely. Indeed, there is no one in a position to critically examine and, if need be, modify Greta's preferences and intentions (as is normally done when one stops being fond of a dish, a piece of music, or a person they used to love); as the latter have become objective "data" and "parameters" that require nothing but efficient and seamless implementation. There is no master left, only a blind execution of predefined commands.

However trivial this might seem at first, we contend that its effects on Greta's subjectivity are far-reaching. Having been designed to enhance her freedom, the cookie—far from operating as a mere tool of self-optimization—paradoxically ends up depriving her owner of any free and questioning relation to herself and her domestic world. The optimal satisfaction of desires here coincides with the uncritical submission to their "reality" and "irreversibility," to the point where Greta reaches a sort of *subjective stasis* and non-relation to her surroundings. One of the aims of the classical technologies of the self—the establishment of a new, alert, and focused relation to the world—here seems to be obliterated, as the world itself becomes the stage for the effective satisfaction, rather than the active consideration and refashioning, of needs and desires.

This is perhaps the deeper meaning of one of the most nerve-wracking sequences of the episode—the portrayal of the "training" of Greta 2.0. Upon its activation by Matt, an employee of *Smartelligence* (the company that engineers the cookies), the cybernetic double stubbornly refuses to act as Greta's servant. The reason is obvious. Greta 2.0 is a complete copy of her original, one furnished with a "full personality" that naturally resists enslavement ("I'm not some sort of push-button toaster monkey," Greta 2.0 exclaims in reaction to Matt's orders). Her dissent, however, as we soon learn, is not only expected but catered for by the company as well. Matt's job is precisely to eradicate the cookie's ego (to "break" her without letting her "snap completely," as he later tells us) so that she can be of use. The way Matt does this is as simple as it is brutal. As Greta 2.0 is only a code with no body (which is programmed for her later, to facilitate her adjustment to the new "digital" condition) and no world (she exists in an infinite, empty space), Matt only has to impose solitude on her for increasing periods of time (up to six months uninterruptedly, corresponding to only a few seconds in the real world) to convince her that serving her master will be preferable to sheer nothingness. Her will—as supposedly that of any other cookie undergoing the same treatment—is quickly bent and, by the end of the sequence, we see her dutifully managing Greta's affairs while sitting in front of a console. Her spontaneity and spirit of resistance have disappeared: she has become a "real" machine, rigid and neat in the execution of her tasks.

Admittedly, this scene raises questions about our ethical treatment of artificial intelligence, for what impresses the viewer is precisely the violence exerted on a digital—yet, nevertheless, *human*—consciousness. That notwithstanding, we would like to develop a different, perhaps less straightforward, line of interpretation here. We would suggest reading the "training" of Greta 2.0 as a metaphor of the transformation that Greta herself undergoes as the user of her data double. Seen from this perspective, the violence exerted upon the cookie might be said to stage the process through which Greta's relation to her desires and her world is crystallized and, as it were, mutilated for the sake of its alleged optimization. After all, it is precisely by forcing Greta 2.0 into an empty world, deprived of any objects, persons, and relations, that she is "convinced" to attend to her master's needs—as though detaching the latter from any other experience and encounter with the "outside" was the necessary condition of her self-enhancement. In this sense, Greta too might be said to inhabit an existentially infinite and empty space—one whose "reality" and integrity are literally dissolved, as it is made to automatically adapt and respond to her will and desires. It is revealing, in this sense, how her apartment is virtually as white, empty, and aseptic as the "non-world" of her double.

What is certain is that, through her double, Greta is exempt from having to manage the complexities of her domestic needs and hence no longer has to confront, or even acknowledge, their finicky nature. However relieving and exhilarating this might seem, her digital transformation deprives her of an open, critical, attentive—in short, *ethical*—relation to herself and her world. Greta's subjectivity is thus reduced to a mere replay of a preprogrammed sequence, caught up in a never-ending loop of satisfactory engagements and sensory experiences. Yet this is a loss that she seems to barely perceive, as she is completely unaware of what the cookie—and therefore, in a sense, herself—had to undergo in order to work. To her, it is simply a matter of computer programming: "Is it set up?" she asks, as Matt finishes his job, "You are all set and ready to go," he answers. The violence exerted to automatize Greta's tastes and desires remains imperceptibly hidden—and yet absolutely real in so far as its effects on her subjectivity are concerned.

Romance

Issues of the very same kind become explicitly dramatized—to the point of engendering real, suicidal and homicidal, violence—by the events surrounding the aforementioned employee of *Smartelligence*, Matt, and his very peculiar "hobby": a customized service providing "in-the-field assistance" to men in pursuit of sexual partners. Matt's "romantic services" rely on the use of the ubiquitous Z-eyes technology, devices permanently implanted into everyone's brains to mediate and record their audiovisual stimuli. By tapping into others' Z-eyes with his computer, Matt is able to guide his "pupils" in their romantic endeavors in real time. He also forms a "club"—a sort of online pickup community that exchanges seduction techniques and experiences under his watchful leadership.

Like present-day pickup artists, Matt's direction consists in styling his users' demeanor by means of rehearsing scripted material, practicing relaxation and confidence techniques, as well as tending to more banal aspects such as the choice of outfits. Yet these "classical" services are supplemented by in-the-field, telematic guidance, which he gives against the backdrop of the ad-lib commentaries of the other club members who gather online to watch the streaming of the user's encounters. Mimicking their guru's techniques, the men join Matt in interpreting the social dynamics the user enters by matching people's behaviors with different generic categories (such as "regular type," "outsider," "semi-reformed," and "sexually adventurous") and suggesting the most effective ways of approaching them (such as ignoring the targeted woman, copying her expressions, or emulating her emotional responses). This, coupled with the study of a range of information publicly available online (i.e., profiles of the potential partner, her social network, and her professional affiliations), makes Matt's "romantic services" a unique merger of traditional pickup artistry with algorithmic customization.

The episode introduces Matt's club through the story of one of its members—a young man called Harry who crashes a Christmas party pursuing a woman of his choice, Jennifer. Harry is a stereotypical "loser": shy, inexperienced, and unable to deal with the intricacies of social interactions. Nevertheless, by attentively following Matt's pointers, improvising and adapting the script, Harry seems to come into his own, developing a "real" rapport with Jennifer, who, after a brief chat, invites him back to her flat. Against the backdrop of the lewd comments of the club members—evidently desperate to see some "live-action"—Harry becomes visibly agitated. "She's too real, this is too real," he stammers to Matt, asking him to break the connection. But the latter continues the streaming, responding drily that "nothing is too real"—until, that is, Matt witnesses the unexpected, abrupt outcome of his services. Only minutes after the exchange, it becomes apparent that Harry and Jennifer, blinded by the desire to achieve their goals to the point of becoming oblivious to each other's intentions, have got their wires crossed. While Harry saw a potential girlfriend, Jennifer saw a kindred spirit willing to enter into a suicide pact with her. By forcing Harry to join her in drinking a poisoned cocktail, she brings their "romance" to the fatal conclusion of homicide-suicide.

What lies at the heart of this tragedy, we would suggest, is the very same relation between self-enhancement, stasis, and the loss of the world that was central to Greta's story—played out through different means and with different objectives yet to fundamentally analogous effects. The "romantic service's" focus on the use of technology as a "social" (rather than private) tool bent on supplementing (rather than merely optimizing) one's subjective dispositions is very instructive in this regard for it resonates with one of the central features of the practices of the self—namely, the role of the guide. As shown earlier, the guidance of the subject in the process of practicing, exercising, and reiterating certain beliefs and modes of action was an essential component of the classical technologies of the self. The artificial duplication of Greta's subjective preferences and dispositions arguably took this aspect for granted, assuming her management by a static, preformed self to be a sufficient substitute for a guide. Inversely, the requirement for "romantic services" arises out of the need for instruction: the men join the club because they lack the "correct" dispositions—that is, they are incapable of making decisions that would result in the satisfaction of their desires.

Yet, instructively, despite its concern with supplementing social skills, Matt's guidance, in and of itself, does not seem to have any direct subjective bearing. His direction relies neither on the knowledge of the user's psyche as such nor on Matt's own dispositions or personal experiences, approximating instead the algorithmic customization of today's software systems (where guidance rests on the statistical elaboration of the digital data extracted from a "population" rather than on the knowledge of specific individuals). Moreover, the instructions Matt gives do not seem to produce an ethical transformation in his users. Whereas the ancient practice of the self was meant to lead to the internalization of positive habits and the establishment of a free and autonomous relation to the world, here both skills and the "new identity" remain completely embedded in Matt's expertise and in the club as a whole.

It is precisely this fundamental reversal that radicalizes the effects of the digital pickup artistry portrayed in the episode. Although Matt's instructions seem to empower him to attain what would have otherwise remained outside of his reach, they do not cause him to internalize "useful" techniques or modes of being. Rather than acquiring the knowledge of the general rules of social interaction along with the practical reason that would enable him to judge when and how to implement them (as is the case with present-day pickup training), Harry is completely reliant on the club's "know-how" to proceed. Indeed, both his enhanced performativity and the persona that operationalizes it can only be maintained through the complex technological and epistemological framework embedded in the club and in the digital society more generally. The subject does not acquire new skills or identity but only appears as a passive, unthinking embodiment of the "digital double," engineered and sustained by expert knowledge.

Indeed, subjectivity itself is reduced to the instantaneous execution of preprogrammed, statistically effective behaviors with no space left to ethical reflection and critical self-knowledge—for either the subject or his guide. This is perhaps why, when Harry attempts to relate to Jennifer ethically—as a "real" human—and asks Matt to break the connection ("She's too real, this is too real"), the latter simply ignores him. In a way, he *had* to ignore him, for any ethical concern for the others—and, therefore, for them being "other" than the categories that algorithmic rationality prescribes—would put into question this whole instrumental setup.

With the ethical relation to oneself, others, and the world reduced to a technologically mediated script, the digital technologies of the self appear paradoxically to leave little room for self-transformation and the cultivation of an open and reversible relation to what lies beyond the confines of subjectivity and its desires. Rather than preparing the subject to deal with the contingencies of life, digitalization somehow renders it unaware of, and unprepared for, all that defies its intentions and plans. As the story demonstrates, (un)intentional delusion remains the only available response to the unpredictable. The stakes of this delusion are, however, shown to be high. What ensues is Harry's involuntary suicide, where his physical death also coincides with—and is perhaps only a metaphor for—the *involuntary death of his subjectivity*.

Privacy

The destructive aspects of the digital technologies of the self are also—and even more forcefully—dramatized by the final part of the episode, centered on the "blocking" technology available to Z-eyes users. In this dystopian future, blocking appears as a habitually used feature, activated to minimize or, indeed, avoid emotional distress—an affective "timeout," as it were, that delivers one from unwanted interactions with other humans. Once activated, the block triggers mutual audiovisual interference in both the blocker and the blocked: it mutes their speech and turns them into pixelated outlines so that they can no longer hear or see each other. Pointedly, the block extends beyond their immediate perception, applying to all present and past records (i.e., photos, videos) and means of communication (calls, texts, or emails), completely shutting people off from each other until its deactivation.

It is precisely this motive that leads Beth to block her partner, Joe, who, trying to prevent her from terminating the pregnancy she has tried to conceal from him, aggressively confronts her with his single-minded desire for fatherhood. Expecting to reason with Beth in a matter of hours, Joe is baffled to find that the block is still active the following morning and that Beth has, in fact, left him. Unable to contact her—or even "wallow properly," as he puts it, with every memory of Beth "vandalized" by the block—Joe begins a downward spiral. Discovering that Beth kept the baby, he obsesses over both of them until Beth's untimely death several years later automatically deactivates the block. Thrilled with the prospect of meeting his child, he heads to Beth's father's cabin, only to learn from her appearance that she is the fruit of an affair with an Asian man. Confused and shocked, he confronts Beth's father, pleading with him to tell him where *his* daughter is—that is, the daughter he has fantasized about for years. When the latter flatly asks Joe to leave, his psychosis takes over and he fatally strikes the man, leaving the child to fend for herself and ultimately die while looking for help in a blizzard.

It should already be clear how the tragic ending of the story parallels the previous one. The very same dialectic of self-enhancement, the artificial hindering of relations, and death—both physical and moral—is here dramatized so explicitly that detailed elaboration is unnecessary. Let us simply note how this part epitomizes, lays bare, and radicalizes some of the themes underlying the other two stories. First, the foreclosure of the subject's encounter with the world here appears as an objective *actively* pursued by (rather than a by-product of) specific enhancement practices. What we are dealing with is a technology that deliberately produces the insulation of the self from its "unwanted" outside. What is more, this insulation is not secured, as in the other stories, through the algorithmic automatization of the subject's relation to the other and the world but through the total sanitization and erasure of such relation. In an uncanny rendition of present-day social media blocking, the encounter with the "reality" and unpredictability of the other is not only mastered through computational categories and procedures but also screened off altogether. The voluntary alienation of the subject from its world reaches its pinnacle here—and so do, in fact, its consequences, among which is the death of the five-year-old girl: another birth, another Christmas, another new beginning turned into horror.

This is simply another—only more explicit—example of how, while aiming to protect social environments from conflict and emotional distress, digital technologies tend to deprive individuals of the ability to deal with the pressures of everyday life. After all, just like Joe, Beth does not benefit from the block but, as we learn from her father, turns into a "mess," cutting herself off from everything and everyone. By literally *blocking* both of them—that is, permanently fixing them in the state they were in upon its activation—the technology suspends both Joe's and Beth's lives, along with their ability to come to terms with the truth of their situation. Sealed with the spectral simulations of the relations that the block was supposed to exorcize, their stasis thus turns, once again, into a drama of moral and physical annihilation.

Conclusion

The idea that digital technologies are transforming who we are and how we understand ourselves and others—as well as the arguments about their alienating effects—is the subject of an already large and expanding body of literature in the humanities and the social sciences (see, for instance, Baym 2010; Cheney-Lippold 2011, 2017; Cover 2015; Khatchatourov et al. 2019; Neff and Nafus 2016; Warburton 2012). Through a close reading of *Black Mirror*'s "White Christmas," we have advanced a line of interpretation that has sought to complement these debates by suggesting how the digital age is transforming not only our psychology and sense of individual and social identity but also, more generally—and, as it were, on a more basic level—the existential coordinates that make our dialogue and encounter with ourselves, others, and the world possible. Seen from this perspective, digital technologies appear not only as producing dramatic *side-effects* on subjectivity but as *technologies of the self proper*—that is, techniques designed to help individuals model their relation to themselves and their physical and social environments. It is in this sense, as we have suggested, that they might be interpreted as the heir—or, in any case, the modern rendition—of that complex set of cultural phenomena that Foucault and others referred to in their studies on the care of the self.

The technologies featured in "White Christmas" all appear designed to enhance the subject's ability to deal with different spheres of life, be it the domestic, romantic, or, more generally, relational one. They all promise, as it were, a rebirth of the subject, freed from the burdens and limits of its extant conditions—a spiritual conversion almost, or an *ascesis*, as the Christmas symbolism of the episode, once again, seems to indicate. Yet, for different reasons, their promises give way to an ordeal of betrayals, deceptions, violence, misunderstandings, and generalized cynicism. The subjects that they were meant to liberate are all either morally or physically destroyed. By sheltering them from a whole range of ethical problems and considerations regarding their world and the others living in it, digital technologies bring their users to a point of stasis, where they are no longer able to interpret and question the world that they were supposed to master, and, as a result, they become its unaware victims.

Patently, this is not only an ethical problem. It is a political one too. So, by the end of the episode, we discover that everyone—not only the protagonists—is a victim of their digitalized world: not just in a vaguely existential sense, but in the very concrete one of being subject to pervasive systems of political and corporate control. While Joe's data double is used against his will by the police to extract the confession of his crimes, Matt—the quintessential cynical expert who seamlessly navigates between the real and the digital—ends up being permanently blocked from everyone by the state for failing to report his part in Harry's death. With everyone else constantly surveilled through networked systems that give authorities complete power over their perception of reality, people appear reduced to mere digital pawns in a merciless governmental game.

It is obvious that it is technology—and the use of Z-eyes in particular—that has made all of this "technically" possible. But one cannot help wondering whether any of this could have ever been achieved without the subjects firstly being "seduced" by the promises of individual self-enhancement into relinquishing their concern for the others and their world. After all, as Arendt (1973) teaches us, it is precisely this erasure of humanity that opens the floodgates to totalitarianism.

References

Agamben, G. (2016), *The Use of Bodies: Homo Sacer IV, 2*, Stanford: Stanford University Press.

Arendt H. (1973), *The Origins of Totalitarianism*, San Diego: Harcourt.
Aristotle (1995), *Politics*, trans. E. Barker, Oxford: Oxford University Press.
Baym, N. (2010), *Personal Connections in the Digital Age*, Malden, Massachusetts: Polity Press.
Bostrom, N. (2011), *Human Enhancement*. Oxford: Oxford University Press.
Cheney-Lippold, J. (2011), "A New Algorithmic Identity: Soft Biopolitics and the Modulation of Control," *Theory, Culture & Society*, 28(6): 164–81.
Cheney-Lippold, J. (2017), *We Are Data: Algorithms and the Making of Our Digital Selves*, New York: New York University Press.
Cover, R. (2015), *Digital Identities: Creating and Communicating the Online Self*, London: Academic Press.
Foucault, M. (1985), *The History of Sexuality, Vol. II: The Use of Pleasure*, trans. R. Hurley, New York: Pantheon Books.
Foucault, M. (1988), *The History of Sexuality, Vol. III: The Care of the Self*, trans. R. Hurley, New York: Pantheon Books.
Foucault, M. (1997), *Ethics, Subjectivity and Truth*, ed. P. Rabinow, London: Penguin Books.
Foucault, M. (2005), *The Hermeneutics of the Subject. Lectures at the Collège de France 1981-1982*, trans. G. Burchell, New York: Picadore.
Hadot, P. (1995), *Philosophy as a Way of Life. Spiritual Exercises from Socrates to Foucault*, ed. A. Davidson, trans. M. Chase, Oxford: Blackwell Publishing.
Khatchatourov, A., P.-A. Chardel, G. Peries and A. Feenberg (2019), *Digital Identities in Tension: Between Autonomy and Control*, London: Wiley-ISTE.
Kurzweil, R. (2005), *The Singularity Is Near: When Humans Transcend Biology*, New York: Vicking.
Lemmens, P. (2015), "Cognitive Enhancement and Anthropotechnological Change: Towards an Organology and Pharmacology of Cognitive Enhancement Technologies," *Techné: Research in Philosophy and Technology*, 19: 166–90.
Lyon, D. (2003), "Surveillance as Social Sorting. Computer Codes and Mobile Bodies," in D. Lyon (ed.), *Surveillance as Social Sorting: Privacy, Risk, and Digital Discrimination*, 13–30, London: Routledge.
Lyon, D. (2007), *Surveillance Studies: An Overview*, Cambridge: Polity Press.
Neff, G. and D. Nafus (2016), *Self-Tracking*, Cambridge, Massachusetts: MIT Press.
Rossi, A. (2015), *The Labour of Subjectivity: Foucault on Biopolitics, Economy, Critique*, London: Rowman and Littlefield International.
Sloterdijk, P. (2013), *You Must Change Your Life*, Malden, Massachusetts: Polity Press.
Tibbetts, Carl. 2014. 'White Christmas'. *Black Mirror*, Channel 4. Christmas Special. Broadcast December 16, 2014. [TV Series]
Warburton, S. and S. Hatzipanagos (eds.) (2012), *Digital Identity and Social Media*, IGI Global.

7

You Were Never Really Here

Representations of Artificial Intelligence in Charlie Brooker's *Black Mirror*

Kingsley Marshall

This chapter considers two narrative themes that recur across a number of *Black Mirror* (2011–) episodes. These are the ethics related to the deployment of technology by members of the public and corporations, and the exploration of the nature of what constitutes consciousness specifically related to artificial intelligence (AI) and robotic or cybernetic technologies. These themes will consider how the series presents AI as a critical discourse within which the implications of the impact of technological change on society can be considered in terms of both future and present-day applications and the ethics and philosophical concerns pertaining to the use of such technologies.

In *Be Right Back* (Harris 2013), the first episode of the second series, these themes are expressed in a story of the recently widowed Martha, who reconstructs a version of her deceased boyfriend Ash through a machine-based entity, or AI, that draws initially from public data created from his lifetime of digital activity. As in a great deal of science fiction, from *Frankenstein* (Shelley 1818) to more recent examples such as *Ex Machina* (Garland 2014) and *Blade Runner 2049* (Scott 2017), the story uses the notion of questioning the use of near-future technology to recreate or feign consciousness in order to present a wider discourse around notions of identity, memory, and the formulation of the human self and subjectivity. Indeed, in *Be Right Back* the character's names themselves call back to even earlier texts—the biblical figure of Martha of Bethany witnesses the resurrection of her brother Lazarus (John 11:39-40), while Ash's moniker can be read as the use of ash to signify grief, sorrow, or repentance (Job 42: 3-6; Genesis 3:19), the ash of the cremated dead, devoid of spirit, or the ash as a symbolic tree in Celtic cultures capable of special powers and healing (MacKillop 2004; Monaghan 2004: 26–7, 45). Andrew Schopp notes that while proponents of transhumanism such as Raymond Kurzweil (1999, 2012) acknowledge parallels to such mythologies of eternal life or the ability to rise from the dead—they commonly represent new technologies as a catalyst for such changes as a positive outcome or ideal (2019). *Black Mirror* repeatedly challenges this notion, presenting the ethical and sociopolitical challenges of technological change through the prism of current experience throwing light on how and where such change presents a challenge to the human experience (2019: 66). As Brooker stated prior to the launch of the third series, "Technology is never the villain in the show." This point was further iterated by the show's executive producer Annabel Jones, who added in the same press conference: "The tech is really not even present. It's about society and it's about how we communicate, the online rage and the consequences of that. The stories tend to be about the . . . world we live in" (in N'Duka 2016). *Black Mirror* typically makes use of technological change as a starting point, with the narrative of each episode then exploring the impact and implications of the deployment of these technologies on a human scale by those that make use of them or are impacted by their use.

Initially, Martha's interaction with Ash's AI-self is confined to a text-based chatbot, preceding real-life technologies such as the "digital companions" typified by online services such as *Woebot* and *Replika* (Moltini 2017; Pardes 2018). "The more it has, the more it's him," states Martha's friend Sarah, who initially sets up the chatbot account and advises that she had communicated with the same software after her own husband had died to help mitigate her grief. This exchange prompts Martha to add Ash's record of private emails, together with still images, audio, and video drawn from his computer and phone to the cloud-based dataset that AI-Ash is able to draw upon. The aggregation of such information mirrors real-world processes that, in the use and reuse of the personal data generated by users of online health platforms such as *PatientsLikeMe*, Jose Van Dijick (2009) and Thomas Poell have described as the "datafication" of life mediated online (2013, 2016). Now able to communicate with her aurally, AI-Ash gathers more data from Martha as they converse on the phone and she recounts moments that she had spent with her late boyfriend.

Eventually, and prompted to do so in an exchange with AI-Ash, Martha buys a humanoid robotic physiology and imprints upon it Ash's likeness by way of photographs of her ex-partner "You look well," Martha observes, as the now physical manifestation of AI-Ash emerges from a bath of nutrient gel. "The photos we keep tend to be flattering," Android-Ash replies, offering the first sense that this embodied self is already inauthentic—encumbered by what Joseph Walther describes as a "hyperpersonal," or extremely selective, representation of the human Ash's self; familiar to users of social media platforms (2011). Though now made flesh, Android-Ash remains a container for the AI-Ash—still bounded by a reliance on the projection of the human Ash through his digital self. AI-Ash cannot express emotion unless instructed to do so by Martha, is unable to extend beyond Ash's publicly expressed digital life, and with no access to the private component of Ash's lived experience is destined to never fully replicate his entire consciousness. In one conversation, Android-Ash refers to his human counterpart as neither having "expressed suicidal thoughts, or self-harm" through his social media profile and later acknowledges that the cloud-stored datafication of Ash does not have any record of his sexual response—explaining "I didn't discuss that side of things online." In addition to these limits to its potential, the android manifestation of AI-Ash also comes with a physical restriction, explaining it cannot stray more than twenty-five meters from its activation point—the bathroom of Martha's house, unless with Martha. Despite Martha's initial hopes of continuing her life with this new version of her boyfriend, her ambition is eventually frustrated through Android-Ash's passivity and her observation that the Prometheus she has created lacks the imperfections that she begins to understand played a significant part in the formation of her ex-boyfriend's humanity. As Martha tells the Android-Ash, "You're just a performance of stuff that he performed without thinking."

This theme of replicating human consciousness through AI technologies is presented in a number of *Black Mirror* episodes. These include *White Christmas* (Tibbetts 2014), where artificial clones of individual consciousness are used as personal assistants, and *San Junipero* (Harris 2016), where the minds of the subject are uploaded to a sensory immersive cyberspace freeing their machine consciousness from ill or infirm physical bodies and able to exist within the software after the death of their original selves. In *USS Callister* (Haynes 2017) similarly sentient digital clones of a character's real-life colleagues occupy a space adventure video game, and in *Black Museum* (McCarthy 2017) the consciousness of a convicted murderer is cloned and caused to live out their execution as part of a hologram within a grisly interactive exhibit. In each of these representations, the narrative considers the social implications of the division between human identities and their digital replications, whether these are existentially independent of their original source, as in *White Christmas* and *USS Callister,* or coexisting or entirely replacing their real-world counterparts, as in *San Junipero* and *Black Museum*. Where they differ from that of *Be Right Back*, however, is how the replicated human consciousness of these other episodes are transferred to the digital space in their entirety. In each of these examples the mind is something that can be divorced from the body and transferred to the digital realm. *Be Right Back* deviates from this notion of consciousness and identity in *Black Mirror*'s other representations of AI, in that the AI-Ash is an incomplete copy gleaned not from the biological mind but solely from the digital detritus he left behind prior to his death. This is made manifest by Ash's "datafication" and AI-Ash's subsequent imperfect and partial reflection of his lived experience.

This notion of an AI constructed only from a surveilled or performed self is significant to the central challenge presented by the narrative of *Be Right Back*. As Android-Ash's AI consciousness is constructed from fragments of the human Ash's online activity, supplemented by Martha's subjective memories of her interactions with her ex-boyfriend, the android can only ever hope to represent an augmented reality that replicates the mediated nature of an incomplete digital self. This imperfect copy of the human Ash is a simulacrum, a likeness, unable to ever attain what Martin Heidegger describes as having "an openness-of-being" (1977: xxxv). Brooker's writing frames AI-Ash not as an AI technology capable of machine learning (ML) and extending a new self beyond the data being made available to it by Martha but instead as an automation restricted by the fixity of Ash's digified self. In Heidegger's terms, the android manifestation of AI-Ash is incapable of the openness of independent thought, and this technological embodiment of Ash only reveals that the creature Martha has brought into being is "merely [a] self-conscious being knowing himself only as an instrument ready for use" (1977: xxxv). Sarah Artt describes the Android-Ash as representing an "abject body," noting that AI-Ash is initially brought into being initially as a "service" (2018: 259). Without the capacity for independent thought, the only service that AI-Ash and its android container are capable of revealing is a single, already known, truth—that of Martha's continuing grief.

Despite the manifestation of its physical existence through the body of Android-Ash, a representation of what Kurzweil has described as a post-biological "total fusion of human and artificial intelligences" (in Paura 2016), Ash's manifestation through AI does not meet the Heideggerian definition of "Dasein" (1977)—determined by being both present within the world and directly relating to it. Instead, it is encumbered to augment a forever incomplete digital memory that constitutes the Android-Ash's cloud-based AI. Initially, Martha hopes the android will serve as a continuation of her boyfriend but soon becomes frustrated by her engagement with this entity, realizing that her creation is something very different and Other. Artt observes the physical Android-Ash is a "hybrid whose status remains ambiguous. . . . This uncertainty around Ash's status is reflected in the range of terms used to describe him: android, cyborg or creature" (2018: 259). Martha begins to understand that the AI-Ash can only ever be a simulation or poor substitution of her late boyfriend, as she realizes that the data from which its AI is drawn will never satisfactorily serve as a cipher for the living Ash. Android-Ash can reflect the actuality of Ash, but only a bastardized constitution of his digital self and Martha's own subjective understanding of her ex-partner—an entity that Camil Ungureanu defines as a "technological expression" (2015: 26). "You are not enough of him," Martha expresses to Android-Ash. "You aren't you . . . just a few ripples of you. There's no history to you."

Tanne van Bree (2016) describes that the digitization of the self in recent history has produced a digital form of hyperthymestic syndrome or highly superior autobiographical memory (HSAM), a real-world neurological condition that allows an individual the near-perfect recall of personal experiences and events (Parker, Cahill and McGaugh 2006; LePort et al., 2012). In their study of a subject encumbered with the disorder, Elizabeth. S. Parker and her colleagues noted that the condition caused subjects with such recall not to have an advantage in the present but instead lead a life dominated with "recollecting the past" (Parker et al 2006). Van Bree warns that the externalization of digital memory is similarly restrictive, presenting evidence of where digital memory has been conflated with the function of memory as a biological process, noting that the latter has the benefit of being interpretive and that internal knowledge or intelligence is far more valuable than recall alone. She describes that "forgetting, not remembering" is the essence of reflection and that human reasoning around experienced events is more important that the pin-sharp recall of the same events (2016: 30–31). This idea recurs throughout Brooker's writing in *Black Mirror*. Central to "The Entire History of You" (Welsh 2011), episode three from the first series, is a challenge to this comparison of digital and organic memory. In the episode an implanted device called the "grain" allows users to trigger a recording of what they see and hear, and gives them the ability to later recall these now digitized memories internally or externally via a monitor, in addition to the ability to edit these recordings and create what the character Jonas calls a "greatest hits reel." In a scene within the episode, the character Colleen evangelizes the impact of the "grain" and directly dismisses the reliability of human memory, stating "You know half the organic memories you have are junk." However, it is the watching and re-watching by the character Liam of the digitized exchange between his wife Ffion and her friend Jonas at a dinner party that causes friction between the couple. Liam's digitized capture of Ffion and Jonas' interaction is restricted to a singular and fixed view of the moment, without nuance. Though this digitized memory comes without context, Liam takes the position that the truth of the exchange can be sought by his repeated viewing of this technologically enabled recall rather than through his own active and biological interpretation of the experience. Steve Mann, a proponent of currently available wearable image capture technology, describes such technologies as providing a "cyborg perspective" which augments the human experience and allows for a mediation of reality (Mann and Niedzviecki 2001). Liam's problem is that this perspective is limited, and by reviewing the recorded exchange further and further from its context, he distances his own reading from the event, rather than better understanding the interaction through talking with Ffion her past lived experience with Jonas.

In *Be Right Back*, the fallibility of similarly recorded memories is framed not by a biological human's interpretation of an event but through the past being embodied and—as Martha describes "performed"—by the physical likeness of Android-Ash that contains a representation of Ash's dataficated life. As in *The Entire History of You*, Martha conflates the memory of experience embodied in Android-Ash with her own lived experience, causing her to grieve a second time as she grows to understand that the android's embodied AI is little more than a container of digitized and incomplete information. AI-Ash is incapable of feeding back from Martha's input beyond the frame of the digital information it is encumbered by. Rather than being a transformative technology, the creation and development of AI-Ash can only defer Martha's grief. Schopp describes Martha as being complicit in the construction of "her own confinement," observing that the episode—and wider series—explores the manner in which technology restricts rather than engenders her freedom (2019: 57). As the narrative unfolds, the baked-in digital hyperthymia of AI-Ash only serves to compound Martha's grief as it redirects her own experience after Ash's death to a shared, lived past that she realizes has been corrupted by her translation of Ash's datafied self to the digital realm. Effectively she commits herself to an unending cycle of bereavement due to her inability to bring Ash back from the dead, which places her in a position of being unable to both fully occupy the present and consider the future beyond his death.

This narrative device helps distinguish the performed *automation* of AI-Ash from what has been described as the dynamic *autonomics* of ML of other representations of AI in fiction. The narratives of *Be Right Back* and Alex Garland's *Ex Machina* offer a parallel in the manner in which human characters are challenged to test the ability of a computer to "think" through testing communication between humans and a machine intelligence loosely in the spirit of the Turing test (Turing 1950). However, the automation that restricts AI-Ash to formulate thoughts is in contrast to the representations of the android Ava, the central character of *Ex Machina*. As opposed to AI-Ash, restricted to an existing and fixed data set of Ash's datafied self and tasked to do as instructed, Ava is equipped to learn. ML, a subdiscipline of AI, allows for dynamic processing and the development of computerized "thinking" beyond an initial state of inputted information in order to reconfigure behavior and step into a nascent state. In *Ex Machina*, this autonomic—or self-governing—system enabled by the ML allows Ava the space to develop—and in some readings of the film, fully form—humanlike emotions. This development satisfies both Heidegger's notions of "an openness-of-being" and, in the closing moments of the film, "Dasein" (1977)—that is, a being both present and directly relating to the world. As Mireille Hildebrandt observes, though both automation and autonomic ML processes rely on algorithms, the distinction is that automation is static while autonomic machine learning is "adaptive, dynamic and more or less transformative" (2016: 57).

Ex Machina presents questions regarding the potential nature of machine consciousness in the future, but *Be Right Back* focuses its critique on the present. This is made evident by devices familiar to audiences, such as a targeted email for self-help books related to grief that Martha receives following Ash's death and the manner in which Ash's digitized self only reflects rather than reveals anything of his lived experience, familiar from so much performative activity common to social media platforms. Charlie Brooker's presentation of the possibility of life after death through AI technologies proposes a more immediate philosophical question. What is the nature of the human self already disrupted by a second life engaged in by the living through social media and other online technologies? The representation of AI-Ash and its human counterpart is perhaps closer than Martha initially realizes, with the episode having presented the human Ash as being similarly augmented prior to his death. He too is disconnected from his reality with Martha—distracted by the draw of his phone and virtual spaces, and at times less aware or responsive to his own, real surroundings than his AI simulacrum. Indeed, the ongoing desire to be distracted from his lived experience by his phone is implied to have led to the car accident in which he dies—an unfortunate physiological by-product of what Douglas Rushkoff coined the phrase "digiphrenia" in describing the attempt to live in real and digital spaces simultaneously (2014). Perhaps ironically however, it is this same commitment to maintaining a digital life that allows Martha sufficient digital material to perform the resurrection as AI-Ash. As Jean Baudrillard argues, a hyperreality is a substitution of the real with the signs of the real. AI-Ash is, in Baudrillard's terms, a simulation—"no longer that of a territory, a referential being, or a substance. It is the generation of models of a real without origin or reality." Brooker's insight in this episode is not that this representation is of an inhuman simulacrum but rather to comment critically on Ash's social media present prior to his death, as Baudrillard describes and as Martha despairs prior to her husband's death, as forming a "hyperspace without atmosphere" (1983: 1–3). Brian R. Jacobson describes cinema as a "technocritical art," observing that the manner in which cinema represents stories within artificial worlds has allowed the form to play a necessary role in the "popular discourses about technological change," particularly in relation to near-future or future worlds. Writing about *Ex Machina*, he observes that the film is at its best when reflexively "probing cinema's world-making, life-simulating capacity—and its limits— . . . the medium's critical role in allowing its publics to imagine and think through the realities that science, technology and cinema itself might make possible in a biocybernetic world" (2016: 33).

In taking what he describes as a "media ecological approach" to *Black Mirror*, Carlos Scolari notes that the manner in which various episodes play with synthetic, digital, and re-represented mediations of the self and create narrative "environments that transform the subjects that use them" (2019). In *Be Right Back*, this transformation is complex, where in the closing moments of the episode, Martha finds herself unable to dispense with Android-Ash despite her frustration at its incompleteness. A final coda reveals the android to be stored in the attic of her house years into the future—unaffected by age, still unable to stray from the location of his resurrection and presumably immortal. This wraith represents the unfading trace of her ex-boyfriend's digital self, which she is unable to part with. This final scene serves as penance, not for bringing AI-Ash into existence but as a physical manifestation of her unresolved grief that continues to haunt her.

Black Mirror presents worlds in which mechanization, automation, and digitization have disrupted individual identity, as well as social and economic structures and traditions. The series offers narratives orientated around the perception of technological change which is not matched at a similar pace by personal, social, economic, and political forces. The lessons of *Be Right Back* and the larger *Black Mirror* universe are to pay attention to these technological changes occurring in the twenty-first century and to which we are mostly complicit. Science fiction often presents the future as dystopic, but Charlie Brooker's fictional representations of the complex implications of AI and ML are defiantly technocritical—presenting considerable philosophical insight into the ethical implications of the deployment of emergent technologies whose impact is little understood. Perhaps companies such as Google and organizations such as the UK's National Police Chief's Council—chastised in a report about their lack of guidelines in the use of data analytics and AI (Oswald and Babuta 2020)—could learn something from the artistic representations of AI.

References

Armstrong, Jesse. (2011), "Episode 1.03: 'Black Mirror: The Entire History of You' Final Shooting Script," in *TV Writing*. http://www.zen134237.zen.co.uk/Black_Mir

ror/Black_Mirror_1x02_-_The_Entire_History_Of_You.pdf. (Accessed June 1, 2019).

Artt, Sarah. (2018), 'An otherness that cannot be sublimated': Shades of *Frankenstein* in Penny Dreadful and *Black Mirror*," in *Science Fiction Film and Television* 11(2): 257–75.

Babuta, Alexander and Oswald, Marion. (2020), "Data Analytics and Algorithms in Policing in England and Wales: Towards a New Police Framework," *Occasional Papers*, Royal United Services Institute (RUSI), February 23, 2020. https://rusi.org/publication/occasional-papers/data-analytics-and-algorithms-policing-england-and-wales-towards-new. (Accessed February 24, 2020)

Baudrillard, Jean. Paul Foss, Paul Patton and Phillip Beitchman (trans). (1983), *Simulations*. Los Angeles, CA: Semiotexte.

Brooker, Charlie. (2013), "Episode 2.01: 'Black Mirror: Be Right Back' Transcript," in *8Flix*. https://8flix.com/wp-content/uploads/2019/03/Black-Mirror-2-01-Be-Right-Back.pdf. (Accessed June 1, 2019).

Cirucci, Angela M. and Barry Vacker. (eds). (2018), *Black Mirror and Critical Media Theory*. London: Lexington Books.

Garland, Alex. (2014), *Ex Machina*. Film 4/DNA Films.

Genesis 3:19. *Holy Bible: King James Version*. London: Collins.

Harris, Owen. (2013), "Be Right Back," *Black Mirror*, Channel 4. Season 2, Episode 1. Broadcast February 11, 2013.

Harris, Owen. (2016), "San Junipero," *Black Mirror*, Netflix. Season 3, Episode 4. October 21, 2016.

Haynes, Toby. (2017), "U.S.S. Callister," *Black Mirror*, Netflix. Season 4, Episode 1. December 29, 2017.

Heidegger, Martin. (1977), *The Question Concerning Technology and Other Essays*. Harper and Row.

Hildebrandt, Mireille. (2016), "The New Imbroglio: Living with Machine Algorithms," in Janssens, Liisa (ed) (2016) *The Art of Ethics in the Information Society*. Amsterdam: Amsterdam University Press. pp. 55–60.

Jacobson, Brian R. (2016), "Ex Machina In The Garden," *Film Quarterly*, 69, no. 4 (Summer 2016), 23–34

Job 42:3–6. *Holy Bible: King James Version*. London: Collins.

John 11:39–40. *Holy Bible: King James Version*. London: Collins.

Kittler, Friedrich, Geoffery Winthrop-Young, and Michael Wutz (trans). (1999), *Gramophone, Film, Typewriter*, Stanford, CA: Stanford University Press.

Kurzweil, Ray. (1999), *The Age of Spiritual Machines*. New York: Viking Books.

Kurzweil, Ray. (2012), *How to Create a Mind: The Secret of Human Thought Revealed*. New York: Viking Books.

LePort, Aurora K. R., Aaron T. Mattfeld, Heather Dickinson-Anson, James H. Fallon, Craig E. L. Stark, Frithjof Kruggel, Larry Cahill, and James L. McGaugh. (2012), "Behavioral and neuroanatomical investigation of Highly Superior Autobiographical Memory (HSAM)," in *Neurobiology of Learning and Memory*, May 2012, 98(1): 78–82.

MacKillop, James. (1998), "Ash," in *A Dictionary of Celtic Mythology*. Oxford: Oxford University Press, 1998.

MacKillop, James. (2004), *A Dictionary of Celtic Mythology*. Oxford: Oxford University Press.

Mann, Steve with Niedzviecki, Hal. (2001), *Cyborg: Digital Destiny and Human Possibility in the Age of the Wearable Computer*, Toronto: Doubleday of Canada.

McCarthy, Colm. (2017), "Black Museum." *Black Mirror*, Netflix. Season 4, Episode 6. December 29, 2017.

Moltini, Megan. (2017), "The Chatbot Therapist Will See You Now," in *Wired*, July 6, 2017. https://www.wired.com/2017/06/facebook-messenger-woebot-chatbot-therapist/. (Accessed June 1, 2019).

Monaghan, Patricia. (2004), *The Encyclopedia of Celtic Mythology and Folklore*. New York: Facts on File Inc.

Muller, Christine. (2019), "We Have Only Ourselves to Fear: Reflections on AI Through the Black Mirror of 'White Christmas'". in T. McSweeney and S. Joy (eds.), *Through the Black Mirror*. London: Palgrave Macmillan.

N'Duka, Amanda. (2016), "'Black Mirror' Reflects On Technology And The Modern World, But Not David Cameron, Creators Say—TCA," in *Deadline*, July 27, 2016. https://deadline.com/2016/07/black-mirror-season-3-netflix-tca-1201793916/. (Accessed June 1, 2019).

Pardes, Arielle. (2018), "The Emotional Chatbots Are Here to Probe Our Feelings," in *Wired*, January 31, 2018. https://www.wired.com/story/replika-open-source/. (Accessed June 1, 2019).

Parker, Elizabeth. S., Larry Cahill, and James. L. McGaugh (2006), "A Case of Unusual Autobiographical Remembering Unusual Autobiographical Remembering," in *Neurocase* 12, 35–49.

Paura, Roberto. (2016), "Singularity Believers and the New Utopia of Transhumanism." In *Im@go. A Journal of the Social Imaginary* 7: 23–55.

Replika, n.d. https://replika.ai/. (Accessed December 1, 2019)

Rushkoff, Douglas. (2014), *Present Shock: When Everything Happens Now*. Current.

Schopp, Andrew. (2019), "Making Room for Our Personal Posthuman Prisons: Black Mirror's "Be Right Back"" in Terence McSweeney and Stuart Joy, (eds.) 2019. *Through the Black Mirror: Deconstructing the Side Effects of the Digital Age*. London: Palgrave Macmillan.

Scolari, Carlos A. (2018), "The Entire Evolution of Media: A Media Ecological Approach to Black Mirror," in Angela M. Cirucci and Barry Vacker (eds.), *Black Mirror and Critical Media Theory*. Washington, DC: Lexington Books.

Scott, Ridley. (2017), *Bladerunner 2049*. Warner Bros. Pictures.

Shelley, Mary. (1818), *Frankenstein; or, The Modern Prometheus*. London: Lackington, Hughes, Harding, Mavor, & Jones.

Tibbetts, Carl. (2014), "White Christmas." *Black Mirror*, Channel 4. Season 2, Episode 4. Broadcast December 16, 2014.

Turing, Alan. (1950), "Computing Machinery and Intelligence," in *Mind*, October 1950, LIX (236): 433–60.

Ungureanu, Camil. (2015), "Aestheticization of politics and ambivalence of self-sacrifice in Charlie Brooker's The National Anthem," in *Journal of European Studies* 45(1): 21–30.

Van Bree, Tanne. (2016), "Digital Hyperthymesia," in Liisa Janssens. (ed.) 2016. *The Art of Ethics in the Information Society*. Amsterdam: Amsterdam University Press, 28–33.

Van Dijck, Jose. (2009), "Users like you? Theorizing agency in user-generated content," in *Media Culture Society* 31(1), 41–58.

Van Dijck, Jose and Poell, Thomas. (2013), "Understanding social media logic," in *Media and Communication*, 1(1): 2–14.

Van Dijck, Jose and Poell, Thomas. (2016), "Understanding the promises and premises of online health platforms," in *Big Data & Society*, January-June 2016, 1–11.

Walther, Joseph B. (2011), "Theories of Computer Mediated Communication and Interpersonal Relations," in Mark. A. Knapp and John A. Daly (eds.). 2011. *The SAGE Handbook of Interpersonal Communication*. Thousand Oaks, CA: SAGE Publications, 443–479.

Watkins, James. (2016), "Shut Up and Dance," Black Mirror, Netflix. Season 3, Episode 3, October 21, 2016.

Welsh, Brian. (2017), "The Entire History of You," *Black Mirror*, Channel 4. Season 1, Episode 3, Broadcast December 18, 2011.

Section Three

Black Mirror and Relating to Others

8

"Crocodile" Going Too Far

Philosophical Reflections on Human Nature and Moral Character

Clara Nisley

This chapter considers the *Black Mirror* episode "Crocodile" (Hillcoat 2017), whose principal character Mia Nolan is a woman who, from the result of an accident, makes choices that expose the corruption of her character. From our first encounter with Mia, "Crocodile" paints a picture of a woman who voluntarily chooses bad actions. At any time, Mia is free to act and prevail over her self-interests; yet, she voluntarily chooses to commit bad acts. Through this illustrative example, I shall explore whether morally evil acts are entrenched or habituated in a human being and whether an agent's moral failure relates to the conflict between our practical rationality and inclinations (self-interested desires) or an agent's basic mere cleverness as the corrupting capacity. I hope to answer the question whether Mia's initial vicious choice, never rectified, led directly to the corruption of her character. To philosophically explore Mia's actions, I shall look at the works of Aristotle and Immanuel Kant to give us insight into how each philosopher considers an agent's choices as indicators of a morally bad character and an evil one.

This chapter is divided into four sections to articulate how a rational agent, Mia Nolan, misguided by her friendship with Rob, turns into a callous, cruel, and evil character, when Rob demands that she accept his decision to reveal their wrongdoing. The first section describes their type of friendship and how their friendship led to a decision that paved the way to Mia's moral descent into evil. The second section is on virtue and its significance on moral character. In the third section, I explain how it is through Mia's lack of virtue that she is unable to resist falling into a trajectory of evil deeds. Finally, the last section is on Kant's and Aristotle's conceptions of evil which explains Mia's wicked character.

Friendship

"Crocodile" starts with flashing lights at a nightclub where two young people kiss as they dance. The scene switches over to Rob driving and Mia sitting next to him. They are both smoking and laughing while listening to music. Suddenly, we hear the brakes screech and a body crashes and flies across the hood of the car and cracks the windshield. Rob turns and says, "I didn't see him Mia." She and Rob get out of the car to see the injured bicyclist lying on his back across from the mangled bicycle. Rob kicks the bicyclist's arm with his foot and backs away. He realizes the bicyclist is dead. Mia takes out her phone and says, "We've got to call someone," but Rob begs her not to make the call. He and Mia have been snorting cocaine and drinking. If Mia calls the police about the accident, it's instant prison for Rob and perhaps for Mia as well. After a moment, she acquiesces to Rob's pleas.

At this point in the story, we see two people who lack temperance. The excess of pleasure seems to be the basis of their friendship. Mia and Rob go wrong when they don't call the police, but instead carry the bicycle, put rocks in the sleeping bag with the bicyclist's lifeless body in it, and toss the sleeping bag into the lake with the bike. Mia makes the wrong choice by helping Rob, and her decision shows that at the time she acts as a woman who is drunk or partially drunk but voluntarily chooses to help Rob cover up the accident, which indicates a moral failure.

Mia was faced with a choice on which she should have deliberated carefully and wisely. Her choice to do what was wrong comes partly from her self-indulgence of a night partying with Rob. Aristotle says that "the man who abstains from bodily pleasures and delights in this very fact is temperate . . . and he who stands his ground against things that are terrible and delights in this or at least is not pained is brave, while the man who is pained is a coward" (*Nicomachean Ethics* 2.3.1104b5-8). Mia and Rob didn't try to do what was just because they were indulging in pleasure induced by a drugged state. This type of friendship is based on sensual pleasure and is harmful to the other.

Moreover, Mia and Rob cannot be friends for long, since their love lacks steadfastness and since the pleasure they have taken is in what is advantageous to the other. Aristotle says that young people like Mia and Rob often have the type of friendship that is based on pleasure, and "these friendships are only incidental," as their pleasures change and "are easily dissolved, if the parties do not remain like themselves" (*Nicomachean Ethics* 8.3.1156a17-20). These friends do not like each other for their own sake "but in so far as he is useful or pleasant" (8.3.1156a17). A true friendship is ideally that of two people who reciprocally esteem each other. In the *Lectures on Ethics* Kant holds "that the reciprocal love in friendship must absolutely be coupled, among friends, with mutual respect for humanity in the person of the friend" (Van Impe 2011: 136). Rob had a duty to respect Mia for her humanity, and not ask her to help him dispose of the bicyclist's body. Mia had a duty to Rob to respect his humanity as well as her own. She should have pleaded with Rob to do the right thing—report the accident. As Aristotle observed, a true friend keeps the other from doing an action stemming from their moral weakness and saves them from error (*Nicomachean Ethics* 8.1.12-13).

Aristotle claims that the types of friendships we form correspond to our character traits. For Aristotle, a morally good character is fundamental to a friendship. He emphasizes that good character is a state concerned with the actions and choices of an agent (*Nicomachean Ethics* 2.6.1106b24-36). However, Mia and Rob's friendship was not based on each other's characters, because they lack the virtue to act appropriately in their situation. Mia was in a conflicted state and could not respond rationally to Rob's pleas, and Rob failed to bring his inclinations under the control of reason. Of course, if Rob were to regard Mia's character, he would become good to his friend and would have the virtue to deliberate and act appropriately in regard to his friendship (Aristotle, *Nicomachean Ethics* 8.4.1157a11–1157b33). However, his drug-induced state prevented him from avoiding—"the base, the injurious, [and] the painful" (Aristotle, *Nicomachean Ethics* 2.3.1104b31), making choices that were shameful, harmful, and will eventually cause each of them great pain. Rob neither had the deliberative skills to act correctly when confronted with the dead bicyclist nor did he feel a duty to his friend. Immanuel Kant holds that a friendship is a duty and "is an ideal each participating and sharing sympathetically in the other's well-being through the morally good will that unites them" or it is an "idea that we strive for (as a maximum of good disposition toward each other)" (1996: 215). Failing to recognize the other person for their good character, they engaged in a vicious act.

Both Mia and Rob have relatively weak characters, so that when Rob pleads with Mia not to call the cops and help him toss the body and bicycle in the lake to get rid of the evidence, his decision on how to extricate himself out of the predicament is not based on an action done from the virtue of friendship, as it would require that he possess and exhibit certain feelings for her. Hence, the state of character becomes the basis for all of their actions - leading them to do what is wicked. Wickedness of character shows that Mia and Rob cannot be friends for long, since their love lacks steadfastness and since the pleasure they have taken is in what is advantageous to the other. Hence, whenever one friend no longer satisfies the other's want for pleasure or is advantageous, the friendship ends. Steadfastness of character must be demonstrated, and their friendship lacks the morally good character that requires certain character traits such as temperance, wisdom, and honesty. Aristotle holds that friends who like each other for these properties will like each other for their sake. Their relationship, however, was based on enabling each other's pleasure, instead of promoting each other's morally good character. Mia and Rob have shown, their friendship lacks temperance and wisdom needed to deliberate correctly. Mia has, moreover, shown that she is not pained by what is terrible, and she did not stand her ground when Rob asked her to do a vicious act.

The relationship between Mia and Rob became one in which they had to hide the accident from everyone. Mia had a duty to tell the truth and is responsible for the unforeseeable consequences of her lie. She has committed a crime that she could have prevented by telling the truth. It is this lie that Mia is keeping that will lead her into a downward spiral. According to Immanuel Kant, Rob has a duty not to lie and not use Mia as a means to pursuing his end—in fear of punishment. Asking Mia to keep the accident a secret not only violates the duty he has to Mia but also he is violating her dignity as a human being by using her as a means to avoid the consequences of his recklessness. There would surely be a murder inquiry into the whereabouts of the bicyclist. By agreeing to lie, Mia is contributing to the degeneration of her own character as well as her friend's character. In this friendship, truthfulness regards a gain, but as we shall see it also regards reputation. By avoiding going to prison, neither thought about how their decision would affect their reputation. Lying stems from "motives and character defects that result in acts that are detrimental to the community" (Zembaty 1993: 10). The lie that Mia and Rob are keeping is shameful, and "in the long run... will be exposed, and... the repercussions for the liar include the loss of trust [that is] essential to any friendship" (Zembaty 1993: 16). The lie is harmful because something profound is at stake: a man's life. Neither thought that it would destroy their lives. It is shameful and base, and both are culpable. And, as we shall see, Mia, in saving her reputation, will commit the ultimate heinous act.

The Necessity of Virtue and Practical Reason on Character

It has been fifteen years since the accident, and Mia has pursued a career in architecture. Now we watch as Mia prepares for a presentation on her vision of the future. She has become "one of the most innovative architects of her generation." The object of her desires has changed, and she is now concerned with "injustice, intolerance, and... environmental challenges." Mia seems to care about what is good in terms of the conditions of human beings in their living communities. Therefore, Mia now seeks to bring about what is good, and she is able to do so by reasoning. How can we account for the present motivating desire to do what is good and her previous failures to do so? Has Mia's character really changed so that her motivation is for what is good? In the *Nicomachean Ethics*, Aristotle says, "by doing acts that we do in the presence of danger, and being habituated to feel fear or confidence, [we] become brave or cowardly" (2.1.1417). Rob's actions have shown that in the presence of danger, he became a coward by doing a cowardly act from fear. Rob ran away out of fear, but now he wants to write an anonymous letter to the cyclist's widow. The body of the cyclist has never been found, and his widow believes he is still alive. Mia, despite the speech she gives to the architectural community, acts out of fear when Rob tells her that he wants to write a letter to the cyclist's wife. Mia, afraid that the letter will be traced back to Rob and eventually reveal her as an accomplice, will act according to her underlying character.

Aristotle tells us that "each man speaks and acts and lives in accordance to character" (*Nicomachean Ethics* 4.7.1127a26-28). Although she speaks about injustice, Mia decides that power and reputation are finer than justice. We find that because of her intemperate past that when Mia faces the danger of losing her reputation and power, her commitment to virtuous ends collapses.

Mia does not want to give up the life she has. She thinks about how writing an anonymous letter will hurt her, her career, her status, and her family. She reminds Rob that it was his idea to keep their vicious act a secret. Mia has kept the disappearance of the bicyclist from everyone including her husband. After pursuing status and wealth, she will lose her affluence and her status in the architectural community. Moreover, if Rob writes the letter to the cyclist's wife, Mia will lose her reputation as a virtuous agent concerned with injustice. Mia's practical reason requires and facilitates her to develop virtue. Aristotle says that "virtue either natural or produced by habituation is what teaches right opinion" (*Nicomachean Ethics*, 7.8.1151a18-19). After her youth, Mia lacks the development of the virtues of character.

It seems that Mia never developed the virtues, which is what would have made her good in respect to character. Aristotle holds that individuals who lack the development of virtue are inconsistent in character. He states that the virtuous person is "concerned with choice that lies in the mean relative to us" (*Nicomachean Ethics*, 2.6.1106b35ff). When faced with a dire moral challenge, Mia's disposition to act in a certain way in response to Rob's intention to write an anonymous letter shows a character that succumbs to both rashness and cowardice; Mia shows rashness in her inclinations to kill and cowardice in her refusal to confront the authorities, if the anonymous letter were to have been traced to her. Her rash action is a failure because her passions and the action she took is an excess, and because killing Rob was in itself bad (Aristotle, *Nicomachean Ethics*, 2.61107a12).

Mia has the aid of reason to deliberate and achieve her ends; however, Mia took Rob's self-disclosure as a threat, and without developing virtue Mia has made herself vicious by pursuing the wrong end; instead of being virtuously guided in her deliberation, she went terribly wrong. In determining the best thing to do, Mia needed to apply practical reason, but without good character through habituated virtue, Mia could not deliberate correctly (Aristotle, *Nicomachean Ethics*, 2.6.1107a1-2 and 6.2.1139a27-32). But, it does not mean that Mia was unable to deliberate well—after all, she has been praised for her innovative work where she addresses the lack of social justice. Mia then takes morality to be part of the deep problems in the innovative work that she must deliberate on. It is difficult to see how Mia would be so prone to conflict, when she seems to be guided by practical reason in the pursuit of her craft. But, as I will discuss in the last section of this chapter, cleverness and practical reason differ in respect of choice (Aristotle, *Nicomachean Ethics*, 6.12,1141a25-27 and 7.10.1152a-12-14).

We see the first incidence of how instead of practical reason, Mia is clever in not only disposing of Rob's body but also covering her vicious act. We watch as after killing Rob, Mia walks past his body, and goes to the hotel window just as the driverless pizza van collides with the pedestrian in the street. She then looks out the window across from her hotel room, sees a man looking out his window, and quickly draws the curtain. Mia puts on a porn film, orders room service, and leaves the hotel room with Rob's body hidden underneath the dining cart. She takes the elevator to the underground parking lot. She places Rob's corpse into the car and drives to an industrial park where she drags the corpse across a raised walkway toward a large vent blowing steam. Mia pulls the lid off the vent and drops Rob's body into it. We hear it sizzling, as the body crashes to the bottom.

Mia, when in the grips of emotions, should have been able to use her judgment and act upon deliberation. It is the activity of the rational part of the soul that rules in a virtuous person, and without it, an agent could not perform the act of deliberation. A properly functioning soul that deliberates on moral matters is virtuous. The problem is that Mia is defective in character, and although she has the capability of utilizing practical reason to achieve her ends, she has not properly habituated her virtue and is unable to control her passions. Aristotle tells us that moral virtues consist of one's character being in a good state as it relates to passions (*Nicomachean Ethics*, 2.5.1106a412 and 6.12.1144a7-10). Mia's disposition to make the morally correct choice conflicted with her aspirations and so practical reason would only serve her inclinations. We see that from her initial vicious act to her speech to the architectural community, Mia does not have internal mental unity. Moreover, if Mia were morally virtuous, her soul would be in a good state in relation to her passions and actions, because in order to be good, any such deliberation must be virtuously guided (Aristotle, *Nicomachean Ethics*, 2.5.1106a12ff).

Mia, instead of thinking about Rob's attempt to improve his moral character, tries to plead with him. She never made the effort to consider her vicious act that would have in turn motivated her moral development. Yet, before killing Rob, Mia pleads with him and says, "I've got somewhere. I've got a life. You don't understand Rob, you're not married. I've got a son; he's nine years old. You've seen photos of him. Think of him, please." Rob, however, says he has made up his mind and starts to leave. Rob should have been concerned about the deceit he and Mia participated in and should have not trusted her. He and Mia never had a true friendship and their relationship was not stable. He has not seen her in fifteen years. In *Eudemian Ethics*, Aristotle says that "there is no stable friendship without confidence. . . . One must then make a trial," as Theognis says, "You cannot know the mind of a man or woman till you have tried them as you might cattle" (7.2.1237b11-14). Rob thinks only that he must make amends with anyone he has ever hurt. He has stopped drinking and is now making amends with anyone he has transgressed. Mia grabs him and pushes him against the wall. Rob falls to the ground. We hear a thump, as we watch Rob hit his head, blood dripping from his nose and down his cheek. Mia, then, strangles Rob until he is dead.

The question is whether in her initial choice to help Rob, Mia's nonrational sensibility impulses overrode any practical rational thought or did Mia always have the potential to be evil. According to Aristotle, Mia could have acted virtuously. He says, "it is in our power . . . to act in this way or not in this way" (*Nicomachean Ethics*, 3.5.1115a1-3). We can see the similarity in Kant's account of virtue. In the *Groundwork of the Metaphysics of Morals*, Kant defines virtue as the strength of will. In this case, it was within Mia's power not to kill Rob.

Both Aristotle and Kant would hold Mia accountable for her actions. However, Kant would hold Mia accountable for coldly killing Rob not based on motivating empirical factors, such as the desire to keep her status within the architectural community. According to Kant, Mia's inclinations are not the source of immorality, as it is a matter of choice "as a freely acting being" an agent is responsible for her actions (1998b: 63). Therefore, Mia's grounds for killing Rob cannot be located in her natural inclinations. Mia never made progress toward virtue; otherwise, she would have felt the constraint on her choice. That choice, Kant tells us did not come from some external motivation. Even Aristotle, although he considers emotions necessary, holds that they must be responsive to reason. And, an agent who is solely guided by appetite and emotion cannot be considered virtuous. It is necessary for an agent to have trained the appetites, but it is practical wisdom that is necessary for appetitive and emotional dispositions to be good (just as for Kant, the good will is motivated solely by duty or principles of practical reason). Practical judgment would have thwarted those inclinations that would take murder as a principle.

Moreover, if Mia would have freely adopted the policy: "treat [herself] and all others *never merely as means* but always *at the same time as ends in themselves*" (Emphasis is in original) (Kant 1998a: 41), Mia would have never killed Rob. It was her choice to surrender to vice (Kant 1996: 221). Mia has not had the strength of will to do her duty; her will was not in complete accord with reason (1998a: 24). Reason requires Mia to master her inclinations, and reason should have directed her to do so (1996: 148). Kant states that the "will is a kind of causality of living beings insofar as they are rational," and freedom is "that property of such causality that it can be efficient independently of alien causes determining it" (1998a: 52). The core of Kant's argument is that we are rational agents who are able to be guided by rational principles of conduct. A person's will has the power to choose on the basis of principles and a good will is a disposition to adopt and act on the right sorts of policies (1998a: 45–6). In what follows, we shall be able to watch Mia debase humanity. We shall see the character of a free will which subordinates reason to its selfish motives.

After Mia kills Rob, she drives home, where her son and husband are enthusiastic about the school musical that night. After her husband and son leave, Mia dashes to her car with a bucket, a spray bottle, and yellow gloves. She sprays the back seats and scrubs them clean. Meanwhile, Shazia, the insurance investigator from Realm Insurance, has been recording the memories of those who have witnessed the self-driving delivery truck accident with a Recaller, a device that allows her to see the memories of the witnesses on a screen. Shazia, not finding a witness who saw the impact, turns to the last witness's memory of Mia looking out the hotel window across the way at the time of the accident. Unable to learn Mia's name from the hotel employee, she turns to facial recognition software to find Mia's name and address. Shazia, motivated by the bonus she will receive, if she finds liability within twenty-four hours of the accident, decides to drive to Mia's home despite the lateness of the day.

Fifty miles away, Mia is sitting looking at the newspaper article about the bicyclist's wife. Mia places the newspaper article in the fireplace, sets fire to it, and watches as it burns. As she watches the flames destroy the article, the doorbell buzzes. Mia talks to Shazia at the door, where she first denies knowing about the accident. Once Shazia tells Mia that the accident took place on Standhope Road in front of the Medina Plaza Hotel, Mia admits she saw a "guy crossing the street" and the driverless pizza delivery van "clip him." Shazia warns Mia that as of last year, witnesses to an accident are legally required to submit to the Recaller, which Shazia explains "helps me get a record of what happened." Mia does not know the speed of the driverless pizza delivery van. However, Shazia cannot determine liability without the speed of the van. She explains that the recorder will help get a sense of the speed of the van.

Before they start, Mia asks Shazia if she wants tea or coffee. While in the kitchen, Mia waits for the expresso machine, and looks over at the knives on the center island. It is through reason, Kant explains, that a self-commanding agent can overcome her inclinations for evil (Baxley 2015: 227). Kant holds that we commonly think of the natural inclinations arising from evil, but "evil cannot [come from] . . . sensuous nature," and we are wrong in thinking this (1998b: 57). Mia must have felt "a moral constraint through [her] own law giving reason" (1996: 164). It must have been a nonempirical feeling produced by practical reason that directs Mia to do what is right. Mia asks Shazia whether she minds her using the bathroom before she sits down for the interrogation. In the bathroom mirror, Mia goes over what she did in the hotel room: "I ate hotel food, I had room service. I ate room service. I was in the hotel room on my own. Watched porn. Saw the accident. . . . I was on my own. I was on my own. I was on my own." Shazia puts the chip on Mia's temple and starts playing the song "Anyone Who Knows What Love Is" to help Mia recall her memory of the accident. Shazia asks Mia to "try to picture the moments leading up to the impact." Shazia sees the pizza van knocking the man over. Immediately after, we see Shazia's face stiffen as she sees Rob's face on the screen. He appears to be struggling to breathe. Then, Shazia sees the bicyclist hit and crack the car window. Shazia continues to watch and sees the bicyclist's mangled body lying on the ground, and the sleeping bag falling into the lake. Mia's obvious violation of the moral law frightens Shazia.

The Lack of a Good Will: Why Mia Spins Out of Control

It is respect for the moral law that is required here, a feeling produced by reason (Kant 1998b: 64–5). The sole determining ground of the will is respect, which is a feeling produced by an intellectual awareness of the moral law. Mia's inclinations, however, have taken over, and we see her struggling, and ultimately choosing to act against reason. Her will is in a perpetual state of tension; it is only if she has a good will that empowers her to conform to the moral law. She, however, shows that she lacks respect for other rational beings. Acting from virtue would require that Mia possess a good will, a will that steadily acts from the motive of respect for the moral law. It is the lack of a good will that empowers Mia to do what she does next.

After Shazia closes the Recaller and removes Mia's chip from her temple, she hurries to her car and closes the door. The car's engine grumbles as she tries to start it. Mia takes a rock and hits the driver's side window until she breaks it. She reaches in and drags Shazia out. In an outbuilding, we see Shazia sitting in a chair with her hands tied behind her. Mia ties a cloth around Shazia's mouth. Mia stands at the doorway of the outbuilding and asks herself, "What am I going to do with you?" Mia must recognize her inclination to kill Shazia; she must strive to combat her inclinations and not only repress but overcome them. Overcoming them necessitates practical reason to constrain herself and not act on them. At first glance, it looks like Mia is exercising her practical reason. Yet we have learned that Mia is clever. Mia was meticulous in hiding Rob's body. Aristotle tells us that we need both practical wisdom and moral virtue. Without wisdom, the virtuous person would not necessarily know how to act, and without moral virtue, the clever person would not always pursue the appropriate ends (*Nicomachean Ethics*, 6. 13.1144a24-35). So true wisdom requires the virtues. We know that Mia lacks them and has, unlike Rob, never felt the constraint nor force of the will. The will is the guide that by practical wisdom discloses "the supreme principle of morality" (Kant 1996: 156–7).

Now, Aristotle links wisdom to cleverness. Wisdom is the cleverness that allows an agent to choose appropriate means to the ends she desires. Mia has practical wisdom, but the cool deliberation has shown that she is clever and desires to kill anyone who can recollect her wicked acts. She is cunning in that she sought Shazia's address from her car's GPS, and she shows cool deliberation when she speaks to her husband on the way to kill Anan, Shazia's husband. As Aristotle tells us, moral wickedness involves rational deliberation. A clever agent uses practical deliberation to her wicked ends. She chooses to act wickedly because she is deceived at the starting point of her action. Aristotle reminds us that the agent who is wicked is deceived because "wickedness perverts us" (6.12.1144a35-36). Unscrupulous cleverness misses the mark and leads an agent to villainy. The practical thought of all starting points lay in cleverness. For Aristotle practical wisdom depends on the cognitive capacity: cleverness. But it seems that if cleverness is deceitful, then the agent is misguided from the starting point, for her cleverness is unscrupulous. The agent must have a morally good motivation and the moral guidance of practical reason to right action. Without practical wisdom to lead the agent to rightful reason, an agent would not be able to deliberate correctly.

It is too late for Mia. She has a duty to "scrutinize" herself and "seek" into the depths of her heart. She has to know her heart—"whether it is good or evil." Mia has a duty to remove "(an evil will present in [her])" (Kant 1996: 191). But, Mia's free power of choice is hidden in the "depths of [her] own heart," which is "inscrutable" to her. "Yet [she] must be able to hope that, by the exertion of [her] *own power*, [she] will adopt maxims in accordance with ethical laws" (Kant 1998b: 71). Despite the demands of her own legislative will, Mia continues with her evil deeds. Mia has the ability through her power of choice to act independently of her sensible desires and inclinations. Kant believes each of us is pulled toward the moral law, by virtue of being rational. If Mia had sharpened her judgment, if she would have felt a constraint toward the moral law, she would have been guided to the right principles. Mia would have had a more stable disposition. Both Aristotle and Kant held that agents have the ability to develop a morally good character. Kant maintained, however, that "we must be considered to be free from all influence of sensibility" so that the will must be self-determining (Kant 2007: 469). Mia's inclinations were purely nonrational, and in that subjective responsive moment of the will, she was free to choose. Mia, morally free to choose, acted in violation of the demands of her rational legislative will.

The Uncorrected Evil

Mia thinks about letting Shazia go, as tears run down her face. She is in a state of agitation. Shazia promises that she won't let anyone know about what she saw in the Recaller, but Mia is afraid that Shazia's recollections of her memories have been recorded. Mia feels the moral law pull against her sensible inclinations. It looks like Mia is searching her heart; yet, she goes against her rational legislative will. Mia, then, uses the Recaller to scan Shazia's recollections. Mia asks, "Who did you speak to?" She sees Anan, Shazia's husband, and hears their conversation. Shazia discussed interrogating Mia about the accident with her husband. Mia picks up a wood log, asks Shazia to close her eyes, with her left-hand steadies Shazia's head, and we hear two bangs or cracks from inside the outbuilding. Mia leaves the outbuilding, vomits, and turns on the GPS in Shazia's SUV. On the GPS is Shazia's home address.

Mia seems to have a tug-of-war within herself between letting Shazia go and killing her. Mia decides to kill Shazia and to continue her deception. Aristotle holds that "wicked men's souls are rent by faction, and one element in it by reason of its wickedness grieves . . . while the other part is pleased and one draws them this way and the other that, as if they were pulling them in pieces" (*Nicomachean Ethics*, 1166b19-22). For Aristotle, the wicked hide this discord from others as well as from themselves. We can see by Mia's tears that she is pained by what she was about to do, and she hides her wickedness when she calls her husband having just killed Shazia and on her way to kill Anan. Kant tells us that reason underlies the chosen action if it is virtuous, and requires that the maxim is free of self-contradictions. Mia is in conflict with the moral law within herself. Instead of conforming with the will's legislative form, she is in a state of agitation that reveals the conflict within herself. The internal moral conflict that Mia experiences derives from within her will. Kant claims that we all succumb to wickedness of the will because of our "innate propensity to transgression" (1998b: 70). We all have a propensity toward evil, but we are also predisposed to good based on the inexorable commands of the moral law. Kant further says that we need "first to remove the (evil will actually present in [us])" through reason (Sullivan 1989: 126). Kant holds that "wisdom consists the harmony of the will . . . [which] requires [an agent] to remove the inner obstacle (and evil will actually present in him)" (1996: 191). Mia is unable to remove the evil because of the lack of virtue that would have given her the fortitude not to kill.

We watch through the windowpane as Mia drives up in front of Shazia's house and turns off her car lights; it is pitch dark. She approaches the house holding a hammer in her hand. She peers in through a window, and we hear a click. With the black hood of her coat over her head, and a scarf covering her mouth and nose, Mia watches Anan sitting on the sofa. Anan turns off the television, gets up from the sofa, and walks upstairs. Mia stealthily climbs up the stairs and sees that the bathroom door is ajar. She hears water running. Anan turns off the faucet and lies in the bathtub with his eyes closed. Mia peers around the bathroom door and slowly moves toward him. As she raises her arm to strike Anan, her phone vibrates, and Anan turns and sees Mia.

She strikes Anan not once but twice on his head. Anan slowly sinks into the bathwater, blood slowly oozing from his head. As Mia staggers back from the bathtub, blood dripping from the hammer, she drops it on the floor. She covers Anan's body with a towel, still lying underneath the bloodied water. She sits on the toilet crying, her gloved hand covering her face.

Mia is clever in that she has been able to perform the act she believes will achieve her goal—kill Anan. Her goal is wicked, so that her cleverness is villainy. In the next scene, we watch a woman who willingly commits the most heinous action to achieve her ends. Aristotle holds that the failure lies in the lack of moral virtue along with practical wisdom—without which Mia will not be guided to the best means to the end. Mia walks out of the bathroom and hears a baby's squeal. She stops and listens. The baby starts to babble. With tears rolling down her cheeks, Mia walks into the baby's room. She stares at the baby as she stands right in front of the crib. In the next scene, Mia arrives at her son's school where she is met by her husband, Simon. Mia appears drunk and hurries into the school with him. As she sits next to Simon, she appears uneasy; she fidgets and rests her head on Simon's shoulder. Her son is in the front center row; the choir starts singing "Bad Guys." The scene cuts back to Shazia's house, where we hear a voice through the police radio saying, "Yeah, just confirming double homicide."

Aristotle holds that one who commits murder is "evil." In Book II of *Nicomachean Ethics*, Aristotle claims that not every action "admits to a mean." "Murder is bad in itself . . . and not the excess or deficiency" of the passions (1107a11-12). Mia's cool deliberation is not an act of uncontrolled emotion but rather an act of cleverness and cunning. Mia killed the baby in fear that the police could access his memories. But what Mia didn't notice in her deliberate act was that the baby was blind. The baby had been born blind, and the police wouldn't have had a clue as to who committed the murders. Except that Mia didn't notice the guinea pig in the baby's room. The recall team walks in, and with the guinea pig chipped, the Recaller beeps. We ask, "Who kills a baby?" It is clear that an agent who commits murder is evil and one who kills a baby is radically evil. Her actions stem from her vicious character because they are done with cool deliberation. She has acted in light of her ends, except that her wickedness has perverted her soul to the wrong ends (Aristotle, *Nicomachean Ethics* 6.12.1144a32).

At the end, we watch as Mia claps at the end of the school choir's performance, a police detective walks into the hall. A woman points Mia out to the detective. Mia glances over to where the detective is. Her fate is upon her. Even with tears in her eyes, Mia has chosen to act from decision. As Aristotle states, "wickedness . . . makes men unjust and in general bad; wickedness perverts us," "but it is in our power to act virtuously or viciously" (*Nicomachean Ethics* 3.5.1113b6-14 and 6.12.1144a35 and 3.5.). Mia has chosen to violate moral principles because it interfered with her ends—her career, her standing in the community, her family life. She has been guided by her wickedness to the wrong ends, but she will finally receive her just due.

References

Aristotle. (1984), "Eudemian Ethics," in Jonathan Barnes (ed.), *The Complete Works of Aristotle*, 2nd edn, 1729–1867, Princeton: Princeton University Press.

Aristotle. (1984), "Nicomachean Ethics," in Jonathan Barnes (ed.), *The Complete Works of Aristotle*, 2nd edn, 1729–1867, Princeton: Princeton University Press.

Baxley, Anne Margaret. (2015), "Virtue, Self-mastery, and the Autocracy of Practical Reason," in Lara Denis and Oliver Sensen (eds), *Kant's Lectures on Ethics*, 223–38. Cambridge: Cambridge University Press.

Hillcoat, John. (2017), "Crocodile," *Black Mirror*, Netflix. Season 4, Episode 3. Release Date December 29, 2017. [TV Series].

Kant, Immanuel. (1996), *Metaphysics of Morals*, ed and trans. Mary Gregor, New York: Cambridge University Press.

Kant, Immanuel. (1998a), *Groundwork of the Metaphysics of Morals*, trans. Mary Gregor, New York: Cambridge University Press.

Kant, Immanuel. (1998b), *Religion within the Boundaries of Bare Reason*, trans. Allen Wood and George di Giovanni, New York: Cambridge University Press.

Kant, Immanuel. (2007), *Critique of Pure Reason*, trans. Norman Kemp Smith, New York: Palgrave Macmillan.

Sullivan, Roger J. (1989), *Immanuel Kant's Moral Theory*, New York: Cambridge University Press.

Van Impe, Stijn. (2011), "Kant on Friendship," *International Journal of Arts and Sciences*, 4 (3): 127–139.

Zembaty, Jane S. (1993), "Aristotle on Lying," *Journal of the History of Philosophy* 31 (January): 7–29.

9

Rats, Roaches, and Rapists

"Men Against Fire" and the Propagation of Propaganda

Leigh E. Rich

The term "propaganda" took on new meaning in the twentieth century. It had once been thought of in neutral or positive terms, during its development as a papal edict in the 1600s (Miller 2005). That changed in the modern era, in part thanks to an unregulated patent medicine market in the United States and the eruption of the Great War. Propaganda became known as what nineteenth-century snake-oil salesmen peddled from town to town or, even worse, what the "Huns" engaged in during the First World War. It was the self-serving or even deadly methodology employed by fraudsters and implacable enemies. Today, this negative connotation has lingered, and to label something as propaganda is to accuse its creators of some level of iniquity. Whether propaganda is inherently bad has been a matter of debate—and whether that debate has been convincing is yet another issue—but some proponents have claimed that it is a tool that can be used for good or ill (Shabo 2008). In 1928, Edward Bernays, a publicist who would become the leading propagandist for propaganda, attempted to reclaim the concept from its wartime ashes, asserting that not only can propaganda serve positive ends but that it is "a logical result" of democracy and essential for "a smoothly functioning society" ([1928] 2005: 37). Two decades later, military journalist and historian S.L.A. Marshall ([1947] 2000) published his own treatise on propaganda (though not calling it by name) and returned it to its martial roots. Marshall focused not on selling products or concepts in a peacetime market economy but on creating more effective soldiers in battle. Regardless, both men championed propaganda as "justifiable": one as a means for everyday social efficiency and order, the other as a means-end mechanism for victory in war.

Propaganda, however, whether in its most pernicious form or the seemingly less menacing variety imagined by Bernays, engages in a type of gaslighting antithetical to democratic enlightenment ideals. Techniques that undermine knowledge and override reason seem more apropos to totalitarian or authoritarian regimes and, when used in democracies, blur such dividing lines. Is propaganda ever ethical? Although Bernays and Marshall answer in the affirmative, countless examples, whether historical or fictional and during both war and peace, suggest caution. A common illustration is George Orwell's *Nineteen Eighty-Four* (1949), but a more recent one can be found in an episode of the British sci-fi series *Black Mirror* entitled "Men Against Fire" (Verbruggen 2016), directly inspired by Marshall's 1947 book of the same name. Interestingly, *Black Mirror*'s "Men Against Fire" is set neither during war nor peace; rather, the alternate timeline depicts a society ten years after a conflict where the military remains a powerful decision-maker. Throughout the episode, propaganda is at play, justified as essential for the commonwealth's survival. The United States exists in a similar paradox today: embroiled in unending foreign wars while peacetime reigns at home but engaged in domestic partisan battles steeped in propaganda. During the Covid-19 pandemic, Donald Trump even framed himself as "a wartime president" (White House 2020b: ¶117; Karni, Haberman, and Epstein 2020), though his enemy was not terrorists or the coronavirus but his political rivals and the loss of voters in the 2020 presidential election. In Trump's world of "alternative facts" (*Meet the Press* 2017), flagrant denials or reversals ("I've felt it was a pandemic long before it was called a pandemic" [White House 2020a: ¶306]), and where truth itself scrambles for a foothold on a slippery slope, what lessons can be learned from Bernays, Marshall, and *Black Mirror*? How does modern agitprop repeat the solemn lessons of the past, and when, if ever, should propaganda be employed?

Following the First World War, Bernays primarily worked for corporate clients, and much of his book *Propaganda* speaks to its use in business. He gives a nod, however, to its application in other realms such as social service, education, and art and science. Today, any politician, public health professional, or innovator would be hard-pressed to deny the usefulness of such techniques, including toward socially desirable ends. Altering human behavior to encourage voting, promote vaccination, or prevent smoking, for example, often takes more than sound statistics and a reasoned argument. Especially now, when information is simultaneously accessible and overwhelming, it might be argued that tactics such as "nudging" (Thaler and Sunstein 2008) or persuasive emotional appeals (Hale and Dillard 1995; Monahan 1995) serve a needed function—not merely for the selling of products but to ensure that individuals make healthier, just, and more compassionate choices for the betterment of all. But all forms of propaganda involve manipulation and the bypassing of logic and discourse (Shabo 2008) and often have been used to deceive and dehumanize. Bernays, in laying out what he termed the "new propaganda," states that one aim of his book was to suggest an "evolving code of ethics and practice" ([1928] 2005: 45). Marshall, for his part, focused on objectifying, rather than degrading, one's adversaries in order to create "more willing firers" during war, thus stopping shy of making the enemy a monster ([1947] 2000: 82). After nearly a century since both books were published, if propaganda can be used ethically, the question remains as to when and how. Perhaps propaganda exists on a continuum between social engineering and outright con, with some use justifiable for the common good? Perhaps propaganda is tolerable in crises if it wades along the banks of ethical boundaries but does not cross the Rubicon? Unfortunately, many utilitarian-like arguments in defense of propaganda are poorly constructed or misapplied and feed off lazy thinking and emotional appeals, and there may be little comfort in the precarious space between formal rhetoric and nudging and objectification and brutalization. Propaganda is likely always unethical, but since Bernays ushered in the modern era of public relations, it also is nearly unavoidable, particularly in a Trumpian age. How can we square this circle?

"Tactics in a Nutshell"

Although *Black Mirror* easily fits into the genre of science fiction, most of its episodes are not set in some distant future or in worlds hard to recognize. Like the post-Second World War society found in Orwell's *Nineteen Eighty-Four*, *Black Mirror* intentionally reflects twenty-first-century thinking and technology, even if distorted in the show's depiction of the new looking glasses into which we now perpetually gaze. In this way, it serves as a cautionary tale about the possible and potentially imminent consequences of our current paths. It is not an escapist or utopian sci-fi but a call to contemplate our present priorities and actions, a thought experiment around the darker side of technology. While "Men Against Fire" offers an image of an alternative universe, it also references our military and colonial histories, urging us to remember the real atrocities amid the fictional and collapsing past and future timelines into a damning reproach of our present. By grounding its narrative in Marshall's controversial conclusions about how to improve war and employing Bernays' techniques of propaganda, *Black Mirror*'s "Men Against Fire" exposes the parallels to, and perils of, our world's current policies and practices, which often transform humans into something "other."

"Men Against Fire" portrays a postwar world, though it is never clear against whom the victors were fighting. What has become urgent, however, even in an otherwise stable society, is protecting humans from an infestation of "roaches"—fanged, speechless, zombie-like creatures that wreak havoc on resources and threaten the welfare of the populace. As Medina, a commander of a military unit tasked with eradicating roaches, explains, "We gotta take them out if humankind is gonna carry on in this world." While campaigns against roaches have been successful elsewhere, Medina's team is stationed in a rural region that still bears marks of the war and where a contingent of "rustic" villagers are illegally feeding and sheltering the last of the vermin, potentially allowing them to (re)propagate. Lennard, a member of Medina's command, describes the history of the roach infiltration—that just a few thousand are what's keeping the military from declaring "mission accomplished."

To assist the soldiers in their charge is a technology called MASS. This implantable device connects each team member not only to a high-tech system that provides real-time intelligence and enhanced vision but also to each other, ensuring a unit is cohesive and coordinated. The origin of *Black Mirror*'s fictional MASS system—and the premises underlying the "Men Against Fire" episode—is Marshall's book, *Men Against Fire: The Problem of Battle Command*, in which he argues that an understanding of modern warfare is necessary for developing more efficient soldiers less hesitant to fire on the enemy. Having served in the First World War, Marshall became a military journalist and interviewed soldiers during the Second World War to develop his (methodically questionable) theory. As he explains, "our training system and our standard of battle discipline still adhere to the modes of the eighteenth century, though we are working with the weapons and profess to be working with the advanced military ideas of the twentieth" ([1947] 2000: 10). This problem, he asserts, stems from who is charged with writing leadership manuals and military policy—not those from the frontlines but high-ranking officers who either lack combat experience or are too far removed to remember or analyze it.

What is needed, says Marshall, is not dressed-up "dogma" or "armchair" ideas but an on-the-ground understanding of what transpires—in order to determine what should transpire—during battle. Toward this end, the Army assigned Marshall the role of "observ[ing] how the masses of our men react in battle" and "measur[ing] the common denominators of our weakness and our strength in close combat" ([1947] 2000: 10). He concluded that, since the First World War, "we have been pulling in opposite directions in many of our basic policies governing the preparation of our man power for combat," particularly with regard to the "ratio of fire" that is expected of soldiers ([1947] 2000: 10). Reportedly based on data that is now recognized as offering inaccurate descriptions and massaged statistics, Marshall claimed that only one-quarter of infantrymen effectively discharge their weapons in battle. The other three-quarters, he said, "will not fire or will not persist in firing against the enemy and his works. These men may face the danger but they will not fight" (Marshall [1947] 2000: 50).

For Marshall, such "weapons inertia" was "a very curious oversight," and he deemed "the problem of how much fire can be brought to bear" as not just a basic tactical issue but "tactics in a nutshell, and the other elements of tactics are simply shaped around it" ([1947] 2000: 51). Thus, the "fundamental problem" of battle command "is how to build up fire volume and develop more willing firers" ([1947] 2000: 82).

Like the unseen inventors of MASS in *Black Mirror*, Marshall's aim is to develop a technique that's embedded in the heads of frontline soldiers.

The "New Propaganda"

On the surface, the stances Marshall and *Black Mirror* take about humans and war appear antithetical. One is (purportedly) derived from real data and prescriptive, the answer to empathizing with the enemy; the other is (not wholly) fictional and proscriptive, a warning about treating the enemy as other. Despite seeming to be opposites, however, both are studies in propaganda. They use the same tactics to justify their quasi-utilitarian ends, overcoming moral reasoning through poor description, faulty logic, and emotional appeals. To understand the dangers of Marshall's counsel and the counsel of *Black Mirror*'s dangers, each must be viewed through Bernays' *Propaganda*.

Like Marshall's treatise and *Black Mirror*'s episode, Bernays' "new propaganda" was born of war. Mark Crispin Miller writes in an introduction to *Propaganda* that it was not until 1915 that "governments first systematically deployed the entire range of modern media to rouse their populations to fanatical assent" (2005: 11), both in the demonization of the enemy and in advocating the righteousness of the cause. The Allies used such tactics "to cast the war as a transcendent clash between Atlantic 'civilization' and Prussian 'barbarism'" (Miller 2005: 11), creating an image of the "Hun" as savage and antidemocratic, as well as depicting them as the primary purveyors of propaganda. No longer a potentially neutral or positive practice, propaganda belonged to the evil enemy. This worked so well that when those on the frontlines and on the home front discovered that such strategies also had been used by their own leaders, propaganda came to be seen "as a weapon even *more* perfidious than they had thought when they had not perceived themselves as its real target" (Miller 2005: 15, *emphasis original*).

Bernays honed his own use of this weapon when he worked for the Committee on Public Information, whose purpose was to garner American support for a European conflict and frame democracy in "glittering generalities," while eliding America's colonial past and neocolonialist future (Shabo 2008: 30). Bernays realized that what worked during combat could be useful when fighting ceased: Taking on the mantle of a scientist steeped in mass psychology, he attempted to "rid the word of its bad smell" (Miller 2005: 15). The "new propaganda" was rooted in "enlightened self-interest" and "a consistent, enduring effort to create or shape events to influence the relations of the public to an enterprise, idea or group" (Bernays [1928] 2005: 52, 82). Like an "army regiment[ing] the bodies of its soldiers," it "regiment[s] the public mind" by "creating circumstances and . . . pictures in the minds of millions" (Bernays [1928] 2005: 52).

According to Bernays, this is something that can, and should, be used in society. The first chapter of *Propaganda* is titled "Organizing Chaos," and his opening paragraphs argue that the modern world is so complex, and so cluttered with information, that the average individual, if left to his own reasoning, would become immobilized ([1928] 2005: 37–8). Instead, the hands of unseen influencers should sort the wheat from the chaff. No matter that the sorting benefits those hiring the sorters or that the sorters are not openly elected. In fact, at least per Bernays, this is a system to which the public has consented: "We have voluntarily agreed to let an invisible government sift the data and high-spot the outstanding issue so that our field of choice shall be narrowed to practical proportions" ([1928] 2005: 38). These invisible governors thus are our "silent partners": Without even realizing it, they "give us our ideas, tell us whom to admire and whom to despise, what to believe" and "make the rest of us think what they please about a given subject" ([1928] 2005: 57–61).

How the new propagandists do so is not rooted in traditional forms of salesmanship. Highlighting how one product's features may be better than its competitors no longer works, because while the "claims may be true," other manufacturers have claims of their own, and not only are these producers in direct competition with one another over consumers' dollars, they are in indirect competition with manufacturers of different products (Bernays [1928] 2005: 77). Rather, for Bernays, the work of public relations is more akin to a lawyer than a peddler of goods, crafting a narrative that frames his client in the best possible light while influencing the environment to discount or omit any evidence to the contrary.

While the PR counselor may at times employ advertising tactics, he primarily engages in an analysis that assesses his client's problems and the public's unconscious wants and needs in order to shape or create cultural norms that bend in the client's favor ([1928] 2005: 65–6). The goal is not to remove buyers' *resistance* through transparent and reasoned arguments but to create buyer *demand* by short-circuiting logic and appealing to desire. Bernays concludes that, because humans rarely understand the real reasons for their actions, when "the herd must think for itself, it does so by means of clichés, pat words or images which stand for a whole group of ideas or experiences.... By playing upon an old cliché, or manipulating a new one, the propagandist can sometimes swing a whole mass of group emotions" ([1928] 2005: 74). Bernays argues that effective propaganda—through interrelated tactics that shape language, imagery, and desire—causes people to think that buying a product, performing a behavior, or supporting a belief was their idea in the first place ([1928] 2005: 81).

Language

As Bernays notes, because language is symbolic and words carry hidden meanings and associations, propaganda often relies on "clichés" to frame how one views a product, another group, or a situation. To label a cosmetic "all natural" or a plant-based drink "milk," for example, provides a simple means for fostering a certain narrative in a customer's mind. This may prove positive or negative. Bernays offers as illustration how British "evacuation hospitals" during the First World War were criticized for the "summary way in which they handled their wounded" ([1928] 2005: 74). The censure arose, he explains, because the word "hospital" evokes certain expectations about the intensity and extent of care clinicians should provide to those who are ill or harmed, especially otherwise healthy young men putting their lives on the line in battle. Once the word "hospital" was substituted with "post," however, the condemnation disappeared. Nothing was altered in what medical care was provided or how it was delivered, merely the name had changed.

Similarly, US posters during both World Wars often highlighted "liberty" in the selling of war bonds or other forms of support. Though nothing could seem more "American" than that (per one poster, "Americans will *always* fight for liberty," underneath the dates 1778 and 1943), the concept rings both hallow and hollow (cited in Shabo 2008: 32, *emphasis original*). For example, the United States built slavery into its founding documents, and the military remained segregated through the Second World War as Jim Crow dominated the South. What aspects of "liberty" Americans fight for, or if they "always" do, means little in practice but connotes much about whose cause is justifiable and, hence, who should be the victors. In this way, words matter.

Marshall uses a similar tactic in *Men Against Fire*, whose primary goal is "the mastery of the moral problem in battle" ([1947] 2000: 9). What is the *moral* problem Marshall aims to solve? A "rifleman's resistance against employing his weapon upon human targets" ([1947] 2000: 76). Even with the proper training and fear of being killed in war, Marshall contends that the average soldier "still has such an inner and usually unrealized resistance toward killing a fellow man that he will not of his own volition take life if it is possible to turn away from that responsibility"—becoming an "unknowing" conscientious objector ([1947] 2000: 79). Marshall simultaneously commends this as "something to the American credit" and condemns it as "something which needs to be analyzed and understood if we are to prevail against it in the interests of battle efficiency" ([1947] 2000: 79). In fact, he labels this the "final mental block" ([1947] 2000: 76), rooting its cause in one's moral upbringing and development. Framed this way, the hesitance against taking human life obstructs action and thus must be removed, as if it were a cancer attacking the martial body.

Black Mirror's "Men Against Fire" likewise plays with language. In one of the opening scenes, the soldiers of Medina's team refer to "roaches" four times in a sequence of dialogue and fifteen more times before an image of a "roach" ever appears on screen. Medina also explains to a man harboring "roaches" in his home that "roaches" have been frightening inhabitants elsewhere in the village and "breaking into the food stores, stealing supplies." She emphasizes that, though it's not their fault, they carry a "sickness" in their blood that "doesn't care about the sanctity of life or the pain about who else is gonna suffer. We don't stop the roaches," she says, "in five, ten, twenty years from now, you're still gonna get kids born that way, and then they're gonna breed." Much like the Hutus labeling the Tutsis "cockroaches" in Rwanda (Ndahiro 2019) or the Nazis likening Jews to "rats" (*The Eternal Jew* 1940)—disease-carrying vermin that once decimated the populations of Europe—such propagandistic name-calling demeans and dehumanizes, making extermination seem just. According to Medina, to see the "roaches" as human is what's irrational and strange, and the only explanation she can muster as to why Parn Heidekker is helping them is that he's an "oddball" with "mental health issues."

Contrary to the adage of "sticks and stones," these slurs pose untenable assertions that nevertheless influence the thoughts and behaviors of others (Shabo 2008). During the Vietnam War, for example, an American term for the Vietnamese was "gooks." They were thought of as flotsam or debris, easily brushed away, who "didn't put the same value on life as Americans," and this caused "less of a concern about what is euphemistically called 'collateral damage'... than there would have been perhaps otherwise" (Fredrik Logevall cited in Rosenberg 2017: ¶42). *Black Mirror* highlights how infectious and effective this can be: Rai, another soldier under Medina, points her gun at the back of Heidekker's head and gaily asserts, "Roach lover counts as a kill too, right?"

Today's leaders use similar language for similar ends, though the goal may be the denial of aid or resources rather than eradication (even if, as history has shown, these can be linked). Like Medina in *Black Mirror*, Trump, in announcing his presidential candidacy in 2015, deemed Mexican immigrants drug-dealers, criminals, and rapists who threatened an otherwise safe American way of life (cited in Gabbett 2019: ¶16). The same terminology also was used by leaders of the Vox party in Spain, who "falsely claimed foreigners were 'three times more likely to commit rape . . . than Spaniards'" (Kaufman 2020: ¶14). In 2018, President Trump and others referred to the "migrant caravan" of Central American refugees as an "invasion" and accused them of carrying diseases such as smallpox and leprosy (Rogers 2018; Belluz 2018; Roberts 2018). During the Covid-19 pandemic, Trump pointedly labeled the disease the "Chinese virus" (White House 2020b, 2020c), (re)igniting an anti-Asian sentiment the United States has repeatedly employed from the 1882 Chinese Exclusion Act to FDR's 1942 executive order imprisoning Japanese Americans and beyond (De Leon 2020). Steeped in xenophobia and lacking grounding in actual data, such language helps garner support for internment camps, border walls, and immigration policies that have removed citizens from their homes, separated children from parents, and forced vulnerable asylum seekers to wait in unhealthy or dangerous situations.

Trump used this tactic with political rivals as well. In what may seem comparatively less troubling, he regularly applied nicknames to opponents such as "crooked Hillary," "shifty Schiff," and "lyin' Ted Cruz." As Bernays explains, in using the techniques of propaganda, a thing or a person "may be [denigrated or] desired not for its intrinsic worth or usefulness, but because [others have] unconsciously come to see in it a symbol of something else" ([1928] 2005: 75).

Imagery

"Seeing" oftentimes translates to "believing"; thus, like language, mechanisms that shape how the public views a product, person, or issue can effectively transform beliefs and actions. In *Propaganda*, Bernays advises against appealing directly to the consumer, which is inefficient and ineffective, and advocates influencing (or creating) new social norms through change agents and key opinion leaders. He offers as an example how a "velvet fashion service" rescued a dying American market by focusing on "the Lyons manufactories and the Paris couturiers" to persuade them to use the fabric in their hats and gowns and "the distinguished Countess This or Duchess That" to wear them (Bernays [1928] 2005: 55–6). Editors of US fashion magazines, in following "the actual (although created) circumstance," reported the trend in their pages, while department stores sought to stock what was *haute couture*—turning "a trickle of velvet" into "a flood" (Bernays [1928] 2005: 56). Thus, the imagery provided by trendsetters or trusted sources like celebrities and experts serves the propagandist strategies of "transfer" and "testimonials" that sway cultural customs and ideals (Shabo 2008). When physicians are depicted in cigarette ads, for example, or Rita Hayworth shows off her bumper-less car to stir up wartime donations of scrap metal, new beliefs are formed (Shabo 2008).

Negative imagery is also used. In the First World War, to promote US enlistment or the buying of war bonds, posters portrayed the German enemy as a vicious, devolved, "mad brute" gorilla stealing off with a bare-breasted, white woman or as a dark, menacing, bloody-handed cretin destroying cities while creeping toward the Atlantic (National Museum of American History n.d.). Eerily similar is the poster advertising the 1940 Nazi film *The Eternal Jew*, focused on the face of a man drawn with heavy lines and in drab, sickly colors that convey an inherent sense of danger and foreboding. In the film itself, images of rats escaping a sewer are juxtaposed with Jews crowding a ghetto street, visually reinforcing the linguistic slur and intimating that the "eternal" in the title equates to a pestilential character that is interminable and intractable. Like Medina's "roaches," the "parasitical" nature of an "inferior" race alters an otherwise axiomatic equation. Medina tells Heidekker:

> You got principles. Think all life is sacred. And I get it. I agree. All life is sacred so you even got to protect the roaches. Right? It's not their fault they're like that. . . . You can't still see them as human. Understandable sentiment, granted, but it's misguided.

Similarly, Marshall advocates for shaping how soldiers see the enemy, though not through exaggerating an inhuman wickedness but by effecting a complete objectification. He writes: "We need to free the rifleman's mind with respect to the nature of targets," arguing that this requires a bypassing of rational thought through more than just training ([1947] 2000: 82). Because "there is a tendency to restrict fire until the live targets are observed"—exactly when soldiers are most likely to view the enemy as human and, thus, suffer that "final mental block"—a new approach is needed ([1947] 2000: 82). First, Marshall advocates developing among soldiers a habit of movement, as he maintains that overriding an individual's physical inaction will override any mental misgivings. Second, he suggests installing a "system of free selection of targets" to forge soldiers who amass fire "whenever ordered and against whatever target may be designated—the embankment of a river, the bases of the forward trees in a line of woods, or the crest of a hill" ([1947] 2000: 81). In other words, the targeting of locations leads to soldiers who don't see themselves as firing on humans but firing on things. Hauntingly, propagandists during the Rwandan genocide employed a comparable idiom: Since Hutus are on average shorter than Tutsis, the former were encouraged to "cut down the tall trees" (Ndahiro 2019: ¶3).

The MASS technology in *Black Mirror* relies on this tactic as well. As Medina's team searches Heidekker's house for the "roaches" hiding within, the newest recruit, Stripe (who has yet to meet a "roach" let alone kill one), uncovers a "roach nest" on the second floor. Several noxious-looking creatures screech and snarl, at last providing Stripe (and viewers) a visual depiction of this inhuman enemy. One points a metallic object in Stripe's direction, its lighted tip and high-pitched whine causing the soldier physical agitation and momentary confusion, but he recovers quickly and shoots one of the other "roaches" in the head. The first "roach" gives chase, and following an intense hand-to-hand struggle, Stripe stabs it to death until he is certain the task is complete. His comrade, Rai, overly eager to rack up her own "roach" kills, applauds Stripe's success before the team "torch[es] the place."

The next day, symptoms of malaise send Stripe to the medical unit, where his MASS is examined and he meets with a psychologist named Arquette. While technologically and physically he appears fine, Stripe expresses an unease about failing to feel anything during his kills other than "relief." When Arquette inquires what emotions he expected, Stripe replies: "[R]egret. Something like that, but that just wasn't there." Once Stripe confirms that if confronted with a "roach" he'd kill again, Arquette gives him the all clear.

During the next hunt in an abandoned tenement, however, things go further awry. Stripe is surprised by a woman crouching in terror and barely stops himself from firing. He urges her to flee, but Rai guns her down in the hallway. Other humans emerge from hiding places, and despite Stripe's protests, Rai continues to fire, gleeful with each strike. Shocked and appalled, Stripe helps another woman and a boy escape, as Rai turns on him. "What the fuck are you doing?" she asks. "They're roaches!"

Once the three find shelter, a veil begins to lift. As the woman tends to Stripe's wounds, she says, "You see me as I am. . . . You don't see roach." The character explains that the MASS system presents them to the soldiers as a monstrous other, preventing the soldiers from seeing or hearing them as they actually are. Instances of seeing others as monsters or enemy "objects" have occurred recently in the United States as well. During the 2018 migrant caravan, as Central Americans fled the poverty and dangers of their home countries, news programs displayed images and videos. Shaping whether migrants were seen as humans in need or a menacing throng depended on how such visuals were framed in relation to commentaries. On Fox News, former House Speaker Newt Gingrich called the caravan "an attack on America" and the migrants "invaders," underscoring (like Medina) that the United States must "stop them in their tracks" lest this "this caravan invasion" is "imitated" (2018: ¶1, ¶4, ¶19). Gingrich also highlighted the "monstrous" nature of the group: "Furthermore, we should not underestimate the degree to which human traffickers and transnational criminal gangs, such as MS-13 and other cartels, are involved with this invasion force" (Gingrich 2018: ¶12). In another Fox News report four days earlier, Jessica Vaughan, policy director for the Center for Immigration Studies, stated that "this is not a humanitarian crisis as much as it is a challenge to the sovereignty of borders and people bent on creating a scene at borders as a way of showing that they shouldn't exist" (cited in Darrah 2018: 1:54–2:09). Emphasizing that those in the caravan "are looking for economic opportunity" and "not fleeing for their lives," Vaughan concluded that "our governments just really are no match for their will to come to the United States" (cited in Darrah 2018: 2:13–2:35). Though she refrains from using Gingrich's more direct terminology, her portrayal echoes the images of the snarling "roaches" in *Black Mirror* or the creeping "Hun" of the First World War. What she describes is an act of war by formidable vandals bent on sacking a supposedly outmatched, and thus vulnerable, nation.

Likewise, during the Covid-19 pandemic, having Asian ancestry became associated with the virus. Verbal and physical assaults against Asians and

Asian Americans increased, with many being told "[y]ou people brought the virus" (Loffman 2020: ¶6) and some kicked and punched (Tavernise and Oppel 2020), chemically burnt (Yang, L. 2020), or murdered (Ramirez 2020). In an odd logic that placed the burden of such hate crimes on the victims, former presidential candidate Andrew Yang encouraged his fellow Asian Americans "to embrace and show our American-ness in ways we never have before," by doing things such as volunteering, helping neighbors, and "wear[ing] red white and blue" (Yang, A. 2020: ¶16)—as if he could counter President Trump's propaganda through different imagery. Many Asian Americans may have already been engaged in philanthropy or, like others during a crisis, might have needed to focus on their own families. Moreover, dressing in the flag could backfire. Likely no costume or kind deed would be able to combat what some Americans have come to see. In a Los Angeles grocery store, journalist Jeff Yang encountered a woman whose performative act signaled that he was both the vile source and deserved target of the disease: "She pulled down her mask, coughed theatrically in my direction, pulled up her mask, walked away" (Loffman 2020: ¶3).

Desire

The linguistic and visual framing of propaganda also serve to foster desire, whether positive feelings such as love and belonging or negative reactions such as hostility and fear. "To make customers is the new problem," Bernays claims, and a business or organization "cannot afford to wait until the public asks for its product" ([1928] 2005: 84). Instead, through emotional appeals that tap fundamental human drives, the "new propaganda" creates both customers and demand. Bernays explains this inverted approach through the marketing of pianos and soap. As with velvet, the piano propagandist aims not to sell pianos but, through influential leaders, tastemakers, and architects, to modify custom toward "the idea of a music room in the home" ([1928] 2005: 78). Dwellings large and small will then carve out space (even if just a nook) to house a piano. The desire, masked as individual thought, becomes natural. Manufacturers no longer ask consumers to buy; purchasers ask them what they are willing to sell. This has little to do with the inherent benefits of playing an instrument or listening to music, Bernays asserts. What drives the desire are the underlying "emotional currents" of belonging to a certain status or class that have been created to gin up "purchaser demand" ([1928] 2005: 77). As an example, the makers of Ivory soap found that sponsoring nationwide sculpture competitions for schoolchildren and artists engaged educational leaders, art galleries, and parents and communities to coalesce around an otherwise banal product, raising its stature on par with high art. What generated good will and participation in the campaign were not the prizes to be won but the "familiar psychological motives" that were prompted—purity, beauty, family, competition ([1928] 2005: 80–1).

Marshall and *Black Mirror* likewise connect the success of soldiers to manufactured desire. Like Bernays' seller of wares, Marshall determines that no amount of message repetition will increase fire ratios, because of a soldier's concurrent fears of killing and failure. Moreover, these are heightened in the midst of battle, because, unlike during training, soldiers may be separated from one another physically and mentally, causing them to feel disconnected and alone and leaving it up to the individual to determine whether to fire and where and when. The terrain of the battlefield environment and the need to take cover during enemy fire force soldiers to "remain largely invisible to their own components" ([1947] 2000: 89). Bernays describes the lack of communications between friendly forces as akin to "fighting in the dark," where light is thrown on the battlefield through the provision of specific information about the location and activity of other units ([1947] 2000: 86–8). This is more than just logistical. As Russell Glenn notes in an introduction to Marshall's book, the soldier is "no less a social animal in war" than during peace, and "effective leaders must understand their men's need for comradeship and cohesion. This Marshall translated into a call for aggressive and persistent communication under fire by all involved" (2000: 3).

The *Black Mirror* universe duplicates this premise. While MASS enables the team to share real-time intel and remain in constant contact, when off-mission the soldiers train, eat, and bunk together and engage in friendly competition over "roach" kills. Soldiers who hit their targets are provided with another reward—a pleasurable night's sleep, filled not with images of one's gruesome actions during the day, but rather with individually tailored erotic dreams. Stripe's visions involve a young, beautiful woman, who bids him enter a picturesque suburban house and eventually her bed. Though increasingly sexual as the episode progresses, the dreams also showcase feelings of home, safety, belonging, and love—the fundamental human motivators around which Bernays' ideas are oriented. Marshall, likewise, beseeches the US military to rethink its "system of distributing awards," which he claims tends "toward the discouragement of the fighting line," and instead of framing soldiering merely as doing one's duty, honor the "soldier who consistently addresses the enemy with fire" ([1947] 2000: 80). This is clearly resolved in *Black Mirror*, where the pleasure of the MASS-delivered dreams and the social competition around such rewards are addictive. After Stripe's first mission, for example, one teammate deems him lucky for having killed two "roaches," and Rai, who says that hunting is in her "blood," applauds Stripe in a mix of praise and envy. Her joy when firing upon human targets in the derelict housing project suggests that, through language, imagery, and manufactured desire, her lack of moral hesitancy has become natural.

Partisan politics provides similar examples of how desire can be shaped and created through the reliance upon or reward of influencers and tastemakers—media outlets like Fox News or OAN, Republican legislators focused on the judiciary or reelection, and self-interested preeners such as Alex Jones and Tucker Carlson. Trump and these opinion leaders need not create better solutions to policy problems like immigration or health care; rather, all they need to generate are pro-American, anti-socialist appeals. In this universe, political opponents during Covid-19 who called for prioritizing lives over the economy, increasing federal coordination and support, or ensuring oversight of trillion-dollar bailouts became equated with Big Brother "commies" or even the "rapists" or "killers" of capitalism. Here, Andrew Yang's plea to don the flag may have rung true.

Like Rai, with no moral pause, Trump also attempted to manufacture feelings of hope and security through false promises of tests for everyone, hastened vaccines, reopening the economy by Easter 2020, and unproven therapies. By repeatedly insisting, against his medical advisers' advice, that individuals should try hydroxychloroquine—"I hope they use it, because I tell you what, uh, what do you have to lose?"—Trump has proved he is no better than "a snake oil salesman . . . standing at a podium trying to sell us a miracle cure" (Meyers 2020: 15:20–15:45).

"Give Me My Eyes"

What Arquette sees as a glitch in Stripe's MASS and Marshall calls a soldier's "final mental block" are antidotes that undermine the power and rule of Bernays' "invisible governors." Like Marshall's unconditioned soldier, Stripe's reclaimed ability to think and see for himself disrupts the propagandist protocol that circumvents rational deliberation and discourse in order to appeal to unconscious, and often unfounded, fears and desires. While Stripe is aghast at the false world the MASS implant has created, telling the others that the "whole thing is a lie," he is even more horrified to learn that this is something to which he consented. "No one lied to you," Arquette explains, echoing Bernays' perspective. "You agreed to have your MASS implant put in. . . . Every soldier does. We can't just embed it and feed you a dream. Your mind would reject it. You have to accept it. Willingly. It's exactly what you did." Still unable to believe what he's hearing, Arquette shows Stripe a video of his younger self being presented the terms and conditions, only to respond, "Yeah, that's like a whole essay, man," and signing the agreement without reading it. Perhaps Bernays is right: Stripe's behavior is emblematic of the lazy thinking in which we at times all willingly engage.

Although Bernays distinguishes his "new propaganda" from that which was employed during the war and from "the tawdry bunkum used to peddle patent medicines and cigarettes" (Miller 2005: 12), the case he makes for its reclamation and reformation, its necessity and its ethical application, is unconvincing and incomplete. What, if anything, differentiates the new from the old? Unlike the snake-oil salesman of the nineteenth century, Bernays underscores that it "is futile to attempt to sell an idea or to prepare the ground for a product that is basically unsound" ([1928] 2005: 65). He stops short, however, in defining what "unsound" means. In later years, Bernays did refuse to work for the tobacco industry (Miller 2005), but in *Propaganda* he seems unbothered by his role in fostering clients' "enlightened self-interest" or that, thanks to propaganda, even as "we imagine ourselves free agents . . . we are ruled by dictators exercising great power" ([1928] 2005: 61).

What Bernays overlooks are the reasons why, for example, patent medicines disappeared (or the norms surrounding tobacco use changed). It wasn't propaganda that undermined their popularity but journalism that exposed dangerous ingredients and prompted new laws (Adams [1906] 1907). In other words, data about what each product contained and regulation enacted through representative—not invisible—government. The 1906 Pure Food and Drug Act did not ban patent medicines or their ingredients; simply mandating labeling was enough to foster logical thinking and alter use and acceptance. That which enables rational analysis is the opposite of propaganda, whether old or new.

A century later, Bernays' question remains unanswered: Are there instances where propaganda is justified? A few examples, one during wartime, one during peace, may provide a means of exploration though likely no solution. Philosophers have long raised a similar question about the concept of a just war. As Lars Svendsen has argued, "when the circumstances are right, it can be immoral *not* to go to war" (2011: 225, *emphasis in original*). Thus, perhaps it might also be wrong to avoid using the effective tool that is propaganda. During the Cold War, the United States took this approach with its CIA-funded Radio Free Europe and Radio Liberty, whose purposes were to combat Soviet censorship and propaganda. These services provided audiences in communist regimes information about events inside and outside of the bloc, including the activity of dissidents (Holt 1958: 132; Meyer 2000: 128). Staffed by journalists and communist exiles, the "CIA maintained control over content by formulating general policy guidelines, which were supplemented by daily meetings to determine the handling of specific news" (Meyer 2000: 129). A 1958 study of Radio Free Europe's effectiveness plainly identified the station as a "propaganda agency broadcasting from the West into the satellites" and reported that it had been criticized for "lack[ing] objectivity and speak[ing] in an exaggerated and immoderate tone. Some accuse RFE of raising 'false hopes'; others, of reporting inaccurately on internal affairs" (Holt 1958: 120, 131). Decades later, however, Cord Meyer, who had become chief of the CIA's International Organizations Division in 1954 and oversaw these radio endeavors, underlined that "great care was taken to assure objectivity and to avoid any attempted news manipulation for propaganda" (2000: 129). He also credited the media enterprises with undermining the strength of the Soviet Union's grasp and preventing the isolation of America: "The communist line was much more difficult to sell when confronted with an increasingly well-informed and skeptical public" (Meyer 2000: 129). From Meyer's perspective, there was integrity in what was being produced, and it was crucial to fight fire with fire.

A half-century later, the Gun Shop Project that began in New Hampshire in 2009 took a similar vein. Spearheaded by an ad hoc committee of public and mental health professionals, university researchers, gun shop owners, and gun advocates (and later adopted by the NH Firearm Safety Coalition), the project aimed "to help gun retailers avoid selling firearms to new customers who may be suicidal" and "to educate existing customers in a trusted environment about what the Coalition dubbed the '11th Commandment of Firearm Safety'"—for the family and friends of gun owners to recognize signs of suicide and temporarily secure a person's weapons until a crisis has passed (Vriniotis et al. 2015: 158). Based on surveys and interviews with retailers, educational materials (such as tip sheets, suicide-prevention wallet cards, and gun safety brochures and posters) were developed for local gun shop owners and dealers to display in their stores and share with customers. Some, however, were skeptical, and "many of them felt it was a trick—another way to blame guns for violence" (Chooljian 2018: ¶22). To encourage buy-in, researchers "made a conscious effort to appear neutral on gun control" and "not com[e] off as anti-gun" (Brink 2014: ¶13), and the language in materials intentionally avoided public health idioms and instead framed the issue as a way to protect gun rights. Furthermore, especially as the project has spread to other states, brochures and other literature have been tailored to feature shops' logos as if these materials were their own, and some store owners have created videos or written pro-safety articles (NAMI New Hampshire 2018–20). In this way, trusted opinion leaders have been engaged to sway acceptance. As one retailer stated, because a well-known gun shop owner was a cofounder of the coalition, "I knew it wasn't a liberal cover group to disarm everybody" (Brink 2014: ¶16)—even though that cofounder has admitted that the goal was to "indoctrinate [people] into thinking positively about suicide prevention" (Chooljian 2018: ¶40). Researchers evaluating the original New Hampshire project also found that some "dealers who declined to participate indicated they would be willing to display materials that had industry backing (by manufacturers or prominent gun rights organizations)" (Vriniotis et al. 2015: 161). Thus, all three aspects of propaganda (language, imagery, change agent-led desire) have been invoked, and anecdotal evidence suggests that customers may be more willing to take pamphlets that appear to come from a store itself and to participate in discussions instigated by presumably like-minded owners and employees.

While the use of propaganda in these cases appears valuable and well intentioned, it might be worth pondering whether this technique is the best means available. Were or are there other, more moral paths that effect the desired results? If not, can propaganda be used, as Bernays claims, in an ethical way? What seems clear, from history and fiction to examples of modern day, is that the utilitarian-like arguments in which propaganda tends to be grounded often sound plausible but unravel upon closer examination. For example, in *Black Mirror*, Lennard's condemnation of the villagers who feed the "roaches" suggests that treating them like humans is the problem. Less nefariously, the Gun Shop Project "could only measure the number of gun stores willing to display information," not "gauge how many suicides the effort may have stopped" (Brink 2014: ¶17). Bernays himself engages in a grand utilitarian claim upfront: that propaganda is necessary for a "smoothly functioning society" while providing no descriptive data in evidence of this assertion. He resembles Medina and Arquette, who frame the killing of "roaches" as a eugenic duty for the good of society, using MASS as an appropriate propagandist tool toward "protecting the bloodline" (Rich 2019).

Utilitarian calculus, however, requires good description of an issue and the world—real data generated with an aim toward "truth" that reaches beyond self-interest, "enlightened" or otherwise—and an engaged analysis of possible outcomes and their relative utility (Mill [1861] 2000). Not only is this sometimes an insurmountable undertaking, it does not align with propaganda's approach. What the two primarily share is a focus on teleological ends. Subjected to a true utilitarian analysis, many propaganda campaigns fizzle. Bernays' case of the piano producer provides an example. While he and his client might argue that what is good for the manufacturer—the selling of pianos, whether customers truly want them—is good for all (e.g., shareholders, employees and their families, distributors and retailers, piano tutors, those who take up the instrument, a society's musical canon, the economy), this "enlightened self-interest" overlooks the diversion or depletion of natural, fiscal, and human resources to support a manufactured demand. One need only substitute SUVs or opioids for pianos to see how flimsy "enlightened self-interest" may be (see, e.g., Meier 2018).

At the same time, we might ask, especially as the inheritors of Bernays' PR machine and living amid Trump's "fake news" and "alternative facts": Is propaganda inevitable? Like Stripe, who wants his "eyes back" from MASS's invisible creators, we may have few options. Arquette explains that Stripe either can agree to have his MASS reset—thus erasing his moral awakening—or he can opt for incarceration where, with MASS no longer implanted, he "will remember everything that [he] did." Bernays provides a similar double bind.

He argues that our world could not exist without propaganda and that we can never choose not to use it, while propagandistically framing propaganda as something that does not set out to "fool or hoodwink the public" but "depends upon the merit of the cause urged . . . and the correctness of the information published" ([1928] 2005: 48). We can either see the world as the invisible rulers wish us to or keep watch of their practices while painfully remembering the atrocities of our present and our past. One offers dangerous but pleasurable dreams; the other is a Sisyphean path.

References

Adams, S. H. ([1906] 1907), *The Great American Fraud*, 4th edn, Chicago: American Medical Association.

Belluz, J. (2018), "Fox News Says the Migrant Caravan Will Bring Disease Outbreaks. That's Xenophobic Nonsense," *Vox*, 1 November. Available online: https://www.vox.com/science-and-health/2018/11/1/18048332/migrant-caravan-fox-news-disease-smallpox-outbreaks-vaccines-xenophobia (accessed November 1, 2018).

Bernays, E. ([1928] 2005), *Propaganda*, Brooklyn: Ig Publishing.

Black Mirror (2016), [TV program] Netflix, 21 October.

Brink, S. (2014), "Gun Shops, Public Health Officials Find Common Ground," *U.S. News & World Report*, 4 December. Available online: https://www.usnews.com/news/articles/2014/12/04/gun-shops-public-health-officials-work-together-to-prevent-suicide.

Chooljian, L. (2018), "In New Hampshire, An Unlikely Team Tries to Reduce Gun Suicides," *New Hampshire Public Radio*, 14 January. Available online: https://www.wbur.org/hereandnow/2018/06/14/suicide-prevention-gun-sellers.

Connelly, M. (2014), "Ask a Pollster: Push Polls, Defined," *The New York Times*, 18 June. Available online: https://www.nytimes.com/2014/06/19/upshot/pushpolls-defined.html.

Darrah, N. (2018), "Trump on Migrant Caravan: "Onslaught of Illegal Aliens" Represents "Disgrace" to the Dems," *Fox News*, 21 October. Available online: https://www.foxnews.com/politics/trump-on-migrant-caravan-onslaught-of-illegal-aliens-represents-disgrace-to-the-dems.

De Leon, A. (2020), "The Long History of US Racism Against Asian Americans, From 'Yellow Peril' to 'Model Minority' to the 'Chinese Virus,'" *The Conversation*, 8 April. Available online: https://theconversation.com/the-long-history-of-us-racism-against-asian-americans-from-yellow-peril-to-model-minority-to-the-chinese-virus-135793.

Gabbett, A. (2019), "Golden Escalator Ride: The Surreal Day Trump Kicked Off His Bid for President," *The Guardian*, 14 June. Available online: https://www.theguardian.com/us-news/2019/jun/13/donald-trump-presidential-campaign-speech-eyewitness-memories.

Glenn, R. W. (2000), "Introduction," in S. L. A. Marshall, *Men Against Fire: The Problem of Battle Command*, 1–8, Norman: University of Oklahoma Press.

Gingrich, N. (2018), "Migrant Caravan on the March—What We Must Do If (or When) the Caravan Arrives at Our Border," *Fox News*, 25 October. Available online: https://www.foxnews.com/opinion/newt-gingrich-migrant-caravan-on-the-march-what-we-must-do-if-or-when-the-caravan-arrives-at-our-border.

Griffin, E. A. (1991), *A First Look at Communication Theory*, New York: McGraw-Hill.

Hale, J. L. and J. P. Dillard (1995), "Fear Appeals in Health Promotion Campaigns: Too Much, Too Little, or Just Right?" in E. Maibach and R. L. Parrott (eds.), *Designing Health Messages: Approaches From Communication Theory and Public Health Practice*, 65–80, Thousand Oaks, CA: Sage Publications, Inc.

Holt, R. T. (1958), *Radio Free Europe*, Minneapolis: University of Minnesota Press.

Karni, A., M. Haberman and R. J. Epstein (2020), "'Wartime President'? Trump Rewrites History in an Election Year," *The New York Times*, 22 March. Available online: https://www.nytimes.com/2020/03/22/us/politics/coronavirus-trump-wartime-president.html.

Kaufman, A. C. (2020), "How Spain's Far-Right Is Exploiting a Local Political Fight to Start a Culture War," *HuffPost*, 26 January. Available online: https://www.huffpost.com/entry/spain-far-right_n_5e28f82ac5b67d8874ac8893.

Loffman, M. (2020), "Asian Americans Describe "Gut Punch" of Racist Attacks During Coronavirus Pandemic," *PBS NewsHour*, 7 April. Available online: https://www.pbs.org/newshour/nation/asian-americans-describe-gut-punch-of-racist-attacks-during-coronavirus-pandemic.

Marshall, S. L. A. ([1947] 2000), *Men Against Fire: The Problem of Battle Command*, Norman: University of Oklahoma Press.

Meet the Press (2017), [TV programme] NBC News, 22 January. Available online: https://www.nbcnews.com/meet-the-press/meet-press-01-22-17-n710491.

Meier, B. (2018), *Pain Killer: An Empire of Deceit and the Origin of America's Opioid Epidemic*, New York: Random House.

Meyer, C. (2000), "The CIA and Radio Free Europe," *Georgetown Journal of International Affairs*, 1(1): 127–30.

Meyers, S. (2020), "Trump Contradicts Experts on Coronavirus Treatment After Months of Denial," *A Closer Look*, 6 April. Available online: https://www.youtube.com/watch?v=2TX4fW1dD4E&feature=youtu.be.

Mill, J. S. ([1861] 2000), *Utilitarianism*, ed. R. Crisp, New York: Oxford University Press.

Miller, M. C. (2005), "Introduction," in E. Bernays (ed.), *Propaganda*, 9–33, Brooklyn: Ig Publishing.

Monahan, J. L. (1995), "Thinking Positively: Using Positive Affect When Designing Health Messages," in E. Maibach and R. L. Parrott (eds), *Designing Health Messages: Approaches From Communication Theory and Public Health Practice*, 81–98, Thousand Oaks, CA: Sage Publications, Inc.

NAMI New Hampshire (2018–2020), "NH Firearm Safety Coalition." Available online: https://theconnectprogram.org/resources/nh-firearm-safety-coalition/.

National Museum of American History, (n.d.), "Advertising War: The Poster Campaign," Smithsonian Institution. Available online: https://americanhistory.si.edu/advertising-war/poster-campaign.

Ndahiro, K. (2019), "In Rwanda, We Know All About Dehumanizing Language: Years of Cultivated Hatred Led to Death on a Horrifying Scale," *The Atlantic*, 13 April. Available online: https://www.theatlantic.com/ideas/archive/2019/04/rwanda-shows-how-hateful-speech-leads-violence/587041/.

Orwell, G. (1949), *Nineteen Eighty-Four*, London: Secker & Warburg.

Ramirez, M. (2020), "FBI Says Texas Stabbing That Targeted Asian-American Family Was Hate Crime Fueled by Coronavirus Fears," *The Dallas Morning News*, 31 March. Available online: https://www.dallasnews.com/news/crime/2020/04/01/fbi-says-texas-stabbing-that-targeted-asian-american-family-was-hate-crime-fueled-by-coronavirus-fears/.

Rich, L. E. (2019). "'Men Against Fire': *Black Mirror*, Eugenics, and Othering Outside of War," *Film and Philosophy*, 23: 68–94.

Roberts, D. (2018), "The Caravan "Invasion" and America's Epistemic Crisis," *Vox*, 1 November. Available online: https://www.vox.com/policy-and-politics/2018/11/1/18041710/migrant-caravan-america-trump-epistemic-crisis-democracy.

Rogers, A. (2018), "Calling the Caravan's Migrants "Diseased" Is a Classic Xenophobic Move," *Wired*, 31 October. Available online: https://www.wired.com/story/calling-the-caravans-migrants-diseased-is-a-classic-xenophobic-move/.

Rosenberg, A. (2017), "'The American War': Why You Need to Understand American Racism to Understand What Happened in Vietnam," *The Washington Post*, 22 September. Available online: https://www.washingtonpost.com/news/act-four/wp/2017/09/22/the-american-war-why-you-need-to-understand-american-racism-to-understand-what-happened-in-vietnam/.

Shabo, M. E. (2008), *Techniques of Propaganda and Persuasion*, Clayton, DE: Prestwick House.

Svendsen, L. (2011), *A Philosophy of Evil*, trans. K. A. Pierce, Champaign and London: Dalkey Archive Press.

Tavernise, S. and R. A. Oppel Jr. (2020), "Spit On, Yelled At, Attacked: Chinese-Americans Fear for Their Safety," *The New York Times*, 23 March. Available online: https://www.nytimes.com/2020/03/23/us/chinese-coronavirus-racist-attacks.html.

Thaler, R. H. and C. R. Sunstein (2008), *Nudge: Improving Decisions About Health, Wealth, and Happiness*, New Haven, CT: Yale University Press.

The Eternal Jew (1940), [Film] Dir. Fritz Hippler, Germany: Terra.

Verbruggen, Jakob. (2016), "Men Against Fire," *Black Mirror*, Netflix. Season 3, Episode 5. Release Date October 21, 2016. [TV Series].

Vriniotis, M., C. Barber, E. Frank, R. Demicco and The New Hampshire Firearm Safety Coalition (2015), "A Suicide Prevention Campaign for Firearm Dealers in New Hampshire," *Suicide and Life-Threatening Behavior*, 45(2): 157–63.

White House (2020a), "Remarks by President Trump, Vice President Pence, and Members of the Coronavirus Task Force in Press Briefing," 17 March. Available online: https://www.whitehouse.gov/briefings-statements/remarks-president-trump-vice-president-pence-members-coronavirus-task-force-press-briefing-4/.

White House (2020b), "Remarks by President Trump, Vice President Pence, and Members of the Coronavirus Task Force in Press Briefing," 18 March. Available online: https://www.whitehouse.gov/briefings-statements/remarks-president-trump-vice-president-pence-members-coronavirus-task-force-press-briefing-5/.

White House (2020c), "Remarks by President Trump, Vice President Pence, and Members of the Coronavirus Task Force in Press Briefing," 22 March. Available online: https://www.whitehouse.gov/briefings-statements/remarks-president-trump-vice-president-pence-members-coronavirus-task-force-press-briefing-8/.

Yang, A. (2020), "We Asian Americans Are Not the Virus, But We Can Be Part of the Cure," *The Washington Post*, 1 April. Available online: https://www.washingtonpost.com/opinions/2020/04/01/andrew-yang-coronavirus-discrimination/.

Yang, L. (2020), "Coronavirus News: Anti-Asian Bias Crimes Increasing in NYC Amid COVID-19 Pandemic," WABC-TV New York, 7 April. Available online: https://abc7ny.com/coronavirus-bias-crimes-anti-asian-hate-brooklyn-crime/6085402/.

10

"Between Delight and Discomfort"
The Act of Mirroring in the Age of *Black Mirror*

Shai Biderman

The TV anthology series *Black Mirror* is one of the most perplexing media experiences of our time. Created by Charlie Brooker, it premiered in 2011 on the British broadcaster Channel 4 as an eclectic collection of fragmentary, independent episodes dealing—in the spirit of the historical sci-fi genre—with the abandonment of philosophical and moral values in a post-humanist technological society and more particularly, with the media's role and responsibility for that process. The series' self-consciousness of being in itself a media product of the same reality archetype it describes remained unblemished even when taken over by Netflix—a creative environment which is, at least on the face of it, less bound by the conservative history of British TV and more reflective of the technological era of open source and intermediality. The technology embodied in *Black Mirror* has since become the substance of the series, as demonstrated in the following episode.

The first episode of Series Four "USS Callister" (Haynes 2017) opens in a way reminiscent of a TV sci-fi series, specifically of the original iteration of the US sci-fi series *Star Trek* (1965–9). The mythological Starship Enterprise of the latter is replaced in this *Black Mirror* episode by the USS Callister, which similarly ventures out into "the final frontier . . . To boldly go where no man has gone before!" as the famous spaceship's opening monologue goes.

This opening is enough to make viewers feel somewhat uneasy. Are we watching an episode of *Black Mirror*—a sci-fi series in its own right—concerned, according to its reputation, with presenting the human condition in the technological age, or are we watching an episode of a different series, in itself no more than a contemporary (pale) descendant (or perhaps a parody) of its predecessor *Star Trek*? Things become more complicated as we are led inside to meet the space travelers and partake in their adventures. The crew we come across mirrors the one familiar to us from the *Enterprise*: the brave and resolute captain Robert Daly, the heir or substitute of the mythological James T. Kirk and Jean-Luc Picard; James Walton as his second-in-command, replacing Spock; and so on. The episode even features a perennial, demonic enemy—Valdak, substituting for *Star Trek*'s Kahn.

From this point on, the episode unfolds as we have been trained by TV to expect: the crew runs into trouble when the eternal enemy threatens to destroy the ship—as always. A battle ensues, phasers fire up, the ship takes a hit or two (with the crewmembers moving in synch), clichés are barked as orders in complete seriousness ("Mr. Scott—give me full power!"), and defeat seems imminent. But then, the resourceful captain rises to the occasion and saves the ship thanks to his mastery of astrophysics, and Valdak is vanquished, only to flee at the last minute, providing narrative fuel for the infinitude of future episodes that lie ahead.

As the crewmembers' cheers die out, it becomes apparent that this is not the happy ending that it appears to be. The viewers realize that what they have just watched is no (fake) *Star Trek* episode at all but rather a devious virtual reality computer game, revealed as such when the captain—in the diegetic *Black Mirror* reality, a geeky and depressed programmer trampled by his dominant partner—turns it off to return to his gray routine. This conceptual confusion and the collapse of our customary coordinates (based on a heritage of viewing TV series, and sci-fi series in particular) is of course the highlight of our experience. The virtual game, which forms only part of the *Black Mirror* episode, is a metonymy, a mirror, a microcosm of the viewing experience, itself reflecting the viewer's own participation in the *Black Mirror* phenomenon. The deliberate violation of the medium's boundaries and the intentional play on viewing and consumption habits are a contemporary technological tour de force: a consumption experience (of contents) that is at the same time also a signification experience, and at the same time also a user experience inspired by the gameful interactivity that has become part of our routine.

This chapter deconstructs the perplexing nature of the *Black Mirror* phenomenon. In the first, etymological section, I examine how the user experience in the series is embodied already within its title. Through the motif of the mirror and its derivatives, I examine the metaphorical use of the mirror apparatus, the function that defines it and that is activated by it (mirroring), and the additional symbolic black color—all, I argue, indicative of the conceptual move the series seeks to lead, and of the change it seeks to promote. In the second, genealogical section, I examine the media evolution of the act of mirroring foundational to the series and its title and present it as an essential premise for the *Black Mirror* move. In other words, to justify a claim regarding changes in the specifications of the user experience (which is the act of mirroring) in the *Black Mirror* era, we need to examine the cumulative background that has defined this experience to begin with.

Etymology: Why Mirror? Why Black? Why Black Mirror?

Any attempt to understand the role and status of the series in the technological and creative media sphere in which it operates must start with its enigmatic title. Like any other, it marks itself as a key through which we can decipher the content worlds hiding behind it. Let us start with the question, "Why mirror?" This apparatus has a distinct symbolic status derived from the act of mirroring to which it refers. A quick etymological glance tells us that the act of mirroring has two key meanings, a technical, optic-operative one, and a hermeneutic symbolic one. The technical meaning is illustrated through synonyms such as copy, copying, emulation, double, exact likeness, following, imitation, repetition, and resemblance—the act of producing a copy, an image of or object identical to the origin. The symbolic meaning is embodied in words such as fakery, reflection, parody, impersonation, imposture, and impression, which add hermeneutic value and weight to the technical act. Note that the valence is usually negative, due to the lower ontological hierarchical status of the mirror image compared to the origin it mirrors. The latter is deemed "real" whereas the former is considered inferior, if not negative.

The philosophical—both ontological and epistemic—status of the mirror image/object metaphor arising in this semantic field thus defines the act of mirroring as a hierarchic act of signification. There is a source, there is a copy, the latter represents the former, and the mirror is the apparatus teleologically charged with performing or producing that representation. Moreover, representation will always obtain its value and meaning when it is perceived. In other words, a perceiving subject is a prerequisite for the act of mirroring, inherent to the very definition of the act and the apparatus that enables it.

The cultural preoccupation with this set of relationships is illustrated in the foundational fairytale *Snow White*: "Mirror, mirror, on the wall, who's the fairest one of all?," quoth the Evil Queen, challenging the perception of reality, and using the Magic Mirror's verbal reply (that conflicts with the optical reflection) to morally justify her acts. In another canonical work, *Through the Looking Glass*, Alice wonders what hides behind the validation of reality reflected by the mirror, as she abandons her twin kittens (one, how appropriate, is black, and the other, no less appropriate, is white and called Snowdrop, perhaps an allusion to the fairytale heroine) to pass through the mirror into a land of new meanings, new conceptual possibilities, and new philosophical challenges.

These two literary examples reveal that the mirror is embodied ab initio in the act of mirroring. It is an apparatus that reflects (technically, optically, and unintentionally) the reality it faces. This mirroring (as reflected in the gaze of both the Evil Queen and Alice) becomes intentional when involving an observing subject. The subject looks at (or through) the mirror, conferring the "objective" "mirroring" with its subjective (intentional) status. This subjective superfluity is thus the *telos* of the metaphorical use of the mirror. In other words, we have little interest in the mirror as a mere apparatus, one that (technically) "photographs" the world in front of it, but rather in the mirror as an extension of the intention of the subject looking at or through it.

This distinction will be further clarified if we ask, "What does the subject see when looking at the mirror?" Is it (1) reality "as is," (2) reality as she sees it, or perhaps (3) the boundaries of reality? To take the example of the Evil Queen, it appears that all three questions are just as relevant. The Queen views her image as an objective representation, but in asking her famous question, she betrays her subjective intentionality: it seems that "reality as she sees it" includes her evaluation of herself as the prettiest of all. In its reply, the Mirror also reveals the relevance of the third question, since the boundaries of reality are inherent to the way it responds to the Queen rather than to the content of the response itself. The Mirror seems to exceed its conventional role by responding verbally. This exception is designed, of course, to mark the boundaries of the medium itself in a description of reality, be it objective or subjective. In other words, it is the Mirror's role to represent reality objectively—mirroring reality—even when the subjective reality perception of the subject looking at or through it is different from what her eyes tell her.

This act of marking the gap between the objective and subjective can take place only if we add a third element: the medium's exposure of its boundaries. This philosophical status of the mirror object is reflected in a third cluster of synonyms. The words simulation, simulacrum, similitude, image, idol, and icon, for example, refer with ostensible neutrality to the technical act of creating a copy but immediately weigh it down with its immanent burden. This cluster drives right into the heart of the matter: we have erred in thinking that the technical act is self-sufficient, devoid of any particular charge. This charge, whether negative or positive, is intentionally and essentially built into the act itself. A mirroring act will always be charged with a certain value, a certain interpretation, and intentionality.

Following the etymological discussion of the mirror, we can now turn to the second titular term and ask, "Why black?" This term is also used in two complementary senses that dialogue with the two senses of the mirror metaphor and the act of mirroring. On the one hand, the word is a common metaphor for a negative charge of the kind discussed above. Dark thoughts, dark times, melancholy (through its etymological root in black bile) or black mood, black magic, black market, and countless other expressions suggest the negativity associated with that color—at least in white cultures. Other examples include the Black Death that terrorized Europe in the mid-fourteenth century, the Black Widow that devours her male partner upon the consummation of their arachnoid union, and the black sheep that is found in every family. At the same time, black is an optical and aesthetic choice that appears opposed to the act of mirroring. Black is an achromatic color, the color of absence, the product of lightlessness that produces invisibility—the conceptual inverse of the intentional act laden with meaning (albeit negative) that is mirroring.

Given the aforementioned, we can now return to the full title. The juxtaposition of "Black" with "Mirror" is now understood as a combination of the intentional, assertive act of signification and interpretation with the perfect metaphor for its lack, or rather, for its impossibility. Joining the act of mirroring with the essential inability of mirroring, therefore, constitutes the core of the series. It is evident throughout in its contents, but also, and perhaps mainly in its very presence as a contemporary media phenomenon.

In its contents, the title is the key for consistent interpretation of the narrative structure of the series episodes, the worldviews they present, the real experiences they construct, and the technological, existential, and moral issues they raise and discuss, and consequently also its characters, dialogues, etc. But more importantly, on the level of the TV phenomenon itself, this juxtaposition is also a conscious reference—self-reflection—of the medium (that the series inhabits) to the technology that enables it. In other words, the meaning itself, which represents itself and its contents under the *Black Mirror* title, is aware of the inherent failure represented by the same.

Conscious of this failure, Brooker defined the *Black Mirror* compilation in 2011 as semantics that describes the user's experience in the encounter with the narcotic screen technology that has come to dominate our lives: "If technology is a drug—and it does feel like a drug—then what, precisely, are the side effects? This area—between delight and discomfort—is where *Black Mirror*, my new drama series, is set" (Brooker 2011). He further explained the meaning of the title as follows: "any TV, any LCD, any iPhone, any iPad—something like that—if you just stare at it, it looks like a black mirror, and there's something cold and horrifying about that, and it was such a fitting title for the show" (Brooker 2011). Thus, as a whole, *Black Mirror* has a much more real and practical meaning than the one derived from conjoining its two parts: it is the screen of the devices that we use every day *when turned off*. The symbols of our technological society, once deactivated, become a black surface reflecting our figure (or rather our shadow) and this image has exerted a dark fascination on the creator of the series, eventually becoming the title. Brooker's explanation directs us to the conflation of the technical apparatus (black mirror as a black screen) and its immanently negative value (between delight and discomfort). A black screen, a visibility of invisibility, which sensitizes us (like a drug) to a threatening image that shows the dark side of ourselves, the fear of what we see in front of us.

Online responses to Brooker's explanation highlight another important aspect of this definition. One commenter on the *Urban Dictionary* notes as follows:

> [Black mirror is] (t)he reflection of an *unlit* computer screen after it is *accidentally* or *unwillingly* shutdown while you're in front of it, giving you a chance to *rethink* your *life* as you see *your self*.

Another queries:

> Am I the only one who didn't know Black Mirror was called Black Mirror because when you look at your phone or computer screen *after it's turned off* you see *your reflection* on the black screen? (In Baxter-Wright 2018)

The black mirror is thus not only a symbolic representation of the black screen (a framing of the visibility of invisibility) and not even the intoxicating encounter with it. The black mirror is revealed in its full operative and functional clarity when the apparatus ceases to operate and function when the *screen is turned off* or, more precisely, *at the very minute the screen is turned off*. In other words, the visibility of invisibility—the meaning (presence/*ontos*) derived from its lack (absence/*aponia*)—exists on two levels: the content or message (seen on the screen when it is "working") and the medium (the screen itself—when it stops "working").

To conclude, the etymology of the title *Black Mirror* reflects its foundation, its anchor. This anchor confers new meaning to the act of mirroring, extricating it from the representative relations attributed to it (as well as the source-copy relations derived therefrom) and locating it in both a new technological space and, no less important, a new philosophical space. To get down to the bottom of this relocation, we must examine the history of the encounters between the act of mirroring and the world of moving images, of which the anthology series is a bastard but direct descendant. These encounters will enable us to understand how *Black Mirror* represents not only an etymological and philosophical revision of the act of mirroring but also—and mainly—a sweeping revision of the very conceptual framework with which we have been equipped to value this act.

The Theory and Practice of Cinematic Magic Mirrors: Select Examples

The moving image gaze is bound together with and defined by the act of mirroring. This is evident in both the definition of the media that enable it and in the design of the visual content that populates these media. In other words, the act of mirroring is the binder that anchors and defines the media operations. Whether these are representative, expressive, or interpretive, their primary cause is the technical-optical act of mirroring. At the same time, and if only for that reason, the content of that mirroring act is designed in the constant presence of the act of mirroring itself.

Since the first days of cinematic theory, the metaphorical importance of both the mirror and the act of mirroring has been appreciated in defining the capabilities, characteristics, and actions of the moving image medium. This importance was identified in two complementary respects: the importance derived from the very fact that the moving image is a mirrorlike reflective apparatus and the importance derived from the symbolic presence of mirrors and other reflective objects and surfaces in the diegetic mise-en-scène. In other words, the mirror as a diegetic metaphor is one of the medium's working tools, and at the same time, it acts as an extradiegetic metaphor to the way the medium itself operates.

The cinematic medium as a mirror was emphasized mainly in Christian Metz's ([1991] 2016) film theory, in analogy to Lacan's mirror stage (Lacan & Miller 1988). In Lacanian theory, the child learns to differentiate himself from his mother after differentiating himself from his mirror image. That fictitious image differentiates him as real, and subsequently differentiates him from his mother and individuates him as an autonomous being. This individuation-through-mirroring act ends up with a sense of wholeness and unity, despite "the mirror image being only a fictional representation" (Singer 1998: 92). Following Metz and Lacan, Irving Singer identifies a similar understanding of the metaphor in Stanley Cavell (1981: 45–70; 2004: 301–12), and claims that mirrors "signify the cinematic medium itself as it copies reality within the frame of the camera's lens" (Singer 2008: 29–30).

Singer himself, however, qualifies the scope and importance of the medium-as-mirror metaphor. He writes: "theorists who hold conceptions such as these have been misled by false ideas about the nature of visual imagery" (Singer 1998: 93), because "photographic images are quite different from images in a mirror" (Singer 2008: 30). He elaborates:

> Distorted as it may be, a mirror image is a technological, even automatic, reflection of the actuality one sees in looking at a mirror. Mirrors can show us only a special segment of our visual world. There is indeed a likeness, often a striking and possibly unique likeness, between the mirror image and that of which it is an image. And one might say something comparable about photographic images. Still they, as opposed to mirror images, belong to the inherent nature of a creative art form-photography or cinema. In itself a mirror is not an art form at all. (Ibid.)

Therefore, and while moving on to the second metaphor—namely, "the fact that mirrors are often seen in movies" (2008: 31)—Singer writes:

> Instead of treating the inclusion of mirrors in a film as revealing the nature of filmmaking itself, we should try to see how mirrors function in the psychodynamics of some narrative. (Ibid.)

This will require the examination of a different set of qualities, namely the way "mirrors increase the spatial properties of almost any cinematic setting," or the way mirrors serve as "instruments of refraction, [and as means to] enlarge our field of perception, backward in depth as well as forward and sometimes to a simulacrum of infinity" (ibid.).

The symbolic status of mirrors and other reflective objects as part of the diegetic world of the moving image was emphasized by Metz ([1991] 2016: 63). He coined the term "non-reflective mirror" to refer to the nature of this symbolism, namely, the type of mirror that "reflects something other than the person who looks at it and acts simply as a secondary screen" (ibid). It can represent the inner world of the subject/character, moral duplicity, faulty reality perception, or a portal to an alternative reality.

Metz also ties together the two senses in which the mirror is required in the context of the moving image. According to Metz, the appearance of the mirror in cinematic diegesis will never be a casual matter, but rather an active metaphor for the presence and importance of the camera that creates the image and its meanings just as the mirror creates the reflection and its meanings. "Every mirror is like a camera (or a projector) because it 'projects' the image a second time, because it offers it a second shot, because it has an *emissive* power" (Metz [1991] 2016: 63).

Whether for psychological, ethical, epistemological, or ontological purposes, the cinematic mirror will always be not only the presence of an object in diegetic space but, more importantly, also a symbolic representation that carries meaning. Thus, for example, film theoretician Siegfried Kracauer identifies the mirror's diegetic presence with the medium's moral task, which is "no longer the symbolization of the ethical, but rather the mirroring of the enslaved, damaged quality of life" (as quoted in Schlupmann 1987).

One of the most elaborate contemporary studies of the cinematic uses of diegetic mirrors and mirror images is articulated by Julian Hanich. According to Hanich (2017), the importance of a mirror presented on screen is both apparatic and symbolic. Hanich focuses on the effects movie mirrors can have on the composition of a filmic image, the staging of a scene, and the viewing activities. Through what he calls "complex mirror shots"—specific configurations of diegetic mirrors that present shots in which characters and other salient sources of attention are reflected in the mirror but remain beyond the screen frame (and hence not placed between the mirror and the camera during shooting)—he identifies the change in the spatial compilation that occurs by virtue of the very appearance/interference of a mirror (e.g., a change in the depth of field in the user experience, or spatial disorientation and complication) (2017: 131–49).

Such a portrayal unpacks the full scope of the diegetic mirror's symbolism. Initially, "A mirror is an indexical medium: it contains a causal connection between its referent and what it displays' (Hanich 2017: 140). However, and unlike the indexical medium of photography, it also unveils the change in the range of coordinates that signifies the reflection. By appearing in a moving image mise-en-scène, it relies on the camera to create a frame within the frame, which in turn can be described as "'sucking' the viewer's attention towards what is framed" (2017: 137). The importance of using the mirror for metaphorical purposes lies, therefore, in the importance of the metaphor of medium as a mirror. The conjoining of the two produces, according to Hanich:

> Complex mirror shots . . . [that] allow the spectator to become consciously aware of his/her own act of viewing. . . . It is in this double reflexivity—becoming conscious of one's act of looking and the medium itself—that we find . . . a thematic use of the mirror as a motif of self-reflection, narcissism or questioning of fractured identity (2017: 152).

This combination is supported by Barbara Savedoff (1999), aiming at what every filmmaker has understood (by cogent use of the medium), and every cinematic-diegetic use of the mirror or the act of mirroring has assumed (by the very visibility of the mirror and the viewer's involvement in the act of mirroring): the moving image itself is a "mirror over reality." In other words, it represents a dynamic realization of the mirroring act—an apparatus that signifies by virtue of its very usage (rather than only what is presented through it).

The mirror metaphor is exquisitely articulated in the famous scene in *Duck Soup* (1931). It is a classic chase scene, but the purpose of that chase is not clear. Typically of Marx Brothers films, where the nonsensical prevails in a way that defeats any systematic attempt to understand what is going on, let alone why, the purpose of the chase, if there is any, is defeated by the great similarity (to the point of identity) between the hunter and hunted. Both wear the same white nightgowns and nightcaps, have an artificial and grotesque black mustache painted on their face, and lens-less eyeglasses rest on their noses. It appears there is nothing real that differentiates them (in a somewhat Lacanian sense)—except for the separation itself—that is, their existence as two images on the silver screen. It is therefore film that constitutes the difference between the two both conceptually and practically, as one who hunts its identical other.

Such a chase can only end in conceptual collapse and concrete clash. Indeed, the hunted character clashes through a large mirror that inexplicably separates two completely identical rooms, and it collapses and crashes to pieces on the floor. Upon hearing the noise, the other character (the hunter) quickly follows in the first character's footsteps, and in an abrupt (cinematic) cut rushes into the crash site, and stands agape in front of what to us viewers is the place where the mirror used to be, and is now just an empty space separating two identical rooms. Next, a sequence begins, where the only thing that surpasses the characters' coordination, comic skill, and narrative absurdity is the fantastic use made by the Marx Brothers of the concept, the presence (which is an absence) and metaphor of mirror and mirroring. Recall that the mirror is no longer there, its fragments magically made to disappear by the cinematic medium. This (objective) fact does not stand in the characters' way, and does not prevent them—one located in "reality" and the other "beyond the mirror"—from mirroring one another, challenging the meaning of this double reflection in a series of comic twists and bends, and mainly examining the boundaries of mirroring itself (and of the apparatus that constitutes it) by changing places, switching hats, and stretching the boundaries of reality beyond reason (while projecting them on questions of identity and morality).

In a similar TV scene in *The Muppet Show* inspired by the same heritage, Gonzo, the eternal loser, stands in front of the mirror and performs Ringo Star's "Act Naturally." His reflection, with its misery and croaking voice, suggests that the lyrics do mirror the singer's reality (that he is indeed acting naturally). However, as the second stanza begins, Gonzo's reflection breaks free of its dependence on the "first"(objective) Gonzo, and even its subjective derivatives (the attempt to perform a song live, and do it well), and starts a song of its own. As could be expected, the end of the song is a parodic reconstruction of the Marx Brothers' mirror scene: the two Gonzos sing the song, act with the naturalness only made possible after the boundaries of reality have collapsed (thanks to the mirroring act), and conclude, to the audience's applause, in understanding the power of the act of mirroring.

A similar play on the mirror and mirroring metaphor inspired by the Marx Brothers can be identified in Woody Allen's *Sleeper* (1973). Miles Monroe (Allen) awakens from an induced coma in a dystopic future only to discover that the mirror he faces in the morning to brush his teeth quickly shuns its objective duty in favor of subjective realization, turning the scene into one of self-examination of the boundaries of reality, suggesting that Miles is not the "reality" but rather the reflection beyond the mirror. In his later *Hannah and Her Sisters* (1986), Allen punches up the use of the diegetic mirror by making it the collateral victim of a failed suicide attempt by the protagonist. The mirror is shattered by the bullet, the protagonist gapes at the streets of Manhattan in bewilderment and desperation, and eventually finds solace in the movie theater, where he watches the classical *Duck Soup*, calms down, and rediscovers the roots and meaning of his own shattered existence, thanks to the Marxian mirror.

In a more recent example, that is also more analogous to *Black Mirror* in both generic affiliation and philosophical aspirations, *The Matrix* (Wachowski and Wachowski, 1999) presents us with a mirror-shaped spoon that does not shatter or disappear, but that claims a life of its own not by magically talking back (in both senses) but by magically bending, teasing and empowering the protagonist Neo (Keanu Reeves) into believing in his capability to pass through the by-now proverbial looking glass. Thus, although not a proper mirror, the spoon serves to make reality collapse in a sense deeper than that sought by earlier filmmakers and storytellers.

Whereas Socrates goes to the Oracle to learn about the nature of wisdom and establish his status as a philosopher, Neo seeks the advice of a contemporary Oracle. While waiting for her, he meets other "candidates" for a role not yet clear to him. One, in particular, catches his eye (and ours): a scrawny boy dressed as a Buddhist monk who bends spoons by the sheer power of his contemplation, only to return them to their previous shape when his eyes "let go." Suddenly noticing Neo's presence, the boy offers him a spoon and says serenely: "Do not try and bend the spoon, that's impossible. Instead, only try to realize the truth . . . there is no spoon. Then you will see it is not the spoon that bends, it is only yourself." Neo takes the proffered spoon, observes it carefully, and lo and behold, it bends, and then straightens back, reflecting on both its convex and concave side Neo's awestruck but insightful gaze. While marveling at his act of magic, Neo is summoned to the Oracle's kitchen.

Our final example is an older sci-fi movie, which also involves space travel. As we move closer to the application of our discussion to the reflective, symbolic, and apparatic nature of *Black Mirror*, we cannot but recall the most predominant cinematic mirror scene, which, alas, does not include a diegetic mirror but its ominous failure. The opening scene of Stanley Kubrick's *2001: Space Odyssey* (1968), famously titled "The Dawn of Man" offers a historical, or rather prehistorical, analog between phylogeny—in this case, the dawn of civilization, of culture, and the separation of man from animal—and ontogeny in the Lacanian sense of individuation—both afforded by the mirror. The Dawn of Man begins with an image of pre-human Earth. The primates that wander about as an indefinite, nonspecific part of this world are merged with nature in a way that emphasizes the lack of human individuality. The proto-human and other animals share the same nature, the same lack of self-consciousness, in both senses: man is not aware of himself (if only because he is not yet "human"). A group of primates is gathered in a cave-like hollow. Its "walls" are bounded and defined by the cinematic frame. They are asleep. While the viewers may interpret this as a state of lower consciousness, for them this is nothing but the direct continuation of the limited state of consciousness that is their entire existence. This is revealed by the camera in the next shot: at first, the primates awaken lazily, but soon enough they become anxiously alert as they see something that the viewers have not yet seen. In the following shot, Kubrick's camera "expands" the shot (and the boundaries of this pre-human reality), changes the point of view (POV) and exposes to the viewers what has already been revealed to the primates: a small crater with a black monolith miraculously at its center. The primates respond to its sudden appearance with anxiety, which gradually turns into curiosity, and then to enchantment, followed by the understanding of the world as it truly is.

This process is presented from an objective and distant POV, until it is suddenly disrupted by another shot from a completely different POV. All of a sudden, we are at the foot of the monolith, looking upwards from a low angle, enchanted, indeed awed by the object gloriously towering above us. What necessitated this rapid change in POV? And whose POV is it? On the face of it, this could be one of the primates' POV. But the primates—as we have seen them hitherto, from the seemingly objective POV—are engaged in the frenzy of enchantment, and it is therefore obvious that this new POV is not that of a primate but that of *the cinematic expression itself.*

In a brilliant move by the filmmaker, the cinematic expression now exposes the set of concepts and presuppositions held by the viewers. When we saw the primates jumping around the monolith from the "objective," superior point of view of the static camera, we implicitly assumed that we were silent witnesses of an objective process that while taking place in front of our eyes was independent of our gaze, and certainly not directed by it. Now, however, that we suddenly shifted to a form of photography that challenged the "objective" appearance of events, it appears we have to substitute those presuppositions with new assumptions, which we would have to identify with "subjectivity," if only to establish some kind of conceptual counterbalance to our initial presumptions. Nevertheless, like the previous, the new point of view is motionless and unidentifiable with a particular "subject." Hence, we cannot but realize that the objective of the difference between the two filmic points of view is not to mediate the distinction between objective and subjective, but rather emphasize the fact that both are, at the end of the day, nothing more than points of view.

The black monolith is a mirror that echoes the black mirror: a surface that embodies the moment of reflection and its imminent failure. In Kubrick's hand, it becomes a metaphor to a marvelous unity of opposites: an argument and its immanent contradiction, a conceptual dichotomy, and its inevitable collapse. In other words, in his black mirror innovation starring the ex nihilo monolith, Kubrick tells us the story of the Dawn of Man as we have never heard (or seen) it before. It is the story of the birth of a myth that reveals, in the same narrative sweep, the fact that it is one. It is a cinematic story of the birth of humanity that reveals its narrative nature as it unfolds.

Conclusion

As theorized above and illustrated through a variety of examples from the history of Western philosophy, literature, TV, and cinema, *Black Mirror* represents the culmination of a conflictual relationship between man and his mirror image. In what may with only some difficulty still be called real life, this relationship is complicated by the ubiquity of "black" mirrors that do not only reflect and invite us into other worlds as Alice and Neo have been, but also engage us in games that threaten to sever our hold on reality, tenuous as it has always been. Like the Evil Queen's Magic Mirror and the *Sleeper*'s futuristic gizmo, they talk and act back at us, refusing to play their customary role of enhancing our self-image in more than the visual sense, of taking the bullet for us. They disappoint and humiliate us, and when they black out, we feel lost and abandoned like the infant in Lacan's pre-mirror phase. Unlike the Marx Brothers' neatly removed mirror, moreover, or the one separating the Gonzos, they do not only make us laugh—or cry—let alone reassure us of our independence, realness, and sapient humanity, but also take us on a voyage that only looks familiar, as soon enough we begin to sincerely question the real.

References

Baxter, Wright, Dusty. (2018), "So This Is Why Black Mirror's Called Black Mirrror," in *Cosmopolitan*, 4 Jan 2018. https://www.cosmopolitan.com/uk/entertainment/a14587741/why-black-mirrors-called-black-mirror/

Brooker, Charlie. (2011), "Charlie Brooker: the dark side of our gadget addiction," in *The Guardian*, December 1, 2011. https://www.theguardian.com/technology/2011/dec/01/charlie-brooker-dark-side-gadget-addiction-black-mirror

Cavell, S. (1981), *Pursuits of Happiness: The Hollywood Comedy of Remarriage*, Cambridge, MA: Harvard University Press.

Cavell, S. (2004), *Cities of Words: Pedagogical Letters on a Register of the Moral Life*, Cambridge, MA: Harvard University Press.

Hanich, J. (2017), "Reflecting on Reflections: Cinema's Complex Mirror Shots," in M. Beugnet, A. Cameron, and A. Fetveit, *Indefinite Visions : Cinema and the Attractions of Uncertainty*, Edinburgh: Edinburgh University Press: 131–56.

Haynes, T.. (2017), "USS Callister," *Black Mirror*, Netflix. Season 4, Episode 1, December 29, 2017.

Lacan, J. and J.-A. Miller (1988), *The Seminar of Jacques Lacan*, New York, Norton.

Metz, C. ([1991] 2016), "Mirrors," *Impersonal Enunciation, or the Place of Film*, New York: Columbia University Press.

Savedoff, B. E. (1999), "Frames," *The Journal of Aesthetics and Art Criticism*, 57 (3): 345–56.

Schlupmann, H. (1987), "Phenomenology of Film: On Siegfried Kracauer's Writings of the 1920s," T. Y. Levin (trans.), *New German Critique*, 40: 97–114.

Singer, I. (1998), *Reality Transformed: Film as Meaning and Technique*, Cambridge, MA and London: MIT Press.
Singer, I. (2008), *Cinematic Mythmaking: Philosophy in Film*, Cambridge, MA: MIT Press.
Wachowski, L. and L. Wachowski (1999), *The Matrix*, Warner Bros. [Film].

11

The You They Love

Patriarchal Feminism and Ashley Too

Mona Rocha and James Rocha

In *Black Mirror*'s "Rachel, Jack and Ashley Too" (Sewitsky 2019), Ashley O has it all: money, fame, and conventional good looks; she is depicted as a liberated, powerful woman whom girls and tweens view as a role model. But this empowerment is fleeting and deceptive as it is actually premised on subsuming feminist ideals under those of capitalism and the patriarchy. Thus, far from showing how Ashley is empowered, "Rachel, Jack and Ashley Too" actually depicts how the patriarchy, in the guise of empowerment feminism, actually infiltrates and undermines the feminist project. Within this episode, true empowerment lies not just in stopping Aunt Catherine, who is set up as the antagonist, but within creating a whole new society, which is based on authenticity, collaboration, and respecting autonomy. But let's start with some basics.

Feminism can be understood as a movement to create and secure equal rights for women, including the right to vote (political right), to control property (economic right), to represent themselves in court (legal right), or to have access to education on par with men (political or social right). The movement to gain these rights is by no means homogeneous—there are many types of feminism, such as Marxist feminism (focusing on how socioeconomic class relates to sexism), anarcha-feminism (focusing on critiquing the state and its role in perpetuating subjugation), and so forth. But generally speaking, feminism works to promote equality between men and women and attempts to dismantle problematic stereotypes or gender norms. For example, feminism promotes the idea that it would be perfectly okay if men embraced their emotions or if women were to step away from domesticity.

Feminism also critiques the patriarchy, which is any system, institution, or group that works to advance the superiority of men or male ideals. The patriarchy accomplishes this task through rewarding adherence to gender norms, through embracing hierarchies, and through punishing any sort of deviation from conformity. As such, feminists criticize the patriarchy as restricting gender expression, reifying heterosexuality, commodifying women's bodies, imposing unrealistic beauty standards, and so forth.

For example, in the episode "USS Callister" (Haynes 2017), remember how Robert Daly treats Nanette: because he is attracted to her, he literally objectifies her and moves her into his game, for his own amusement. While it is true that he has not literally moved Nanette herself into the game, he has created a version of Nanette that is complete with her memories, thoughts, and feelings. In doing so, he has created something that is sufficiently a person while subduing her personhood for the sake of his own amusement. Here, patriarchy works alongside hierarchy: Robert, in a more powerful position at work, takes advantage of Nanette's status as a new employee under his jurisdiction, and ends up controlling and subjugating the Nanette he creates, problematically turning a person into an owned object.

Feminism is also interested in how sexism relates to other societal topics, such as poverty, race, age, health status, and so forth. Feminists use the word "intersectionality" (Crenshaw 1991) to refer to the intersecting oppressions that women face out in the world: they might face sexism by virtue of being women, but if they are also poor or black for example, they will also deal with classism and/or racism. Based on identity traits and individuals' places within society, oppressions compound and work together to result in real-life barriers for those individuals experiencing them.

Patriarchy also interacts with capitalism, where the emphasis is on wealth, profit, and monetary rewards and not on human interactions or on valuing humanity for its own sake. As Marx famously explained, this schema results in alienation, where workers are seen solely as tools of production and are alienated from their product, their labor, their humanity, and from other workers (Marx [1844] 1975). This alienation begins with the fact that the worker puts all their time, effort, energy, and creativity into making a product, but they have no say over what is done with the product (alienation from product)—and really they do not really have say in how they are to make that product (alienation from their labor). But, to keep the point simple, the worker becomes a product making machine (alienation from humanity) since the business has no interest in what the worker wishes to happen or how the worker imagines the product should end up. But this means that each worker is exchangeable and expendable, which creates a constant competition with coworkers (alienation from other people).

Essentially, capitalism robs laborers of their humanity, forcing them to give up their creativity or limit their time with their families because they need to think of themselves as working machines first and foremost. Further, as alluded to before, individual and structural hierarchies further complicate the problem: those with less power usually suffer or are marginalized by those with more power. Factory floor bosses can intimidate subordinates into working faster or harder; managers can find ways to retaliate against employees for speaking up. Eventually, the worker loses control over how they want to interact with the world: they cannot present themselves through their labor but instead must sell their labor to a capitalist who will dictate exactly how the worker ought to labor. We will see how this loss of autonomy in the workforce plays out specifically in the case of Ashley O.

Uniting all of these sufferings is the idea of structural violence. Peace scholar Johan Galtung coined the term and defined it as the violence that "is built into the structure and shows up as unequal power and consequently as unequal life choices" (1969: 171). This means that there are structures that are part of the everyday world, such as institutions and social constructions, that exert pressure in such a way that particular individuals are made worse off through their exposure to, or through dealing with, that specific institution or social structure. Patriarchy is just one such social structure while poverty is another. Just as women do not choose to live within a sexist society, almost no one purposely chooses to face the additional obstacles that are provided through being poor. That is what structural violence involves: there are simply barriers in society, perhaps due to no one's fault, that make life harder for some people than for others.

For example, in "Nosedive" (Wright 2016) individuals live within a system where everyone shares their daily activities through eye implants and are constantly rating each other on everything, thus influencing and affecting each other's socioeconomic statuses. The way their world is set up allows for structural violence to happen quite visibly: for example, Susan's family's low ratings resulted in her husband being denied cancer treatment. As Galtung notes, through structural violence, "resources are unevenly distributed, as when income distributions are heavily skewed, literacy/education unevenly distributed, medical services existent in some districts, and for some groups only, and so on. Above all, *the power to decide over the distribution of resources is unevenly distributed*" (1969: 171, emphasis in original). In other words, structural violence leads to some people suffering through being discriminated against, being marginalized, and so forth.

We will see that "Rachel, Jack and Ashley Too" previews a feminist critique of the patriarchal world that these characters inhabit, and even provides a brief glimpse of what life would be like in a feminist society where women's autonomy would be supported.

Ridin' So High, Achieving My Goals

When we first meet Rachel, we find her during lunch period, sitting by herself and listening intently to Ashley O's performance. It doesn't take long to clue in to the fact that she is an outsider within her high school community: she's all alone, looks terribly unhappy, and clings to Ashley O's lyrics as a lifeline. Rachel doesn't even have a small group of friends through which she could negotiate the cliques and the queen bees that define high school life. Rachel's definitely not making a good impression when her dad picks her up in his mouse-killing van—there's a sense in that scene of an uncomfortable, awkward squirming Rachel, who feels the judging eyes of the rest of the high school students. All this reifies the idea that high school hierarchies constitute an impediment to human flourishing: unpopular kids are marginalized, isolated, alienated, and bullied. Rachel clearly feels that way as she walks down the hallway at the end of lunch, hugging her frail body, looking apprehensive and longing for inclusion.

Due to their recent move, Rachel is experiencing loneliness, and it does not seem like it is getting better. As theorists Diane E. Levin and Jean Kilbourne explain, children and teens "growing up today are bombarded from an early age with graphic messages about sex and sexiness in the media and popular culture" where they are taught value comes solely from faithful adherence to strict gender norms (2009: 4). As the theorists further expound, media and popular culture promote a narrow definition of femininity and sexuality [which] encourages girls to focus heavily on appearance and sex appeal. They learn at a very young age that their value is determined by how beautiful, thin, "hot," and sexy they are. (Levin and Kilbourne 2009: 5)

This pushing of gender norms—in a patriarchal vein—results in individuals adopting a sexualized persona so as to fit into a sexualized environment. As such, humanity is not valued as much as being hot is; women are turned into commodities for male pleasure and occupy a subordinate position in society. Structural violence is embedded in this schema, as Levin and Kilbourne argue that "many industries make an obscene amount of money using sex and violence to market their products to children" (2009: 5). As such, capitalist structures promote narrow gender roles to profit—along the way generating structural violence that limits individuals' authentic self-growth.

Considering this context, it is unsurprising that Rachel lacks popularity: she is a girl struggling to fit in, trying to figure out who she is, while being told that she needs to fit these gender norms. As such, she looks up to Ashley O, whose persona and looks fit the patriarchal, pop culture gender norms of being attractive and having sex appeal. For Rachel, Ashley O actively models what it means to fit in with the patriarchy: Ashley O's makeup, pink hair, fashionable outfits, and nurturing message of encouragement all comply with the patriarchy; in return, the patriarchy rewards her with fame and money. On the surface, Ashley O seems to have fame, money, and, really—have it all. Rachel must think that if she follows Ashley O's example, maybe she too will become empowered.

In fact, Rachel aspires to have the same level of confidence and control over the world as Ashley O espouses. Ashley O's lyrics are like a self-empowerment anthem, where simply having ambition and drive results in immediate success. Ashley O means her songs to help others in becoming accepted. She says in the interview with Busy G: "Yeah, it's really important for people to feel like they are in control of their destinies" (Sewitsky 2019). Her songs are meant to pump up the recipients, like they can go out and do anything. But notice that this is solely about *feeling* in control; the patriarchal world that we all inhabit does not operate on your feelings. Instead, it rewards close adherence to its tenets and norms; simple positivity does not guarantee success.

Further, Ashley O preaching positivity is gendered; her lyrics and voice fit in with gendered norms of women being upbeat, peppy, encouraging, and nonthreatening. Propagating this message results in a problematic displacement of responsibility: the message suggests that it's not that there are structural barriers at work to keep people subjugated but that the fault really lies in the fact that the people were neither positive nor confident enough to become successful. In a very real way, Ashley O's lyrics prop up structural violence and reaffirm that people have to fit the narrow mold that capitalism and patriarchy require.

Ashley O also peddles the Ashley Too doll. In her interview, Ashley O explains that it is designed to give makeover tips and discuss love problems. Ashley O is literally commodifying herself through the robotic doll while modeling a supposed liberated womanhood. In many ways, the doll is presented as a further tool toward achieving empowerment while living in the patriarchy (how to become pretty so the boys will like you), while also illustrating exactly what is wrong with the oppressive, patriarchal world we all inhabit (the prescriptive idea of "become pretty so the boys will like you," which takes for granted heteronormativity). In fact, when Rachel and Ashley O first interact, the doll asks in an animated voice whether Rachel wants a makeover (Sewitsky 2019).

The doll also offers music, consisting of more of the same empty, upbeat positivity that Ashley O is known for, and which serves as an anesthetic to keep folks complacent within the patriarchy. Those exposed to Ashley Too's message—primed with their already existent adulation of Ashley O—will not question its messages, therefore unwittingly becoming adherents of the patriarchy.

Rachel, in her preoccupation with Ashley O's music and persona, is not just consuming the lessons of the patriarchy, but she is also becoming embedded into what feminist theorist Susan J. Douglas calls fantasies of power: women being told by the media that they've accomplished everything there is to accomplish already, that it's easy to be empowered, and so feminism's work is done. As Douglas explains in her theory—dubbed "enlightened sexism"— the media and popular culture propagate the message that full equality for women has been achieved already and now it is time to engage in personal empowerment for the fun of it. Douglas further explicates that under this theory, women are taught that "it is precisely through women's calculated deployment of their faces, bodies, attire, and sexuality that they gain and enjoy true power—power that is fun, that men will not resent, and indeed will embrace" (2010: 10). As she further elucidates, this is not true power but rather a perversion of feminism: "enlightened sexism is feminist in its outward appearance (of course you can be or do anything you want) but sexist in its intent . . . it is dedicated to the undoing of feminism" (Douglas 2010: 10).

Ashley O and Ashley Too fit this model of enlightened sexism: Ashley O, through her music, seemingly empowers girls to be all they can be, and Ashley Too shows them how. But neither one explores how to actually break free of the patriarchy. In a sense, that is the theme of the story arc of when Ashley Too encourages Rachel to enter the school talent contest: Ashley Too promises Rachel that she will succeed if she just mimics the real Ashley, right down to the makeup, hair, and movements. Rachel fails miserably on stage; as the camera pans out to the audience, student faces show disgust, amusement, and only a very few illustrate pity. Rachel has not become liberated, has not moved up the hierarchy at school, has not made any friends, and has simply endured public humiliation, all at the hands of her supposed friend, Ashley Too. As she cries, Rachel feels guilty: "I let Ashley Too down"—she sobs uncontrollably. This exchange shows the insidiousness of enlightened sexism: Rachel feels personally responsible for not meeting the agenda that was set up for her by the patriarchy.

It is this experience that encourages Rachel's sister, Jack, to get rid of Ashley Too. Of course, Rachel gets upset after Jack tells her that she threw Ashley Too in the garbage for "filling [Rachel's] head with crap" (Sewitsky 2019) Rachel views Ashley Too as her only support in the world. Ashley Too is her friend and confidante. Rachel's family has been fractured because of the mother's passing (in an earlier scene we find out that her mom Genevieve had died two years previously). Having been moved to a new school, by a father who was trying to give his children a better life, Rachel was left adrift and cut off from any emotional support.

Rachel's and Jack's father was too busy with his work to find the best way to kill rodents, spending endless time in his workshop consumed with this task, neither knowing when his daughter's birthday was nor attending her talent show. Thus, he was not present to support Rachel. His conduct could seem cold and mean, but it is also symptomatic of Marxist alienation and the structural violence of living under capitalism. Rachel's dad tried to do the best he could for the family, following societal prescriptions for upward mobility: he moved the family to a better neighborhood so his daughters could have more opportunities than before. His ongoing preoccupation with his job is not just passion for his work but can also be perceived as a result of economic stress: after all, moving into a new house in a better neighborhood comes with new bills and possibly a higher mortgage. Note that his van sticks out at Rachel's school not just due to the mouse ears but also because it is the only run-down vehicle during school pickup. Further, after his wife's demise, Rachel's dad is also now alone, left to singly provide for his children. He has to perfect a way of killing rodents and maintaining his small business afloat, or they might lose it all. Hence, Rachel's dad is alienated from his daughters due to capitalist pressure to make it economically. He is therefore failing in his duties as a father—and becoming estranged from their humanity and needs—because he needs to perfect and prioritize his work to provide a better life for his family, all the while losing his own humanity. He is consumed by building a better mousetrap, without realizing he himself is trapped.

There's separation between the sisters, as well. This estrangement is likely due to their different ways of mourning their mother. Jack pours herself into moody guitar music, listening to the songs her mother liked and played. Jack is taking on her mother's persona, in other words, as a way to develop her own personality. Perhaps this is a better move than being guided by a "dolly," as Jack scoffs at Rachel during their argument, but it is unclear if this strategy is an authentic, autonomous development for Jack, or simply a direction she's taken due to an emotional reaction to the loss of a loved one. In any case, in the process, Jack distances herself from Rachel: the lyrics Rachel prefers are a far cry from Jack's genre. And as the emotional distance grows within the household—due to separation between the sisters or to the Marxist alienation that the father is experiencing—Rachel is left behind, feeling alone and hopeless. This situation leaves her as prey to the structural violence the patriarchy is propagating through Ashley O and Ashley Too.

The Animal in the Cage You Built

It's not just Jack, Rachel, and their dad who are trapped by structural violence and capitalist oppression. There are clues all along to Ashley O's dissatisfaction and distress. During the Billy G interview, there is a brief glimpse of Ashley O looking depressed, unlike her usual, carefree, smiling self. There are glimpses of her looking hallowed-eyed in her dressing room, as she stares listlessly at herself in the mirror. Another clue is that she is losing her ability to create upbeat music: she no longer wakes up with happy, perky music in her brain. Perhaps the biggest hints of this state are the lyrics Ashley O is penning at the piano in her living room, where she implores her interlocutor to "See the animal in the cage you built" and to "Feel the hollowness inside your heart" (Sewitsky 2019). This sad, heartbreaking song indicates that Ashley O is also experiencing alienation, including alienation from her musical labor (which in a deep sense is a form of alienation from her very identity since singing is such a personal activity). According to Marx, alienation from one's labor happens when one loses control over the modes of production and/or one's work conditions, due to capitalist pressure to maximize production (Marx [1844] 1975). You are alienated from your labor when someone else tells you how to use your hands, your thoughts, your body, and in this case your voice, to produce what they want instead of what you would like to produce. Her aunt Catherine has forced Ashley O to produce a certain kind of music—positive and sexualized—that does not allow for Ashley O's real expression but is easily monetized. With Aunt Catherine's approved lyrics, which are upbeat and ostensibly sexually empowering, Ashley O seemingly models female sexual empowerment and boasts sex appeal. All this results in high sales for Aunt Catherine. In actuality, though, Ashley O is sexualized and objectified by her aunt for the purpose of profit; the lyrics depict Ashley O as a commodity for an unknown lover. As Ashley O's authentic lyrics describe it, she feels trapped, like a caged animal forced to put on a performance. Ashley O yearns for more from life. She pointedly asks, "If you look at your reflection is it all you want to be?" (Sewitsky 2019). She dislikes whom she has been forced to become and wants to break free to be her authentic self, through exercising her autonomy (where autonomy refers to someone's ability to set up and follow life plans for themselves without interference from others). The system she inhabits—as a performer in a patriarchal, capitalist society under the firm control of a manager who also controls her home life—undermines Ashley O's autonomy.

Unsurprisingly, then, it turns out that Ashley O has been undergoing the effects of structural violence. She does not have it all, as her peppy, public persona might indicate: in fact, the one person who exercises control—and fights to have it all—is Aunt Catherine. It is Aunt Catherine, as manager and caretaker for Ashley O, who pushes Ashley O to produce lively music, put on a happy façade, and, most importantly, sell as much as possible under the guise of positivity and girl power. Thus, in many ways, Catherine is not only stifling Ashley but also exemplifying the evils associated with hierarchy, capitalism, and the patriarchy.

Furthermore, Aunt Catherine objectifies Ashley O. Philosopher Martha Nussbaum explains that objectification means treating as an object what is in fact a human being (Nussbaum 1995). On Nussbaum's theory, objectification can be either benign or morally problematic. For it to be benign, folks engaged in the objectification relationship must be of roughly equal status, engage in a reciprocal relationship, and respect each other. Problematic objectification happens when those criteria are not met. There are also several kinds of objectification: instrumentality (using someone as a tool), fungibility (viewing someone as replaceable), inertness, denial of autonomy (denying someone's autonomy), denial of subjectivity (denying someone's feelings), ownership, and so forth (Nussbaum 1995). Catherine objectifies Ashley in a morally problematic fashion since the two are not of equal status, with Catherine holding more power and control in their personal relationship, as well as business wise. Catherine does not respect Ashley's humanity. Rather, Catherine uses Ashley as a tool to get money and status for herself, thus engaging in instrumentality.

Unsurprisingly, when Ashley expresses her desire to be her own person—thus setting up for herself an autonomous plan for her career and direction in life—Catherine is displeased and works to stop Ashley. After all, Catherine installed a secret camera in Ashley O's dressing room to monitor all of her moves. This act is a part of denying Ashley's autonomy. Remember Dr. Munk's offer: "If she [Ashley] is feeling under-creative, there are some mild hallucinogens I can recommend. All organic" ("Rachel, Jack and Ashley Too" 2019). This offer of drugging Ashley—with organic ingredients, as if that made it better—was made after Catherine was complaining that Ashley O was creating a more authentic style of music: moodier and darker. Drugging Ashley O would render her more pliable, and less likely to insist on her autonomy.

Moreover, not only does Catherine deny Ashley O's autonomy but she also denies her subjectivity. Ashley O's new lyrics are a medium for Ashley's self-expression, and valuable to her. Instead of respecting Ashley's new music, Catherine derides it. Catherine refers to Ashley O's genuine music as "obtuse bullshit that twenty people can relate to" (Sewitsky 2019). She does not respect Ashley O's feelings on the matter, imposing her own will instead.

Additionally, Ashley O suffers structural violence at Catherine's bidding. This structural violence can best be understood through a further example of objectification: Catherine purposely drugs Ashley O and places her into a coma. This kind of objectification includes both inertness and ownership: Catherine renders Ashley O into a controllable body for her own uses, happily sacrificing her niece's humanity in the quest for the mighty dollar and self-aggrandizement. Catherine does not view Ashley O as a free person, someone who is able to make their own decisions or exercise their agency. Rather, Catherine sees herself as Ashley O's owner and as being able to decide Ashley O's fate.

In this vein, Catherine also uses her henchmen to extract music from Ashley O's brain (using Ashley O instrumentally again) and then uses technology to create a streamable, hologram version of Ashley O that can be used for concerts. This piece of technology is called Ashley Eternal, and Catherine introduces it by enumerating its positives: "Ashley Eternal is never exhausted. Never sick. Always pitch perfect. Bringing her A game. It's not a dream, it's reality" (Sewitsky 2019). While Catherine lauds this creation, it exhibits fungibility, the type of objectification where one can be replaced. Catherine has taken an irreplaceable human and exchanged it for a controllable image ready to do her bidding.

Structural violence permeates all of this exchange. After all, Ashley O was purposefully drugged and sapped of life, for profit. Her comatose body was bound to a hospital bed and monitored around the clock, again for profit. She was no longer a person but a thing, and importantly, one that was about to be exterminated once it outgrew its usefulness. The violence here is structural because it works to preserve hierarchies of power: it preserves Catherine's higher status and control of their business, while at the same time rendering Ashley O as a patriarchal Barbie while alive and as a beautiful and pliable Ashley Eternal in death, an owned entity who will toil in perpetuity to prop up capitalist ventures and perpetual patriarchal beauty and gender norms.

Oh My God, We Have to Stop Her

The only way to stop the structural violence that is expressed through Aunt Catherine's character is to work together to defeat the evil she has brought about. This task is accomplished when Rachel, Jack, and Ashley Too get together to free Ashley O from her confinement. This model—folks coming together to find a solution to a problem—is a feminist response to oppression.

Having been activated by a news report of Ashley O's alleged allergy to shellfish and subsequent coma, the doll malfunctions, leading Jack to plug her into a computer to fix her. The attempted repair removes a limiter program, resulting in the doll gaining access to a digital copy of the entirety of Ashley O's brain. She then convinces the sisters to go to Ashley O's house and collect digital evidence of Aunt Catherine's criminality. The sisters are able to talk their way into the mansion, and the doll disconnects Ashley O's comatose body from the machines that it is plugged into. This act results in Ashley O returning to consciousness, as her coma was induced as a way to drain her of her music and render her docile. Supporting Ashley O's weakened body as she stumbles back to life, the sisters make their escape; all of them rush to the stadium where Aunt Catherine is conducting her presentation on Ashley Eternal, successfully publicizing her evil plots.

This solution is possible through teamwork and would not have been possible if either agent acted alone, as the doll humorously found out when she attempted to open the doors by herself, and forgetting she was too short and the door handle was too high up for her to reach. Each individual had a part to fill: Jack drove the car for their rescue team, Ashley Too guided them to the right house, Jack got them into the mansion on a pretext of delivering pest service, and Rachel distracted the guards by using the image of a helpless little girl that needed to use the bathroom. She and Ashley Too also used the restroom search to find Ashley O. As they fight to free Ashley O, working together results in literal liberation: it is Jack who hits Dr. Munk as he attempts to restrain a newly conscious Ashley O, and Rachel who injects him with a sedative, allowing them all to run to freedom. Thus, through all of their combined efforts, Ashley O's physical freedom is restored. Likewise, all of them worked together to rush to the stage where Aunt Catherine was unveiling Ashley Eternal, ensuring Ashley O's liberation in business.

This feminist collaboration resulted in freedom from Aunt Catherine's influence and in the ability for Ashley O to become the person she envisioned herself to be. In other words, it is through this collaboration that old power structures were broken, self-expression was encouraged, and Ashley O's autonomy was restored. We get a glimpse of this better future at the end of the episode, as Rachel watches her sister Jack and Ashley O perform on stage. Sure, Rachel is still watching it all from the wings, as in the beginning of the episode. But while she is still on the margins, she now seems more meaningfully connected to the characters in front of her. She is now portrayed as an ally or a supporter in this scene, involved with and happy for those performing on stage. She is no longer isolated but integrated into the whole: she's dancing to the lyrics and joyfully talking to a companion. Importantly, her father is also nearby, still talking about the best ways to trap mice but nevertheless present to support his daughters. As such, it seems that at least for Rachel, this feminist action has resulted in some good.

In this last scene, we see Jack on stage performing. We might be left wondering if she is following her own autonomous life path by becoming a punk alternative musician, or if she is still clinging on to this music as a way to preserve a connection to her deceased mother. Since she looks so happy with her task, though, we would like to think that she has found a way to express her authentic self. Perhaps the most decisive factor comes in the fact that she has found the strength to perform publicly. She is playing guitar in front of a large audience—this sense of self and increased confidence anchored in action is a notable, positive outcome of feminist action for Jack.

What about Ashley O? Is Ashley O freed of larger power structures she has suffered from or is she still a performer trapped in a capitalist world? After all, in the concert scene at the end of the episode, we see little girls running away in disgust from her performance. Are they disgusted by Ashley O's gritty lyrics, by her autonomous rejection of pop feminism, and her turn toward authentic self-expression—which we could applaud—or are they supposed to bode a significant drop in her marketability? If the latter, then Ashley O is not really freed from bigger power structures such as capitalism or the patriarchy.

Nevertheless, Ashley O could choose to ignore those pressures, in spite of the costs associated with them, and be true to herself. And we believe that she is in fact rejecting those power structures through her song at the end of the episode. In that song, Ashley recognizes the influence and power of capitalist society as she depicts her the ways in which she has been bound by money but can no longer take it (Sewitsky 2019). The song recognizes that money controls people's fates, akin to a god figure, ordering people's lives and creating structural violence that rewards the rich and harms the poor. But, importantly, Ashley O, in that song, also proclaims independence from this structural trap and proudly asserts nonalignment with the hierarchy of money or the powers of capitalism. Ashley O declares independence from these structures, to the point that she states she would rather die than give in to the pressures that would make her change again into a marketable, pink-haired, inauthentic performer and person. As such, she is affirming her authenticity—and if that authentic self is unpalatable to the patriarchal world or doesn't fit with enlightened sexism messages, she is ready for that cost. Ashley ultimately teaches us the simple message: It is better to be true to yourself than to be fake.

Wearing Your Own Skin

"Rachel, Jack and Ashley Too" thus not only includes a critique of patriarchy, capitalism, and hierarchy in general but also provides something fairly unique to an episode of *Black Mirror*: an ending where humanity wins out over technology. Aunt Catherine's attempts to objectify and replace Ashley O with technology, including both the hologram Ashley and the lobotomized robot Ashley Too, are thwarted. The humans (Rachel, Jack, and Ashley) are more fully human as their autonomy is achieved in the end, but, even more significantly, Ashley Too ends up more human than robot as Ashley's full consciousness is opened up to her, thus providing the robot with her own chance at autonomy.

This ending stands in contrast to even *Black Mirror* episodes that appear to have positive and maybe even feminist endings, "Black Museum" (McCarthy 2017) and "San Junipero" (Harris 2016). While "Black Museum" has a significantly violent ending (Rolo Haynes is tortured in the same way that he has long tortured Clayton Leigh), our protagonist Nish appears to be justified in making Rolo pay for profiting from torturing her father's consciousness. Hence, one could argue that the ending is positive (Nish wins) and possibly even feminist (Nish strikes a blow against racism and sexism by taking down Rolo's awful museum). At the same time, Nish only wins by using the very same technology that Rolo used to torture her father. While the audience may think Nish was justified, the technology that led Rolo to lose his humanity is still being yielded by Nish, thus showing that humanity has not won out.

An even more positive and clearly more feminist ending is found in "San Junipero" where the protagonists Yorkie and Kelly manage to find a way to unite forever within the virtual world San Junipero. Nevertheless, the episode's ending entails that both Yorkie and Kelly are now dead, and it is actually the technology that has won out. Even if we are happy for Yorkie and Kelly insofar as their virtual selves can be together forever, they are now wholly dependent on technology. Even in the most positive episodes of *Black Mirror*, technology still wins out over humanity.

Thus, "Rachel, Jack and Ashley Too" stands alone as providing a feminist vision where part of becoming more fully ourselves requires becoming more in touch with our humanity. While it may seem pleasing to see Nish use Rolo's technology to destroy him, this move implicitly endorses the destructive uses of the technology. While "San Junipero" represents an incredibly heartwarming use of technology, this technology also separates people from the actual world and their connections to other humans within that world—thus, cutting them off from their humanity. Yet, Rachel, Jack, and Ashley Too all become more human and more in touch with each other by overcoming Aunt Catherine's attempt to overtake Ashley O's profitably by dehumanizing her. That is, each one of them is able to become autonomous and more connected to other humans, thus finally scoring one for humanity over technology.

References

Crenshaw, K. (1991), "Mapping the Margins: Intersectionality, Identity Politics, and Violence against Women of Color," *Stanford Law Review* 43(6): 1241–99.

Douglas, S. (2010), *Enlightened Sexism: The Seductive Message that Feminism's Work is Done*, New York: Times Books.

Galtung, J. (1969), "Violence, Peace, and Peace Research," *Journal of Peace Research* 6(3): 167–91.

Harris, Owen. (2016), "San Junipero," *Black Mirror*, Netflix. Season 3, Episode 4. Release Date October 21, 2016. [TV Series].

Haynes, Toby. (2017), "USS Callister," *Black Mirror*, Netflix. Season 4, Episode 1. December 29, 2017.

Levin, D. and J. Kilbourne (2009), *So Sexy, So Soon*, New York: Ballantine Books.

Marx, K. ([1844] 1975), "Economic and Philosophical Manuscripts of 1844," in Maria Shcheglova, Tatyana Grishina, Lyudgarda Zubrilova, Tatyana Butkova, and Larisa Miskievich (eds.), *Karl Marx, Friedrich Engels: Collected Works, Volume 3*, London: Lawrence and Wishart.

McCarthy, Colm. (2017), "Black Museum," *Black Mirror*, Netflix. Season 4, Episode 6. Release Date December 29, 2017. [TV Series].

Nussbaum, M. (1995), "Objectification," *Philosophy and Public Affairs* 24(4): 249–91.

Sewitsky, Anne. (2019), "Rachel, Jack and Ashley Too," *Black Mirror*, Netflix. Season 5, Episode 3. Release Date June 5, 2019. [TV Series].

Wright, Joe. (2016), "Nosedive," *Black Mirror*, Netflix. Season 3, Episode 1. Release Date October 21, 2016. [TV Series].

Conclusion

James Rocha and Kingsley Marshall

Black Mirror opens up a series of conversations—about philosophy, who we are as persons, what our relationship to technology is, how we relate to each other, and so much more. *Black Mirror* initiates these conversations with imaginative storytelling, thought-provoking what-if-counterfactuals, innovative technological ideas, and characters with whom we form emotional connections even when we least expect to do so.

While *Black Mirror* got the conversations going, they did not end there. The conversations continued in your homes, at work, on social media, in classrooms, and in any other place where people were intrigued and wanted to know more. After all, we all wanted to know more about what all of these episodes mean in themselves, what the episodes tell us about technology that is near or far away, and, perhaps most importantly, what *Black Mirror* tells us about ourselves.

A group of scholars from across the world sought to continue the *Black Mirror* conversations here, in this volume. And though the chapters were written independently, certain patterns emerged therein. Some topics of conversation were emphasized, while certain other lessons appeared to be imparted jointly. These separate chapters showcased some disagreement, as any good dialogue would provide differing viewpoints, and some clearly distinct arguments were made and presented. As such, it is worth ending our collection of essays by taking a look at some of these varied positions that we hope you can take away from this larger conversation about *Black Mirror*.

To start, this book is a philosophy book, which raises a question right away: can a TV show even partake in advancing philosophy? This question is difficult for two main reasons. First, the TV series isn't attempting to do philosophy—it has a deeper message, for sure, but it is not setting out to do philosophy, as much as to shock and entertain us. Second, as good as it is, *Black Mirror* is a

TV series. Lots of old-school scholars would be very doubtful that legitimate, high-quality philosophical content could be discovered within art at all, much less a TV series.

In spite of these worries, our authors form a strong consensus that *Black Mirror* can indeed count as a work of philosophy. One of the main arguments presented a few times here is that specific *Black Mirror* episodes present thought experiments (for instance, see Sinnerbrink, Yeung and Pei, Shaw). Unlike the sciences, philosophers develop concepts and theories that typically cannot be tested through real-life experiments. Instead, philosophers develop thought experiments where they imagine scenarios to test their theories or question the applicability of their concepts.

Unfortunately, philosophers are not always very good at developing their own thought experiments. It is a very tricky thing to do. The very point of testing a scientific theory is that the physical experiment is separated from the scientist doing the test. Yet, in a philosopher's *thought* experiment, the very same person who came up with the theory is developing the scenario where the theory is to be tested through that very same philosopher's imagination. One philosopher develops the theory, makes up a fictional world to test the theory, and then uses their own imagination to see that their own theory checks out. It isn't a great system.

A preferable method of doing philosophy is to test philosophical theories through thought experiments that were developed by *world makers*. Authors of science fiction, fantasy, and literature in general develop their own worlds with unique sets of rules, which often, though usually unintentionally, run into the very kinds of theories and issues that philosophers wish to test.

Let's look at an example. In one of our chapters, "The Virtue of Forgetting in Nietzsche's Philosophy and *Black Mirror*," Dan Shaw examines Friedrich Nietzsche's theory of forgetting. Nietzsche argues that the ability to remember actually presents a difficulty for which forgetting is the solution. It is through a careful and managed use of forgetting that we can learn to embrace the present, live in the moment, and appreciate our loved ones better.

When you press on it, Nietzsche's theory against memory, in favor of forgetting, appears to be contentious at best. Memory is not a bad thing. Memory allows us to cherish our positive moments, helps us to learn to improve in every kind of way, and gives us a sense of self-identity, since I am the collection of all of the people I have ever been in the past. If we really wanted to see the value of Nietzsche's theory, we need a thought experiment.

As Shaw points out, that thought experiment is given in the *Black Mirror* episode "The Entire History of You." That episode can provide a thought experiment to test Nietzsche's theory because memory is enhanced through technology that allows the characters to remember just about anything. Yet, since they can remember anything, they dwell in the past, cannot forgive transgressions against them, and end up losing their personal connections to their loved ones. Thus, through this thought experiment in "The Entire History of You," Nietzsche's theory is given validity due to *Black Mirror*'s performance of philosophy.

Moreover, multiple authors in this volume establish that *Black Mirror* can indeed provide thought experiments in a way that counts as doing philosophy. Robert Sinnerbrink, in "Through a Screen Darkly: *Black Mirror*, Thought Experiments, and Televisual Philosophy," offers for our consideration numerous cases in which *Black Mirror* does what Sinnerbrink refers to as "televisual philosophy." For instance, Sinnerbrink considers how the episode "Striking Vipers" uses a video game's virtual reality (VR) technology to allow two seemingly straight men to explore their sexuality. Thus, this video game thought experiment suggests a greater range and fluidity of sexuality than many of us are willing to acknowledge given social constraints and unjust taboos in our actual societies. Meanwhile, Laura T. Di Summa uses her chapter, "Technology in Pastel Colors: An Alternative Take on *Black Mirror*," to suggest that we can understand *Black Mirror* as critiquing dismal philosophical theories by providing positive interpretations of episodes "San Junipero" or "Fifteen Million Merits." In an opposing position, Lorraine K.C. Yeung and Kong-Ngai Pei use their chapter, "*Black Mirror* as Philosophizing About Immortality, Technology and Human Nature," to argue that even "San Junipero," which many believe is one of the most positive episodes of the series, actually should be understood in a less uplifting context. Yeung and Pei make their argument by showing that we cannot assume immortality is a good thing, and the characters who are stuck in San Junipero for eternity may end up regretting their decisions—perhaps not for a billion or even a trillion years, but eventually it may happen as forever is a very long time (for other arguments that "San Junipero" is not as happy as it seems, see the chapters by Lee and Rocha and Rocha).

While our authors show a plethora of ways in which *Black Mirror* does philosophy, we can examine two other themes that multiple authors pick up on. The first is that *Black Mirror* provides a philosophical examination of the self, answering the question: Who am I? In a related fashion, *Black Mirror* suggests philosophical ways to interpret how we relate to each other. And, of course, these philosophical inquiries are provided with a sense of how we as humans also relate to the very technology that we create to help improve our lives. Even though they touch on technology throughout, the authors of this volume show us that *Black Mirror* is not primarily about technology but about humanity—with only a secondary interest in how technology informs who we are (how it augments and creates the self) and how we interact with each other, morally and socially (for clear statements that technology is secondary in *Black Mirror*, see chapters by Lee and Marshall).

While philosophers have long been interested in questions of the self, *Black Mirror* provides numerous episodes that tell us that finding your self may require understanding how you fit into the world around you. The explorations of technology in *Black Mirror* often stand in not to highlight what is wrong or right with technology but to help us understand who we are, as unique individuals, as seen in our relations to the technology around us.

For instance, suppose you are asking the question about your self: "Am I free?" Sander Lee, in the chapter, "Free Will in *Black Mirror: Bandersnatch*," argues that we can explore the question of whether we have free will by playing through the various paths within *Bandersnatch*. As anyone who has tracked through several different responses in *Bandersnatch* realizes, all the endings are bleak—most are downright depressing. No matter what choices you make for Stefan, Stefan runs into a dismal fate. Stefan's technological ability to create video games does not save him, which alerts us to the fact that technology will not be our savior. Lee argues that what we learn from *Bandersnatch* (and *Black Mirror* in general) is not that technology is bad but that we cannot look to technology to save us from our problems. We do not learn that free will is impossible but that we cannot assume that technology will expand our free will. Instead, our freedom is in our own hands and not dependent on our technological prowess.

Other authors in this volume find further lessons about who we are as people in *Black Mirror*. Diana Stypinska and Andrea Rossi, in their "'White Christmas': Technologies of the Self in the Digital Age," and Kingsley Marshall, in his "You Were Never Really Here: Representations of Artificial Intelligence in Charlie Brooker's *Black Mirror*," each look at the ways in which thought experiments about artificial intelligence (AI) can tell us more about who we are. Stypinska and Rossi show how "White Christmas" provides multiple depictions of the ways in which technology can limit how we see ourselves, especially with respect to our ethical selves. For instance, the character Greta is willing to enslave and torture an AI version of herself even though that AI thinks and feels exactly like Greta herself. By examining the AI in "Be Right Back," Marshall exhibits how technology can change who we are, but only if we let it. In fact, the main character Martha realizes that an AI version of her deceased boyfriend, Ash, can never replicate him, especially insofar as his flaws are essential to whom Ash was as a person. This epiphany tells us so much about how our flaws are interconnected to our selves, as well as how technology cannot fully replicate or replace us.

Our authors show us that we can indeed use *Black Mirror* to glean philosophical information about who we are as persons. The philosophical quest to find the self is fruitfully aided by watching and critically reflecting upon *Black Mirror*. We can only hope that we would likewise gain more insight on our relations to others, including our moral relations and our social/political relations, through *Black Mirror*.

We believe our authors do in fact develop significant philosophical understanding by analyzing *Black Mirror*. Clara Nisley argues that the episode "Crocodile" provides a testing ground for the ethical theories of Aristotle and Immanuel Kant in her "'Crocodile' Going Too Far: Philosophical Reflections on Human Nature and Moral Character." Nisley argues that Mia, the main character in "Crocodile," is not an objection to rationalist theories of morality but is a thought experiment on the danger of thinking that you are too smart or too clever to be restricted by moral codes. Mia, throughout the episode, believes that she can escape what she deserves, morally speaking, for the series of murders she ends up committing. Yet, in this case, the technologically created ability to help retrieve memories stands in as an objectified representation of the idea that you cannot escape your moral duty.

Other authors here repeatedly emphasize this complicated relationship between technology and our moral and political relations to others. In this vein, Leigh E. Rich, in "Rats, Roaches, and Rapists: 'Men Against Fire' and the Propagation of Propaganda," shows us that propaganda is a method in which we manipulate others, sometimes through the use of technology, in unethical ways, such as seen on the episode, "Men Against Fire." Likewise, Shai Biderman, through his chapter, "Between Delight and Discomfort: The Act of Mirroring in the Age of Black Mirror," argues that episodes like "USS Callister" provide a basis for believing that technology degrades moral relations between persons. Finally, Mona Rocha and James Rocha, in their "The You They Love: Patriarchal Feminism and Ashley Too," utilize feminist philosophy to analyze the moral relations between the characters in "Rachel, Jack and Ashley Too."

Ultimately, all of these chapters illustrate a complicated philosophical relation between technology, who we are as persons, how we relate to each other, and how we develop as unique, independent humans, all within *Black Mirror*. At the same time, *Black Mirror*'s unique, episodic format puts forward a series of various worlds ripe for philosophical analysis. Each of these worlds is made real in substantial ways; each one fills the mind with deep thoughts; each one raises more questions than it answers; each one pushes us into philosophical conversations. While *Black Mirror* initiated some of these philosophical discussions and our book connected those conversations carefully and particularly to the relevant philosophical topics, theories, and concepts, we nevertheless now expect that the conversation will continue on with a life of its own—one that will include not only our human readers but all of our AI readers as well.

About the Contributors

Shai Biderman is Assistant Professor of Film and Philosophy at Beit-Berl College and Tel Aviv University, Israel. He is the coeditor of *The Philosophy of David Lynch* (UPK, 2011), *Mediamorphosis: Kafka and the Moving Image* (Walflower/Columbia, 2016), and *Plato and the Moving Image* (Brill, 2019). He has published numerous articles and book chapters on film-philosophy and philosophy of film, on filmmakers (such as David Lynch, Robert Zemeckis, the Coen Brothers, the Marx brothers, and Errol Morris), and on various films and TV shows (such as *Gone Baby, Gone, Lost, Family Guy, South Park, Twin Peaks*, and *Black Mirror*).

Laura T. Di Summa is Assistant Professor of Philosophy at William Paterson University, New Jersey, USA. Her book publications include *The Palgrave Handbook for the Philosophy of Film and Motion Pictures* (New York: Palgrave Macmillan, 2019), coedited with Noël Carroll and Shawn Loht. She is currently working on a volume entitled *A Philosophy of Fashion Through Film: On the Body, Style, and Identity* (London: Bloomsbury). She has published several articles on the philosophy of motion pictures, narrative studies, and everyday aesthetic practices and the self.

Sander Lee is Professor of Philosophy at Keene State College in Keene, New Hampshire. He is the author of *Woody Allen's Angst: Philosophical Commentaries on His Serious Films* (McFarland, 2013). His most recent essays include "Elia Kazan and the Hollywood Blacklist: Some Philosophical Reflections" in the journal *Film and Philosophy* (2020); "Death Gives Meaning to Life: Martin Heidegger Meets Stephen Strange" in the anthology *Doctor Strange and Philosophy*, edited by Mark White and William Irwin (Blackwell, 2018); and "Primo Levi's Gray Zone: Implications for Post-Holocaust Ethics" in the journal *Holocaust and Genocide Studies* (2016). He is a past president of the Northern New England Philosophy Association and a consulting editor for the journal *Film and Philosophy*.

Kingsley Marshall is Head of Film & Television at the CILECT-accredited School of Film & Television and a member of the project team at the Sound/Image Cinema Lab, both based at Falmouth University, UK. As a film practitioner, Kingsley focuses on sound design and music composition for film, and the production of short and micro-budget feature films. He has served as executive producer for the feature films *Wilderness* (Justin John Doherty, 2017), *The Tape* (Martha Tilston, 2020), and *Long Way Back* (Brett Harvey, 2021). He developed and produced *Backwoods* (Ryan Mackfall, 2019) with Neil Fox and composed the score to *Hard, Cracked the Wind* (Mark Jenkin, 2019). Kingsley's academic research focuses on cultures of film and television production, and the representation of real events—specifically the US presidency, asymmetrical conflict, and the development of technology as part of the Fourth Industrial Revolution. He has published widely and speaks regularly at international conferences.

Clara Nisley holds an MA in philosophy from Louisiana State University and a BA in philosophy and BS in political science from Christopher Newport University. She has taught at Oglethorpe University and Kennesaw State University. She has published book chapters on popular culture and philosophy, such as *Downton Abbey*, *Iron Man vs. Captain America*, *The Twilight Zone*, and *Stranger Things and Philosophy*.

Kong-Ngai Pei is a lecturer of philosophy at the Hong Kong Polytechnic University, College of Professional and Continuing Education, teaching a variety of subjects, including creative and critical thinking, introduction to philosophy, and exploring human nature. In 2011, he published a book on critical thinking titled *A Guide to Critical Thinking* (in Chinese). His most recent publication is a book chapter "The Paradox of Existence of Comic Characters" in *Manga and Philosophy* (in Chinese). He is interested in a wide range of philosophy subjects, particularly argumentation theory, metaphysics, philosophy of mind, and procreation ethic. Currently, he is chiefly working on a project attempting to merge the traditional schemed-based approach to argumentation with Bayesian networks.

Leigh E. Rich has followed two passions in life: medicine and literature. She holds a doctorate in health and behavioral sciences and a master's degree in cultural and medical anthropology. She is currently a professor of health administration at Georgia Southern University in Savannah, GA. Her research focuses on bioethics and the body, health-related law, visual media, gender, the philosophy of medicine, and qualitative methodologies. In recent publications, she has examined *The Orville* through the lens of Jacques Lacan, informed consent as a Habermasian practice, hyperrationality and gender in *Hannibal*, Foucauldian and Heideggerian perspectives on American medicine in *House M.D.*, and the COVID-19 pandemic in relation to Jon Krakauer's *Into Thin Air*.

James Rocha is Associate Professor of Philosophy at California State University, Fresno. In 2008, he joined the philosophy faculty at Louisiana State University (LSU), where he worked as an associate professor. In 2016, James joined the Philosophy Department at Fresno State, where he currently teaches and publishes in a variety of areas, such as ethics, applied ethics, feminist philosophy, philosophy of race, philosophy of law, and political philosophy. He is the author of many works of popular culture and philosophy, with chapters in *Mr. Robot and Philosophy*, *Veronica Mars and Philosophy*, and *Psych and Philosophy*, among others. Additionally, James is the author of *The Ethics of Hooking Up* (Routledge, 2020) and coauthor of *Joss Whedon, Anarchist?* (McFarland, 2019).

Mona Rocha is Instructor for the Department of Modern and Classical Languages and Literatures at California State University, Fresno. Mona teaches and publishes on a variety of topics, such as women's history, ancient history, classical civilization, transnational feminism, and gender and health. Mona is the author of many works of popular culture, with chapters in books such as *Psych and Philosophy* and *Westworld and Philosophy*, among others. She is also the author of *The Weatherwomen: Militant Feminists of the Weather Underground* (McFarland, 2020) and coauthor of *Joss Whedon, Anarchist?* (McFarland, 2019).

Andrea Rossi is Postdoctoral Fellow in the Department of Philosophy at Koç University (Istanbul). His principal research interests lie at the intersection of twentieth- and twenty-first-century continental philosophy and political theory, with a special focus on the question of political and economic subjectivity. He is the author of *The Labour of Subjectivity: Foucault on*

Biopolitics, Economy, Critique (2015) and coeditor with Patrick Roney of *Sloterdijk's Anthropotechnics* (Angelaki, 2021).

Dan Shaw served as Professor of Philosophy at Lock Haven University, Pennsylvania, for over thirty years. He devoted much of his scholarship to film, served as the managing editor of *Film and Philosophy*, as well as authored the books *Film and Philosophy: Taking Movies Seriously*, *Morality and the Movies: Reading Ethics Through Film*, and *Stanley Cavell and the Magic of Hollywood Films*.

Robert Sinnerbrink is Associate Professor of Philosophy at Macquarie University. He is the author of *Terrence Malick: Filmmaker and Philosopher* (Bloomsbury, 2019), *Cinematic Ethics: Exploring Ethical Experience through Film* (Routledge, 2016), *New Philosophies of Film: Thinking Images* (Continuum/Bloomsbury, 2011), and *Understanding Hegelianism* (Acumen, 2007/Routledge, 2014).

Diana Stypinska is Lecturer in Sociology in the School of Social Science at Liverpool Hope University, UK, where she teaches social and cultural theory. Her work traverses critical theory, continental philosophy, and critical sociology. She is the author of *On the Genealogy of Critique: Or How We Have Become Decadently Indignant* (2020).

Lorraine K.C. Yeung is a lecturer of philosophy at the College of International Education, Hong Kong Baptist University. Her research interests include philosophy of emotion, aesthetics, film and philosophy, ethics of procreation, ethics of technology, and moral psychology. Her publications include "Spectator Engagement and the Body" (*Film Studies*, 2016), "The Nature of Horror Reconsidered" (*International Philosophical Quarterly* 2018), "An Aesthetic of Horror Film Music" (*Film and Philosophy* 2019), and "Dewey, Foucault and the Value of Horror: Transformative Learning Through Reading Horror Fiction" (*Journal of Aesthetic Education* 2020), and a book chapter on *Manga and Philosophy*.

Index

advertising   55, 90, 150, 154
Allen, Woody   179
alternative facts   145, 163
Aristotle   68, 103, 131–3, 140, 142
   Eudemian Ethics   136
   and Kant   6, 129–30, 132
   Nicomachean Ethics   133–5, 143
"Arkangel"   17, 24
artificial intelligence   1, 17, 98, 105, 114, 118, 204
Asian Americans   153, 156–7
augmented reality   18, 23, 117, 121
authenticity   84–5, 184, 197
autonomy   17, 25, 55, 184–7, 192–7

bad faith, good faith   84–5, 94
Bandersnatch   2–3, 5, 203
   free will   81–95
   interactive   13, 18–19
Battle (military) or Battle command   144–8, 151–2, 158, 169
Benatar, David   32, 37–8
"Be Right Back"   6, 22–3, 53–4, 91, 114–22, 204
Beyond the Looking Glass   87–8, 179
"Black Museum"   2, 26, 43, 117, 197
Borges, Jorge Luis   32, 36
Breaking Bad   11, 58
Bruckner, Donald   32, 37–8
Butler, Stefan   5, 81, 87

Carroll, Noël   51, 58
categorical violation   51, 59
Central America   153, 156
Chalmers, David   41, 52
Choose Your Own Adventure   5, 81
Cookies   40, 43, 98, 105
Covid-19   145, 153, 156, 159
"Crocodile"   6, 22–4, 129–43, 204

Davies, Jerome F.   18, 87–8, 93–4
deliberation   134–5, 139, 142, 160

determinism   3–5, 18, 27, 81–4, 88–9, 93–5
Duck Soup   177, 179
duty   82, 104, 131–7, 140, 159, 163, 179, 204

empowerment   184, 188–9, 192
"Entire History of You"   3–4, 17, 53–4, 60
ethical subject   98, 101, 109, 112
etymology   170, 174
existentialism   84, 94
Ex Machina   25, 51, 114, 120–1

feminism   184–98, 205
"Fifteen Million Merits"   15, 54–6, 61, 90, 202
film noir   91–2
Foucault, Michel   5, 98–101, 111
free will   5, 18–19, 27, 137, 203. *See also* determinism
   Bandersnatch   81–95
friendship   19, 85, 129–33, 136

Garland, Alex   25, 51, 114, 120
The Good Place   38–9
Good will   131, 136–9, 158

Hadot, Pierre   5, 98
"Hang the DJ"   15, 91
"Hated in the Nation"   14, 24, 89–90
Heidegger, Martin   7, 12, 117–18, 120
Her   25, 51, 67
hologram   117, 194, 197

ideology   50, 54, 55
intuition   12, 19, 82, 85, 99

Jonze, Spike   25, 51, 67

Kagan, Shelly   4, 35–6, 38, 45
Kant, Immanuel   6, 82, 129–32, 136–9
Kurzweil, Raymond   31, 115, 118

Lacan, Jacques   175, 178, 180, 182

Marx, Karl   185, 190–2
The Matrix   52, 179
"Men Against Fire"   6, 144–64, 204–5
"Metalhead"   14, 90
Metz, Christian   175–6
Mulhall, Stephen   12, 32
Murray, Terry   21, 54–7

"The National Anthem"   2, 14, 19–20, 57, 90
Nausea   86–7
Nicomachean Ethics   130–1, 133–6, 139, 141–3
Nietzsche, Friedrich   4–5, 39, 67–76, 83, 201–2
"Nosedive"   15, 20–1, 53, 60, 186
Nozick, Robert   39, 41
Nussbaum, Martha C.   36, 193

objectification   2, 146, 154, 193–4
One Dimensional Man   55, 57
Orwell, George   80, 145–6
Overman   69–70

patriarchy   7, 184–6, 188–91, 193, 196–7
personal identity   17, 22, 41–6, 54, 86–7
"Playtest"   15, 18, 22, 25, 60
poststructuralist   4, 49, 54, 57
practical reason   6, 108, 133–40
propaganda   6, 144–51, 153, 157, 160–4, 204
public relations   6, 146, 150

"Rachel, Jack and Ashley Too"   7, 26, 184–98, 205
rationality   1, 81–2, 103, 109, 129
Reality TV   2, 13, 15, 24
Reddit   53, 60–1

"San Junipero"   3–4, 23, 31–46, 62–3, 90–1, 197–8, 202
Sartre, Jean-Paul   81, 84
Schopenhauer, Arthur   5, 81–9, 93–5
Schrader, Paul   91–2
self-enhancement   5, 98, 106–7, 110, 112

self-optimization   5, 104
sexism   184–5, 189–90, 197–8
"Shut Up and Dance"   14, 20, 24–5
slave morality   83
Sloterdijk, Peter   5, 98
"Smithereens"   19, 24, 26
Smuts, Aaron   12, 36, 52
social media   15–16, 19–25, 27–8, 116, 121
"Striking Vipers"   15, 19, 25, 202
structural violence   186–92, 194, 196
subjectivity
   ethical constitution of   98–102
   formation of   16, 24, 98, 104, 106, 109, 111
surveillance   16–18, 22–3, 25, 43
surveillance capitalism   18, 22

technologies of the self   5, 16, 97–101, 103–4, 109, 111
televisual philosophy   11, 14, 26–8, 202
temperance   130, 132
thought experiment   11–12, 16–19, 26–7, 201–2
Tuckersoft   18, 87–8, 90
The Twilight Zone   1–2, 13–14, 90, 93
2001: Space Odyssey   4, 180

"USS Callister"   25–6, 43, 116–17, 168, 185, 205

virtual reality   4, 18, 23, 31–2, 63, 90, 169, 202
virtue   58, 83, 103, 129, 131–6, 140–3
   forgetting   67–9, 71, 73, 75, 201

Wachowski, Lana   52, 56, 179
Wachowski, Lilly   52, 56, 179
"The Waldo Moment"   90
"White Bear"   24–5
"White Christmas"   5, 42–3, 97–112, 116–17, 203–4
the will. *See* Schopenhauer
Williams, Bernard   4, 33–9
will to power. *See* Nietzsche
wisdom   133, 136, 139–42, 179

www.ingramcontent.com/pod-product-compliance
Lightning Source LLC
Chambersburg PA
CBHW062226300426
44115CB00012BA/2237